International Library of Psychology
Philosophy and Scientific Method

ETHICS AND THE HISTORY
OF PHILOSOPHY

International Library of Psychology, Philosophy and Scientific Method

GENERAL EDITOR—C. K. OGDEN, M.A. (*Magdalene College, Cambridge*)

Asterisks denote that other books by the same author are included in the series.

ETHICS AND THE HISTORY OF PHILOSOPHY

SELECTED ESSAYS

by

C. D. BROAD

Litt. D (Cantab.); F.B.A.

Fellow of Trinity College, Cambridge;
Knightbridge Professor of Moral Philosophy in the University of Cambridge

NEW YORK
THE HUMANITIES PRESS INC
LONDON: ROUTLEDGE & KEGAN PAUL LTD
1952

Printed in Great Britain
by Latimer, Trend & Co. Ltd., Plymouth

To

GEORG HENRIK von WRIGHT

Fennis mira feritas . . . nec aliud infantibus ferarum imbriumque suffugium quam ut in aliquo ramorum nexu contegantur. . . . Securi adversus homines, securi adversus deos, rem difficillimam adsecuti sunt, ut illis nec voto quidem opus esset.

TACITUS: *Germania*

INTRODUCTION

T HE present volume consists of a selection of the public lectures which I have given on various occasions and the articles which I have contributed to various periodc als during the last twenty-five years. If it should be found to appeal to a tolerably wide circle of readers, I hope that it may be possible to publish a further selection, covering a somewhat different range of subjects, at a later date.

My first duty is the pleasant one of gratefully acknowledging the permission to republish which has been so readily granted by the several persons and institutions concerned. The lecture on Sir Isaac Newton and the obituary notices of McTaggart and of W. E. Johnson appeared originally in the *Proceedings of the British Academy*, and I have to thank the Council of the Academy for allowing me to reprint them here. To the editor of the *Hibbert Journal* I am indebted for permission to reprint the following papers, viz. the essays on John Locke and on Henry Sidgwick, the lecture on Egoism as a Theory of Human Motives, and the article entitled 'Ought we to fight for our Country in the Next War?'. The lectures on the Philosophy of Francis Bacon and on Determinism, Indeterminism, and Libertarianism were held publicly before the University of Cambridge and were afterwards issued as pamphlets by the Cambridge University Press. They have been out of print for many years now. I am grateful to the Syndics of the Press for allowing them to be made available again in the present volume. For permission to reprint the lecture on The New Philosophy: Bruno to Descartes, and the papers on Leibniz's last Controversy with the Newtonians and on Conscience and Conscienti-

vii

ous Action, I have to thank the editors of the *Cambridge Historical Journal*, of the Swedish journal *Theoria*, and of *Philosophy*, respectively.

The various articles appear in their original form, save for a few slight verbal changes necessitated by the lapse of time since their first publication. I have divided them into three sections, under the headings *Biography*, *Philosophy of Science*, and *Ethics*. If a further selection should be published later, it would cover the topics of *Psychical Research*, *Religion*, and *Politics*.

It may not be out of place to make a few introductory remarks about some of the essays which follow. In doing so I will take the contents of the three sections in turn.

As regards the essays in the Biographical Section the following remarks may be of interest. The lectures on Sir Isaac Newton and on Henry Sidgwick and the article on Locke were all written in connexion with centenaries of their subjects. In Newton's case the event commemorated was the bicentenary of his death, in the cases of Locke and of Sidgwick it was the tercentenary and the centenary, respectively, of their births. The Newton lecture was the Annual Master Mind Lecture of the British Academy for 1927. The lecture on Sidgwick was given in Leeds under the auspices of the University in 1938.

McTaggart and W. E. Johnson I knew well, first as teachers and later as friends and colleagues. I am most deeply indebted to both of them.

McTaggart was my Director of Studies when I studied Moral Science as an undergraduate at Trinity College; he was one of the examiners of the dissertation on which I was awarded a Fellowship of the College; he presented me for my doctor's degree; and it was largely through his influence that the college appointed me as his successor when he retired from his Lectureship. He did me the honour to make me his sole literary executor and one of the two executors and trustees under his will. It fell to my lot, in the former capacity, to arrange the publication of the second volume of his *magnum opus*, *The Nature of Existence*, which he had left in typescript. Some years later I wrote and published an elaborate critical commentary on the two volumes of that work under the title *Examination of McTaggart's Philosophy*.

I have sometimes been twitted with the allegation that my

final estimate of McTaggart's philosophy is much less favourable than that which I wrote in the obituary notice for the British Academy. Anyone who cares to test the truth of this assertion can do so by taking a look at the last four or five pages of the *Examination*. For my own part I do not think that there is much in it. But, if there were, my withers would be unwrung. In the first place, I might quote Dr. Johnson's remark: 'In a lapidary inscription a man is not on his oath.' And then I might add that philosophers, unlike politicians, are permitted and even expected to *learn* as well as to *live*, and to alter their opinions in view of relevant changes in their knowledge.

Turning now to the section entitled *Philosophy of Science*, I will make the following remarks. The lecture on the Philosophy of Francis Bacon was given in the Senate House at Cambridge on 5th October 1926, when the University celebrated the tercentenary of Bacon's death. It ends with a phrase, which I have often seen quoted and not seldom misquoted, about inductive reasoning being still 'the scandal of philosophy'. It is fashionable at present in some quarters to insist that the question: 'How, if at all, can induction be justified?' is in some sense a meaningless or improper one, which can be asked only under a misapprehension and therefore needs no answer. I take this opportunity of saying that I have seen no argument which seems to me to establish this contention. I am glad to find that Mr. Kneale, in his admirable book *Probability and Induction* (1949), shares my opinion in this matter.

The lecture entitled *The New Philosophy: Bruno to Descartes* was delivered in Cambridge on 4th March 1944. It was one of a series, given by various members of the University, which was arranged by the History of Science Committee under the title *Science in the Sixteenth and Seventeenth Centuries*. In the last paragraph but one of this lecture there occurs the following sentence about Descartes' theory of the human mind and body: 'The human soul becomes a kind of Thomistic angel, doomed for a time to haunt a penny-in-the-slot machine, and permitted very occasionally and within very strict limits to interfere with the works.' In his book *The Concept of Mind* (1949), Professor Ryle has used the phrase 'the theory of the ghost in the machine' to describe the same doctrine, and this phrase has been much quoted. I do not doubt that Professor Ryle means much the same by his 'ghost' as I meant by my 'Thomistic angel'. But I cannot refrain from pointing out that the latter phrase is a much more accurate description of Descartes' theory than is the former. A ghost is *not* conceived as a purely mental unextended substance, but as an *embodied* mind with a peculiar kind of body, viz., one that is only occasionally visible and seldom if ever tangible. For the Thomistic-angel theory there is little to be said. But there are plenty of fairly well attested facts which afford *prima facie* empirical evidence for the ghost-in-the-machine theory, if 'ghost' is used in its proper sense. I allude to the ostensibly paranormal phenomena known as 'astral travelling', 'out-of-the-body experiences', 'haunting', 'bi-location', 'materialization', etc. These alleged phenomena fall within the field of psychical research, and Professor Ryle, in common with most other philosophers, has left the contents of that field altogether out of account in speculating on the mind-body problem. If there should be good evidence for a 'ghost in the machine', in the present sense, that problem will be doubled. For we shall then have to consider, in the case of each living person, *two* relationships, viz., (1) the relation of his mind to his ghostly or 'astral' body, and (2) the relation of the latter during his normal waking life to his ordinary physical body.

The lecture on Leibniz's last Controversy with the Newtonians was delivered before the Philosophical Faculty in Uppsala on 8th October 1946, and was afterwards discussed at a *seminar* there. I gladly take this opportunity to express my thanks to my many friends, graduate and undergraduate, in Uppsala. Their kindness and hospitality have made every one of my numerous visits to their ancient and famous town and University a delightful and a memorable experience. I cannot but feel honoured and touched at the way in which they have taken a foreigner and a stranger to their bosoms and made of him an alumnus of their University and a member of one of its Nations.

I come finally to the section entitled *Ethics*. The essay on Determinism, Indeterminism, and Libertarianism was the inaugural lecture which I delivered in 1934 on becoming Knightbridge Professor of Moral Philosophy in Cambridge. All that I need say about it is to record the remark make to me at dinner the same evening by a colleague, of another faculty, who had been present at the lecture. 'If that is what you really believe about your subject', said he, 'I should think that, if you *had* any duties, the first of them would be to resign the Chair.' I can see what he meant, but I have seldom allowed conscientiousness to degenerate into fanaticism and I have continued to draw my salary ever since.

The paper on Egoism as a Theory of Human Motives was delivered as the Marrett Memorial Lecture at Exeter College, Oxford, in 1949. I remember with pleasure and gratitude the hospitality of the Rector and his wife and of the Fellows of the College on that occasion.

The two remaining essays—Ought We to Fight for Our Country in the Next War? and Conscience and Conscientious Action—deal with a subject which must inevitably be very much in the minds of thoughtful and sensitive young men at times when their country seems to be on the brink of a major war. I am not responsible for the title of the first of these papers. I was asked to take part in a symposium with this title in the Audit Room of King's College, Cambridge, some years before the outbreak of the second World War. One of my fellow symposiasts was a sincere and intelligent pacifist, for whom I felt great respect; the other was a clever-silly left-wing intellectual, who provided the dialectical firework display that was expected of him. At that time it was common form in left-wing circles in England to anticipate that the next war would be an attack, engineered by a reactionary English government, on Holy Russia. These circumstances explain, and may in part excuse, a certain acerbity in the tone of my contribution.

The second of these papers was written early in 1940. Holy Russia, hand in glove with Nazi Germany, had by then stabbed Poland in the back and wantonly attacked Finland. Very soon we were to be fighting for our lives. By that time most of those who had declared that they would not fight for king and country were either doing so or preparing to do so; many of them were to display heroic courage and to suffer dreadful injuries; and not a few were to make the supreme sacrifice.

C. D. BROAD

Trinity College
Cambridge
June 1951

CONTENTS

xiii

SECTION I

BIOGRAPHY

SIR ISAAC NEWTON

O N 25th December (O.S.) 1642, in the manor-house of
the small hamlet of Woolsthorpe in the parish of Colsterworth in Lincolnshire, some six miles south of
Grantham, a widowed mother was delivered of a frail and puny
child in whose honour we are assembled here this evening. This
child, in spite of the inauspicious circumstances of his birth,
was destined to live for eighty-five years, and to spend seventy
of them in the most strenuous intellectual and practical activities. He was partly to make, and wholly to consolidate, the
greatest revolution in human thought about external nature of
which we have any record. And, as Bacon had anticipated, this
theoretical insight into the structure of the material world has
extended men's practical control over matter to a degree which
seems almost miraculous.

Newton's father, Isaac the elder, was a small landed proprietor whose family had farmed the estate of Woolsthorpe for
several generations. His mother was Hannah Ayscough of
Market Overton in Rutlandshire, the owner of a small estate
at Sewstern in Lincolnshire; and she had lost her husband a
few months after her wedding. In 1645 Hannah Newton made
a second marriage, with the Rev. Barnabas Smith of North
Witham, a neighbouring village, whither she went to live, leaving young Isaac at Woolsthorpe in the care of his maternal
grandmother. Newton's relations on his father's side seem to
have taken little interest in him; but his mother's brother, the
Rev.William Ayscough of Burton Coggles looked after his welfare.

Newton's education was begun at neighbouring village
schools at Stoke and at Shillington. When he was twelve years

B   3

old he was sent to the King's School at Grantham; and, while he was there, he lodged at the house of a Mr. Clark, an apothecary, and his wife. Newton was not an infant prodigy. The tradition is that he first gained self-confidence through winning a fight with an older boy who had bullied him, and that, after this episode, he began to make steady progress both physical and mental. His taste for experiment and his skill with his hands were early shown by his favourite hobbies. He was a good draughtsman; he made paper kites, and frightened the yokels by setting these kites free at night with lighted lanterns fastened to their tails; he constructed sundials which were treasured for many years; but his greatest achievement at this time was a model windmill worked by a mouse hidden within it.

In 1656 Newton's stepfather died, leaving his mother with three young children. Newton's education was, for a time, interrupted by his being brought home to learn to manage his mother's estate. But it was evident that his heart was not in this, and his relatives at some sacrifice sent him back to school at Grantham. They also took the wisest course which relatives can take by entering him for Trinity College, Cambridge. He remained at Grantham from 1658 to 1661 preparing for the University; and, by the end of that time, he had become head boy of the school and had won a considerable local reputation in his work.

In 1661 Newton was admitted to Trinity as a sizar. The first book that he read carefully at Trinity seems to have been Kepler's *Optics*, and it is noteworthy that Newton's first important published work dealt with this subject. At this time geometry was the weakest string to Newton's mathematical bow. He is said to have first realized his ignorance in this department when trying to read a book on astrology which he had picked up at a fair near Cambridge. He thereupon bought and studied a copy of Euclid's *Elements*, but was at first rather unfavourably impressed with it. It seemed to him then, as it seemed to so many of us at school, that Euclid was merely labouring the obvious. In 1664 he competed in the Trinity scholarship examination. One of his examiners was Isaac Barrow, a geometer of the highest rank, who was destined to exert a great influence on both Newton's mind and his fortunes. The examiners recommended him for a scholarship, but commented on his weakness in geometry as compared with the other branches of mathematics. Newton had the good sense to attend to their criticisms; he returned to the study of Euclid and began to admire the rigour which he had formerly taken for mere verbosity.

By 1665 Newton was doing original work of the first order in both pure mathematics and physical optics. He had discovered the Binomial Theorem and had begun to experiment with prisms. This was the year of the Great Plague. By August the epidemic had become so serious that the College was dismissed. Newton was away from Cambridge with short intervals till 1667. Those of us who were at the University in August 1914 or May 1926 can form a pretty accurate picture of the feelings of Newton and his contemporaries; though this kind of interruption was of course far less disturbing to intellectual work than the European War or the General Strike. It cut short Newton's optical experiments, but it did not require him to waste his time as a soldier or a special constable; and, in the rural solitude of Lincolnshire, he was able to make great progress in pure mathematics and in theoretical physics. It was during this period that he first discovered the Method of Fluxions and began to apply it to various problems. In 1666 at Woolsthorpe he also had the first notion of his theory of universal gravitation, and made certain deductions which seemed at the time to be inconsistent with the facts. The seeds of most of Newton's greatest achievements were thus sown during the plague year; but he kept his mathematical discoveries to himself, and he set his gravitational speculations aside as being contrary to experimental facts.

By 1667 the plague had abated. Newton returned to Trinity early in the year and was elected a Minor Fellow. He went down again soon after his election, and was in Lincolnshire from December 1667 to February 1668. In March 1668 he returned, took his M.A. degree, and was elected to a Major Fellowship. He spent the August and September of that year in London collecting materials for renewing the optical experiments which had been cut short by the plague. He now settled permanently in Trinity on that distinguished staircase, E. Great Court, between the Great Gate and the Chapel. At first he kept in the rooms on the left-hand side of the ground floor;

but he soon moved to those on the right-hand side of the first floor, in which the present lecturer is his unworthy successor:

Aetas parentum, peior avis, tulit
Nos nequiores, mox daturos
Progeniem vitiosiorem.

Newton had devoted himself to researches on light and colours. In consequence of his discoveries in this field he concluded that it was useless to attempt further improvements in the very imperfect refracting telescopes of the period. He thereupon invented and constructed a telescope on a wholly different principle, viz. one which worked by reflection from a mirror instead of refraction through a lens. His first small model, about six inches in length, was completed towards the end of 1668 and was perfectly successful. In 1669 Barrow retired from the Lucasian Professorship in order to devote himself wholly to theology. He and Newton had become close friends, and Newton had helped in the publication of Barrow's *Optical Lectures*. On Barrow's nomination Newton was appointed his successor in the Lucasian Chair. He began by lecturing on optics, but later on he lectured on algebra and gravitation. The optical lectures were published many years later, after he had resigned the Chair and left Cambridge.

In January 1672 Newton was elected a Fellow of the Royal Society. At their request he made for them a bigger and better reflecting telescope, which is still in their possession. In February 1676 he published the results of his optical researches on colours and the spectrum in the *Proceedings* of the Society. Unfortunately this extremely important paper led to the first of a long series of controversies with Hooke, a great, but erratic and irascible, genius. Newton was abnormally sensitive to criticism and disliked taking part in controversy, and his experience over his first scientific paper made him afterwards most unwilling to publish his results. This policy, so far from protecting him from controversy, was the main cause of the very unedifying dispute which broke out later between him and Leibniz about the discovery of the Differential Calculus.

At this time Newton's financial position was far from easy. The salary of his Professorship was small; he was always generous in gifts and loans to his relatives and friends; and he had spent a good deal of money on his scientific experiments. In March 1673 he wished to resign from the Royal Society, ostensibly on the ground that the distance of Cambridge from London made it impossible for him to attend the meetings regularly; but really, there is little doubt, because he found the weekly payment of a shilling a heavy burden. In 1675 Newton, together with Hooke and some others, was granted exemption from this payment at the instance of Oldenburg, the secretary of the Royal Society. In the same year his financial prospects were somewhat brightened by the action of Charles II, who, with the kindness and good sense which he always displayed when his own comfort was not at stake, permitted Newton to continue to hold his Fellowship without taking Orders.

From 1678 to 1687 Newton was mainly occupied with his epoch-making work on the laws of motion and the law of gravitation. This culminated in 1687 in the publication of the immortal *Principia*. In this connexion the scientific world owes a debt of gratitude to Halley, the astronomer. It was he who in 1684 stimulated Newton to reconstruct a proof, which he had made some years earlier and lost, of the proposition that a body, attracted to a centre with a force inversely proportional to the square of its distance therefrom, would describe an ellipse about this centre as focus. Halley next induced Newton to embody this in a short tract, *De Motu*. This was received by the Royal Society in February 1685. In April of the same year Newton began a larger treatise with the *De Motu* as its basis. In a year's time Halley was able to announce to the Society that the treatise was ready for press, and a week later the manuscript (which in fact contained only Book I of the *Principia*) was presented to them. Halley now pressed the Council to undertake the publication, and in May the Society decided to publish the book without delay. But their funds had been depleted by another recent venture; and nothing was done till June, when they empowered Halley to see the book through the press, and accepted his most generous offer (for Halley was not a rich man) to print it at his own expense.

The usual controversy with Hooke now began. Hooke complained that he had suggested the inverse square law to Newton. Newton was furiously angry; and, carrying the war into his enemy's country, suggested that Hooke himself had got the idea from a letter which Newton had written to Huyghens through Oldenburg in 1673, a copy of which Hooke, as successor to Oldenburg in the secretaryship of the Society, must have seen. Reacting very much as he had done in his former controversy with Hooke in 1672, Newton now wanted to suppress Book III of the *Principia* altogether. Halley now played the moderating part which Oldenburg had played then, and induced Newton to alter his mind and to acknowledge that the inverse square law had been suggested independently by Hooke, Wren, Halley, and himself. This difficulty having been removed, Samuel Pepys, who was then President of the Society, gave his *imprimatur* in July 1686, and printing began two weeks later. Book II reached the Society in March 1687, Book III in the following month, and the completed work was published in July 1687 as a quarto volume of five hundred pages at the price of nine shillings.

In the meanwhile Newton had been drawn into the exciting political events of the time. In February 1687 the Vice-Chancellor of the University of Cambridge had refused to break the law at the behest of James II by conferring the M.A. degree on a Benedictine monk. He was summoned to London to appear before the High Commission, and was accompanied thither by eight members of the Senate, of whom Newton was one. They were bullied by Jeffreys, and returned to Cambridge with the royal displeasure concentrated upon them. But the glorious Revolution was at hand, and a Protestant wind was shortly to waft the Dutch deliverer to our shores. Newton was a convinced supporter of that great party which counts St. Thomas Aquinas and Locke as its political philosophers and the Devil as its first member. He was elected for the University to the Convention Parliament, and recorded a series of silent votes from January 1689 to February 1690. We may complete our account of Newton's activities as a politician by mentioning that he sat again for the University from November 1701 till the dissolution in July 1702. He did not then seek re-election. But in 1705, soon after he had been knighted by Queen Anne in the drawing-room of the Master's Lodge at Trinity, he stood again and was disastrously defeated in the Tory reaction of that year. This was the end of his parliamentary career.

The period from 1687 to 1696 was not an altogether happy

one for Newton. It is true that his ideas spread quickly in England. Within three years of its publication the doctrines of the *Principia* were being officially taught in the Universities of Cambridge, St. Andrews, and Edinburgh; and before long they had penetrated even to the Home of Lost Causes. On the Continent the Newtonian theory had a much harder fight against the predominant Cartesian cosmology and the opposition of Leibniz based on mainly philosophical grounds. To put against his scientific successes Newton had personal bereavement and financial worry. His mother became seriously ill while he was a member of the Convention Parliament, and died, in spite of the skill and devotion with which he personally nursed her. Moreover, he was still comparatively poor, and the efforts of Locke, Pepys, and Charles Montagu to secure some remunerative office for him were at the time unsuccessful. He was nominated for the Provostship of King's, which had fallen vacant; but, as he was neither an Etonian, a Kingsman, nor a clergyman, his chances can never have been great.

Newton fell into a state of ill-health and nervous depression. He felt that he had been neglected. Always inclined to be difficult in his personal relations, he now began to tax his friends with indifference or treachery. On the Continent it was believed that he had gone mad; and, in the best traditions of Cartesian physics, the misreported facts were ingeniously accounted for by the false hypothesis of the dog *Diamond* and the burning of Newton's manuscripts. At this time Newton devoted a good deal of attention to alchemy and theology, in both of which subjects he had always been keenly interested. In 1690 he wrote, but did not publish, a tract on *Two Notable Corruptions of Scripture*, in which he displays the strongly Arian tendencies which he unhappily shared with Milton. He also wrote on the *Prophecies of Daniel* and on the *Apocalypse*, to which subjects he returned in later life. At this time Bentley, then at the beginning of his turbulent career, was preparing to give the first course of *Boyle Lectures*, and proposed to use the Newtonian cosmology as the basis of an argument in favour of Theism. Newton corresponded with him during the composition of these lectures, and, in answering certain questions which Bentley had raised, brought out clearly his own views on the theological implications of his system,

9

BIOGRAPHY

If any one be left so steeped in the scientific orthodoxy of the eighteen-seventies as to consider an interest in theology or alchemy to be a clear sign of mental decay, he may be reminded that Newton was also engaged at this time in working out the detailed theory of the moon's motions, which is admittedly one of the hardest parts of gravitational astronomy. From 1694 to 1696 he was in constant correspondence with Flamsteed, the Astronomer Royal, about the positions of the moon, and the corrections to be made in astronomical observations on account of the refraction of light by the earth's atmosphere. The co-operation of Newton and Flamsteed. though of the utmost value to science, was a source of constant irritation to both of them. Both were in bad health, poorly paid, and suffering from a feeling of neglect. They contrived to quarrel over Halley, who was rightly regarded by Newton as his friend and benefactor, and was disliked on theological grounds by Flamsteed, who was rather narrowly orthodox. In 1698, when Newton tried to carry his work on lunar theory still further, he resumed collaboration with Flamsteed, but again there was trouble. It will be as well to anticipate a little here in order to finish the unsatisfactory story of the relations between these two great but ill-assorted scientists. Prince George of Denmark, the Consort of Queen Anne and the father of her nineteen children, in the scanty leisure which his conjugal duties allowed him, could be induced to take some interest in science. He was an admirer of Newton, and was a Fellow of the Royal Society while Newton was President. George offered to defray the expenses of publishing Flamsteed's collected observations; and he asked Newton, Wren, and some other Fellows of the Society to act as referees. By the beginning of 1705 the committee reported and the printing began. The first volume was published in 1707. There was then a long series of delays, owing to difficulties with Flamsteed, and at the end of 1710 a committee was appointed to inspect the apparatus at the Royal Observatory and to report on its condition. With great lack of tact Newton was made chairman of this committee. Flamsteed took this as a vote of censure on himself; and the breach between him and Newton became absolute, and was not healed at Flamsteed's death in 1719.

The year 1696 saw the end of Newton's financial anxieties and the beginning of a wholly new mode of life for him. His friend Charles Montagu became Chancellor of the Exchequer in 1694, and the Whig ministry decided to call in and re-coin the silver currency, which had become incredibly debased. It has never been part of the Whig theory of government that political virtue should be its own sufficient reward, and, when the Wardenship of the Mint with a salary of £500 to £600 a year fell vacant in 1696, King William offered it to Newton, who at once accepted it and took up his work without delay. The office was no sinecure. The recoining was equivalent to a process of deflation, and this generation knows from bitter experience what hardships that necessary transaction inflicts on many innocent and deserving persons. The discontent thus inevitably engendered was fomented and used factiously by the Opposition; and, if Newton under Jeffreys had been called upon to withstand the *vox instantis tyranni*, he and Montagu had now to meet the full blast of *civium ardor prava iubentium*. The appointment was a great success. Newton took his duties very seriously. He was absolutely incorruptible, and he brought all his great intelligence and his admirable practical ability to bear on his new work. He so stimulated the process of recoining that by 1699 it was completed. In that year he was rewarded for this distinguished public service by being made Master of the Mint at a salary of £1,200 to £1,500 a year. This office he held till his death.

Newton now lived in London, where his niece, the beautiful and accomplished Catherine Barton, daughter of his step-sister Hannah Smith, kept house for him. Catherine married in 1717 John Conduitt, who succeeded Newton in the Mastership of the Mint. She had been greatly admired by Montagu, who, at his early death in 1715, had left her £5,000. Her daughter, Catherine Conduitt, born in 1719, married Viscount Lymington and became the ancestress of the present Earl of Portsmouth.

The rest of Newton's life was spent in dignity and prosperity. He became President of the Royal Society in 1703, and was knighted by Queen Anne in 1705. It was a period of steadily growing influence and peaceful development of the scientific ideas which he had excogitated in his earlier years. In 1704 Newton published the lectures on *Optics* which he had delivered in Cambridge many years before. He had delayed publication till after the death of Hooke in 1703, in order to avoid stirring the embers of the old controversy. The first edition of the *Optics* contained bound up with it two important but disconnected tracts on pure mathematics. The first was on the application of Fluxions to the rectification of curves, and the second was on the classification of the seventy-two kinds of cubic curve. In 1714 a second edition of the *Optics* appeared. The mathematical tracts were now omitted, and Newton appended a series of *Queries* in which he gave free rein to those physical, philosophical, and theological speculations which he had so sternly bridled in the main body of his works.

It was a remark by Leibniz in an unsigned review of the first edition of the *Optics* in the *Acta Eruditorum* which started the dreary controversy about the invention of the differential calculus. Leibniz hinted that Newton had simply taken his own published work and translated it into the fluxional notation. John Keill of Oxford replied in 1708, and hinted in turn that Leibniz had got the idea of the calculus from some of Newton's manuscripts to which he had had access. Leibniz sent a vigorous protest to the Royal Society, and demanded that Keill should be made to withdraw his accusation. Instead of doing so Keill particularized. He drew attention to the insinuation made in the review in the *Acta Eruditorum*, and explained that Leibniz could have constructed the calculus from what he had seen of Newton's letters to Oldenburg. Leibniz was naturally unappeased. He stated publicly that the views expressed by the writer in the *Acta Eruditorum* were fair. In 1712 the Royal Society appointed a committee to investigate the question. The committee seems, on the whole, to have tried to be just; but Leibniz could hardly be expected to accept as judicial the findings of a body which included so strong a partisan of Newton as Halley. It gave a balanced report in favour of Newton; and, on its advice, the relevant letters and papers were published in 1713 under the title of *Commercium Epistolicum*. The controversy dragged on till Leibniz's death in 1716; but we need not rake this unsavoury dust-heap further.

The accounts which it has been necessary to give of Newton's quarrels with Hooke, Flamsteed, and Leibniz would produce a highly distorted impression of his character if they were not qualified by reference to special extenuating circumstances and balanced by some account of his many acts of kindness to other scientists. Undoubtedly Newton had faults of temper. But it is equally certain that both Hooke and Flamsteed had corresponding defects which made serious friction almost inevitable. The latter part of Leibniz's great career was very far from happy or prosperous, and the unmerited neglect which he experienced at the Hanoverian Court after the accession of George I cannot have improved his temper. Accusations of plagiarism were extremely common in the seventeenth and early eighteenth centuries, owing to the lack of scientific journals and to the habit of partially disclosing and partially concealing scientific discoveries in letters which were circulated from one hand to another.

Among the mathematicians whom Newton befriended, the most important are Roger Cotes, Henry Pemberton, Colin Maclaurin, and James Stirling. Cotes was a brilliant young mathematician, a Fellow of Trinity, and the first holder of the Plumian Professorship, which he obtained at the age of twenty-five. From 1709 to 1713 he occupied himself in bringing out the second edition of the *Principia*. This contained improvements in lunar theory and in the theory of the precession of the equinoxes. Newton also added to it his famous *General Scholium*, in which he discusses the theological implications of his system. Cotes was an admirable editor, and his correspondence with Newton is copious and valuable. He died very young, to the great regret of Newton and the great loss of mathematics. The third edition of the *Principia* appeared in 1726. It was admirably edited by another young man, Henry Pemberton, who discussed every point in it with Newton. Newton gave Pemberton 200 guineas for his trouble. After Newton's death Pemberton played a prominent part in the valuable controversy about the logical principles of Fluxions which was started by the publication of Berkeley's *Analyst* in 1734. Colin Maclaurin, the discoverer of Maclaurin's Theorem, was a mathematician of the first rank. In 1717 he was appointed Professor at the Marischal College, Aberdeen, at the age of nineteen. In 1725 he wanted to move to Edinburgh in order to get the reversion of the Chair there which was then held by James Gregory. Newton supported him, and, on Newton's recommendation, he was made assistant and successor to Gregory. Newton rendered this

13

arrangement possible by offering to contribute £20 a year to his salary. Maclaurin succeeded to the Chair in 1726. His *Treatise on Fluxions*, published in 1742, is probably the most logically perfect and rigorous treatment of the calculus on Newtonian principles; but it is unfortunately so prolix as to be almost unreadable. James Stirling, commonly called the 'Venetian', had a most romantic career. Whilst an undergraduate at Oxford he became entangled in Jacobite plots in 1715, and had to flee to Venice. There he discovered the secret of making Venetian glass, and had again to flee because the manufacturers of that material were plotting to murder him. He was a pure mathematician of great ability, and Stirling's Theorem is of constant use in the theory of statistics. Newton arranged for the publication of Stirling's work during his exile, and in 1725 got permission from the Government for Stirling to return to England. Stirling afterwards made a great name for himself in Scotland as manager of the Leadhills mines, and the city of Glasgow honours him as the man whose engineering ability first made it a great seaport.

In 1722 Newton began to suffer from his last illness. By taking precautions he kept fairly well till 1724, when his disease revealed itself as a stone in the bladder. By 1726 it was evident that he was breaking up. He died painlessly, after a period of considerable suffering borne with great courage and patience, between 1 and 2 a.m. on Monday, 20th March 1727. His body lay in state in the Jerusalem Chamber and was buried in Westminster Abbey. He bequeathed the family estates at Woolsthorpe and Sewstern to John Newton, his paternal uncle's grandson. John was a wastrel, and sold the property to Edmund Turnor of Stoke Rochford, whose lineal descendants hold Woolsthorpe to this day. Newton left, in addition, personal estate to the substantial amount of £32,000 to be divided between his eight living nephews and nieces, the children of his half-brothers and sisters, Mary, Benjamin, and Hannah Smith. He had already provided handsomely for his Ayscough relations.

Having completed my sketch of the main events of Newton's life, I will now give some account of his chief scientific discoveries. These may first be subdivided into optical and non-optical. Under the latter head we shall have to consider three closely connected subjects, viz. the Principles of Dynamics, the Law of Gravitation, and the Theory of Fluxions.

Optical Discoveries. Undoubtedly Newton's greatest achievement in optics was his experimental proof that white light is not homogeneous but consists of a mixture of lights of various colours, and that light of each colour has its own characteristic degree of refrangibility which is constant for a given medium. Before Newton's time there was very considerable scientific knowledge of the geometrical side of optics, but practically no scientific knowledge about colour.

Now Newton saw that the fact which he had discovered enormously complicates the problem of making satisfactory optical instruments. What is wanted in such instruments is that a set of parallel rays after refraction shall all be accurately focussed at a single point. This would be hard enough to secure even if the light were all of one kind. Descartes knew that it could not be accomplished by a lens bounded by spherical surfaces, and he showed what kind of lens would be needed; but all non-spherical lenses are extremely difficult to grind. But, since white light is a mixture of lights of different refrangibilities, any lens which solved the problem for one of its constituents would fail to solve it for the rest. In technical language, Newton saw that chromatic aberration must be avoided as well as spherical aberration. It seemed to him that no solution of this problem with lenses was possible, and therefore he turned his attention to constructing optical instruments which worked by reflection instead of refraction. Here Newton was mistaken. He failed to recognize that different kinds of glass refract light of the same colour to different degrees, so that it is possible to make a compound lens which shall be approximately achromatic by cementing together lenses constructed of suitably different glass. It is true that a reflecting telescope had already been proposed by Gregory; but Newton was the first to construct one. It is interesting to notice, on the other hand, that Newton first proposed the plan of the instrument which we now call a 'sextant', and that this was rediscovered and one was first constructed by Hadley in 1730.

Newton's other great contribution to optics was his researches on the colours of thin plates and films, such as soap-bubbles. The best means of studying this phenomenon experimentally is still that which is known as 'Newton's Rings'. Here, as always, he was not content with merely qualitative results. He measured the radii of his successive rings of light and darkness, and found that they were proportional respectively to the square-roots of the odd and even integers.

The phenomena in question are particular instances of what we should now call 'interference', and should explain by the reinforcement or annulment which takes place when two trains of light-waves pass through the same point, according as two crests or a crest and a trough arrive there at the same time. Now the theory that light consists of trains of waves in an ethereal medium had been suggested by Hooke and by Huyghens. Newton definitely rejected this theory, and we must now ask ourselves why he did so, and what exactly he believed on the subject. He rejected the wave-theory on two grounds. The first was that it seemed inconsistent with the fact that light does not pass round opaque obstacles, as sound-waves or waves in water do. The objection is an extremely plausible one. The answer to it is twofold. If the obstacle be small enough, viz. of the order of magnitude of the wave-length of light, light does to some extent lap round it. And the reason why this happens as a rule to so slight an extent is the extremely short length of light-waves as compared with waves in air or water. Newton's second objection was that the wave-theory, in the form in which Hooke and Huyghens had formulated it, was inconsistent with the phenomenon of the polarization of light, which Huyghens had discovered in connexion with the double refraction of crystals such as Iceland Spar.

Now this second objection was perfectly correct. Hooke and Huyghens had conceived light-waves as longitudinal, like sound-waves, i.e. as consisting of alternate compressions and rarefactions executed *in* the direction in which the beam is travelling. Now this entails that a beam of light is symmetrical about its direction of propagation. Newton clearly saw that the fact of polarization implies that a beam of polarized light has not this kind of symmetry. What he did not see was that this could be explained by the supposition that the oscillatory motions in the case of light are executed *at right angles* to the direction of propagation. In ordinary light these oscillations take place indifferently in all the planes which intersect each other in the line of propagation; in plane-polarized light they are confined to a certain one of these planes.

It is commonly thought that Newton accepted the emission theory of light. This is true; but it is liable to be very misleading unless it be carefully qualified. (1) In rejecting the wave-theory he was no doubt committed to some form or other of the emission-theory. But he was most careful not to tie himself to any particular form of this hypothesis, though most of his followers assumed that a beam of light consists of a shower of corpuscles. (2) Like most of his contemporaries he had no doubt of the existence of an elastic and pervasive ether. And he was inclined to think that vibrations in this medium play an essential part in the complete explanation of optical phenomena. His final suggestion is that the ether is very much rarer in the pores of bodies than it is outside, and that the density diminishes continuously but very quickly in the region just outside the bounding surface of a body. By this hypothesis he could explain the bending of light when it strikes a body at an angle and is transmitted. He could also explain the diffraction which takes place when light grazes the edge of a small obstacle, such as a thread. Moreover, he thought that the disturbances produced in the retina when light strikes it are conveyed to the brain by vibrations which they set up in the ether contained in the pores of the optic nerve. In terms of the corpuscular form of the emission-theory what appears to us as light of a certain colour consists, outside our bodies, of particles vibrating in a characteristic way. When such particles hit the retina they set up a vibration of a corresponding period in the ether contained in the pores of the optic nerve. This vibration travels to the brain, where the mind in some quite unexplained way perceives it as a certain colour. (3) In order to explain the interference-phenomena which he investigated Newton had to postulate something which bears a formal analogy to the notion of wave-length in the undulatory theory of light. If a very thin transparent film of wedge-shaped cross-section be viewed by reflected monochromatic light the thinnest part will appear black, then will come a coloured band, then another black band, and so on alternately, passing from the thinner to the thicker part of the film. Newton interpreted this fact by suggesting that a beam of light has 'fits of easy reflection and easy transmission', and that these 'fits' are of characteristic length. Thus, up to a certain thickness light is easily transmitted and the film looks black by reflected light. Between this thickness and a certain greater one light is easily reflected and the film looks brightly illuminated. It is evident that this theory of 'fits' recognizes a certain characteristic length associated with light of a given colour, and a certain periodicity in the properties of light with respect to this length. It is in this sense that there is a formal analogy between the concept of 'fits' in Newton's theory and that of wave-length in the modern theory.

Non-optical Discoveries. In order to understand and appreciate Newton's achievements in non-optical matters it will be necessary to explain briefly the position which science had reached on these subjects by his time. Newton's astronomical and mechanical structure was built on two great pillars, the work of Kepler and that of Galileo.

Kepler had shown that the apparent daily and yearly movements of the sun, the stars, and the planets could be accounted for most simply and to a very high degree of approximation by supposing that the earth rotates on its own axis every twenty-four hours, and that it and the planets all describe ellipses of various eccentricities and with various periods about the sun as a common focus. The latter part of this proposition constitutes *Kepler's First Law*. Inspired by beliefs which now appear highly fantastic, Kepler had sought for quantitative regularities in the planets' motions, and had discovered two of the highest importance. The first is that the line joining any planet to the sun sweeps out in any given time an area which is characteristic of the planet, proportional to the time, and independent of the planet's position in its orbit. This is *Kepler's Second Law*. Lastly, Kepler had discovered a most curious relation connecting the periods with which the various planets describe their respective orbits. He found that for any two planets the squares of their periodic times are to each other as the cubes of their mean distances from the sun. This is *Kepler's Third Law*. By Newton's time these three laws were generally accepted, and it was felt that there must be some explanation of them, though no one knew what the explanation could be.

We must next consider Galileo's work on falling bodies and on the motion of projectiles. Galileo had shown that when a body is allowed to fall to earth its velocity increases uniformly with the time that has elapsed since it started to fall, i.e. that it falls with a constant acceleration. The velocity of a body thrown vertically upward diminishes according to the same law. He had also shown that this acceleration is the same for all bodies in the same neighbourhood, and is quite independent of their shape, size, weight, or materials, provided the resistance of the air be allowed for. He next considered the path of a projectile shot into the air at an angle between the vertical and the horizontal. With wonderful insight he recognized that, when a body is given a velocity in a certain direction, this velocity does not die away automatically and need constant renewal. On the contrary, it remains unchanged in amount and direction unless some external cause operates to modify it. This very far from obvious fact constitutes the *Law of Inertia*. Next he recognized that the velocity of a body in any direction can be regarded as compounded of two velocities of suitable magnitudes in any pair of directions at right angles to each other. This is the *Principle of the Composition of Velocities*. With these two principles the problem of the motion of a projectile, apart from air resistance, can easily be solved. The velocity of projection at an angle to the earth can be regarded as composed of a certain velocity vertically upwards and a certain other velocity parallel to the earth's surface. The latter, on the Principle of Inertia, will remain constant throughout the whole course of the projectile. The former will first diminish to nothing and then increase again to its original amount in the opposite direction, exactly as if the projectile had been shot vertically upwards and had then fallen back again. Galileo proved that the path, on these assumptions, would be a parabola; and he experimentally verified that this is in fact the case. Lastly, it is important for our purpose to notice that Galileo invented and constructed the first telescope; that with it he discovered Jupiter's moons; and that it was known by Newton's day that the periodic times of Jupiter's moons in their revolutions about Jupiter obey Kepler's Third Law, with the mean distances of the moons from the planet substituted for the mean distances of the planets from the sun.

Newton's work on the principles of dynamics may fairly be described as a generalization of the results which Galileo had reached in connexion with the special case of falling bodies and projectiles in the neighbourhood of the earth's surface. Expressing ourselves in terms of conceptions which we owe to Newton, we may say that Galileo was dealing with dynamical transactions subject to the following very special simplifying conditions. (1) They took place in a field of force of a single kind, viz. gravitational force. (2) This field of force was practically uniform. (3) The force itself was of a very peculiar kind, which was not fitted to disclose the fact of *mass* as distinct from that of *weight*. For, since the gravitational force on a body is *directly* proportional to its mass, whilst the acceleration produced in a body by any force is *inversely* proportional to its mass, bodies of all masses will fall with the same acceleration in the same gravitational field. (4) The fact that the earth was rotating on its axis and moving round the sun with Galileo and the bodies on which he was experimenting was of negligible importance in these experiments.

Now Newton's great achievement was to formulate a set of principles which apply to *all* motions whatever, no matter whether they be caused by gravitational, electric, magnetic, or any other kind of force, or by impact. The first need was to clear up certain points about space, time, and motion which had been left vague by Galileo. A body which is moving in a straight line with a uniform velocity on the surface of the earth is describing a very complicated path with a variable velocity with respect to the sun. Again, a body whose velocity is uniform when duration is measured by the amount of water that has flowed from a tank will be moving with a non-uniform velocity when duration is measured by a pendulum clock. It is therefore useless to put the Principle of Inertia in the form that a body, unaffected by external causes, will continue to move with uniform velocity in a straight line, unless we state what is to be our standard of straightness and what is to be our standard of equality of duration. To meet this difficulty Newton postulated two entities which he called 'Absolute Space' and 'Absolute Time'; and he formulated the Principle of Inertia in terms of motions which describe equal distances along straight lines in Absolute Space during equal lapses of Absolute Time. It is generally admitted that this expedient is neither theoretically satisfactory nor practically useful. Absolute Space and Absolute Time are very mysterious entities which give rise to grave metaphysical difficulties. Even if they exist, they cannot be observed. And, although Newton gave a test for distinguishing between absolute and relative *rotations*, there is no available test for absolute *translations* which does not involve a reference to force and thus render the Principle of Inertia tautologous. In practice the Principle of Inertia has to be formulated in terms of motions which are rectilinear with respect to the fixed stars and uniform with respect to standard time-measurers constructed to certain assigned specifications.

The term 'Force' can now be defined, or described, generally by the statement that a body is said to be acted on by a force when and only where there is a change in the magnitude or the direction of its velocity.

The next important advance is the introduction of the concept of Mass, and its clear distinction from Weight. It is found that precisely similar bodies, made of different materials, e.g. a sphere of wood and an equal sphere of lead, when placed in exactly similar circumstances, undergo different changes in their velocities. The same blow, e.g. will accelerate the wooden sphere much more than the equal leaden sphere. This fact is expressed by saying that all bodies have masses, and that the accelerations produced in different bodies by the same force are inversely proportional to their masses. The force acting on a body at a given moment is now measured by the product of the mass of the body into the acceleration produced in it by the force. Now bodies of all masses at the same place on the earth's surface fall with the same acceleration, as Galileo had shown. It follows that the gravitational force on each must be proportional to its mass. Hence at any given place weight is proportional to mass, and can be used for comparing masses; for weighing just consists in balancing the gravitational forces on the bodies in the two scale-pans.

No further concepts are needed in formulating the principles of dynamics. But there is need of one further principle, and this Newton recognized and formulated in his *Third Law of Motion*. Suppose a body *A* exercises force on a body *B*. Then, Newton saw, this is only one side of a mutual transaction. The body *B* must exercise on the body *A* a force which is equal in amount and opposite in direction to that which *A* exerts on *B*. An extremely important corollary was deduced by Newton from this law. The mutual actions of a set of particles cannot alter the rest or motion of their centre of gravity, and so the centre of gravity of an isolated system must be either at rest or in uniform rectilinear motion.

Newton's formulation of a complete set of principles, applying to all motions, would no doubt have been impossible without the previous work of Galileo. But, allowing for this, it remains one of the most magnificent achievements of the human mind. Considering the difficulty of the task, and the way in which principles which seem to contradict ordinary experience had to be extracted by insight and reflection from experience, it is not surprising that two such intellects as Galileo's and Newton's were needed to complete the undertaking.

We are now in a position to understand Newton's discovery of the Law of Universal Gravitation. Since the planets move round the sun, and our moon moves round the earth, and Jupiter's moons move round Jupiter, there must in each case be some force which continually acts on these moving bodies and prevents them from flying off with uniform velocities in straight lines. And it is very easy to show that Kepler's Second Law (i.e. the description of equal areas in equal times) will be satisfied if and only if the force acts along the line joining the moving body to the body about which it revolves. Three questions at once suggest themselves. (1) Is it the same force in each case? (2) If so, how does this force vary with the distance between the moving body and the central body? And (3) can this celestial force be identified with any force that we are acquainted with on earth?

Now the fact that Kepler's Second and Third Laws are obeyed by Jupiter's moons in their motions about Jupiter as well as by the planets in their motions about the sun at once suggests that the same force is acting in both cases. Again, although the planets move in ellipses with the sun as focus, and not in circles with the sun as centre, it happens that the ellipses are very nearly circular and consequently that the focus is very nearly central. And, although the velocity of any planet is not exactly the same at every point in its orbit, it is approximately so. Lastly, although the sun and the planets are not mere points but are large bodies, still their distances apart are so enormous compared with their radii that we can begin by treating them simply as massive points. So, as a first approximation, we can suppose that the sun and the planets are massive particles and that each planet moves in a circle about the sun with a characteristic constant velocity. Now, on this simplifying assumption, it is very easy to show that the periodic times of the planets will be connected with their distances from the sun in the peculiar way which Kepler's Third Law asserts, if and only if the force which attracts each planet to the sun be directly proportional to the product of the masses of the two bodies and inversely proportional to the square of their distance apart. Obviously, then, this suggested law is worth following up.

The next step was as follows. Might not the force which keeps the planets in their orbits about the sun, and Jupiter's moons in their orbits about Jupiter, and our moon in its orbit about the earth, be identical with the force which we are acquainted with at the earth's surface as gravitation? Newton proceeded to test this suggestion by working out its consequences for the case of the moon. On this supposition, if the earth can be treated as a particle with all its mass concentrated at its centre, the gravitational force at the earth's surface will be directly proportional to the earth's mass and inversely proportional to the square of its radius. The gravitational force due to the earth at the moon will be directly proportional to the earth's mass and inversely proportional to the square of the distance between the centres of the earth and the moon. Now the gravitational force at the earth's surface is known, and so are the earth's radius and its distance from the moon. Consequently we can at once calculate what force the earth would exert on the moon on the hypothesis which is being tested. And from this we can easily calculate what should be the period in which the moon revolves about the earth, on the simplifying assumption that it moves uniformly in a circle, which is approximately true. If the calculated period of the moon should agree exactly with its actual period, the hypothesis is presumably true, and we can identify the force which keeps the moon and the planets in their orbits with the force which makes unsupported bodies fall to the earth.

Now the whole of this argument was worked out by Newton at the age of twenty-three with the numerical data then available to him while he was compelled to rusticate at Woolsthorpe owing to the Plague in 1666. On these data the calculated period of a complete revolution of the moon is about 23·3 days. The actual period is about 27·3 days. So the difference was about 16 per cent. Newton thought that this was too great, concluded that his hypothesis must be wrong, and dismissed the whole subject from his mind for the next sixteen years. But, in June 1682, at a meeting of the Royal Society, conversation turned on Picard's measurement of the earth's radius. Newton's attention was now called to the fact that the true radius of the earth is 3,956 miles, instead of 3,440 miles as he had assumed in his Woolsthorpe calculations. He repeated his calculations on his return to Cambridge. With the amended value of the earth's radius the calculated period of the moon becomes 27 days, as against the actual value of 27·3 days, a difference of only a little more than 1 per cent.

The hypothesis that the force which keeps the moon and the planets in their orbits is the same force which we experience on earth as gravitation had now become extremely plausible. But a very difficult bit of work remained. Newton had now to take into account the fact that the earth, the sun, and the planets are not really mathematical points, and that the planets really move in ellipses with variable velocities about the sun as focus and not in circles with uniform velocities about the sun as centre. He succeeded in proving the extremely beautiful theorem that the attraction produced by a sphere composed of matter which attracts in accordance with the inverse square law is exactly the same at any external point as if all its mass were concentrated at its centre. Thus the first simplifying assumption turned out, not to be an approximation at all, but an accurate account of the facts. And he succeeded in proving that a body moving round a centre to which it is attracted in accordance with the inverse square law will describe an ellipse about that centre as focus. This is the proof which he had made and lost, and which he reproduced in 1684 in answer to a question by Halley.

Kepler's laws were now completely accounted for, and Newton's hypothesis that every material particle attracts every other with a force directly proportional to the product of their masses and inversely proportional to the square of the distance between them was firmly established. This is the first, and perhaps the greatest, of the three supreme triumphs of the human mind in physics. The other two which deserve to rank with it are Maxwell's correlation of all the phenomena of electricity, magnetism, and light in a single set of differential equations; and Einstein's General Theory of Relativity, in which Newton's theory of gravitation is absorbed, transformed, and generalized. The rest of Newton's work on gravitation was twofold. He applied his law to explain certain terrestrial phenomena due to the gravitational influence of the heavenly bodies on the earth, e.g. the tides, and the precession of the equinoxes. And he applied it to account for minor anomalies in the motions of the planets, and more especially of the moon, which are due to the fact that each body is attracted to some extent by all the other bodies in the solar system.

In comparing the achievements of Newton with those of Maxwell and of Einstein we must bear in mind that he had to invent and construct the mathematical instrument which he needed for working out his physical ideas, whilst they found the pure mathematics that they required ready to hand. This brings us to the last of Newton's great scientific discoveries which we have to consider, viz. the Method of Fluxions, which is his form of the Differential and Integral Calculus.

Let us first consider what Newton had to do in order to calculate the gravitational force exerted by a solid sphere at a point outside it. He had to regard the sphere as composed of a very large number of particles so small that each could be treated as approximating to a point, to compound together the very small attractions which each of these particles would exert at the external point in question, and to determine the limit to which this total force would approach as the particles were made smaller and smaller and their number was made greater and greater. This is what we should now call a problem of integration. Let us next consider the problem of determining the path of a particle projected with a certain initial velocity and then left to move under the gravitational attraction of a centre of force. The dynamical principles required are precisely the same as those which Galileo used in dealing with the path of a projectile. But the problem is far more complicated. In Galileo's problem the force acting on the particle was constant in magnitude and direction throughout the whole transaction. In Newton's problem the force is continually altering in magnitude, since it depends on the distance of the particle from the attracting centre, and this is constantly changing. And the force is continually altering in direction, since it acts along the line joining the particle to the centre, and this line moves round in space with the particle. Newton had thus to deal with velocities which varied from moment to moment in both magnitude and direction, and, moreover, with the variations of their variations from moment to moment. In every dynamical problem, in fact, we require the notions of momentary velocity and momentary acceleration. It is obvious that these are extremely difficult and sophisticated notions. If we confine ourselves literally to a single moment and a single position, the particle is not moving at all. And, if we consider the history of the particle throughout any interval, however short, there is in general no one magnitude and no one direction which can be ascribed to its velocity. It is such concepts as these, and their laws, which Newton had to define and determine in his Theory of Fluxions.

Particular problems in integration had been solved long before Newton's time by special devices, particularly in connexion with determining the lengths of curves and the areas enclosed by curves or the volumes enclosed by surfaces. But each problem had been solved by some special trick whose discovery depended on the insight or luck of some individual mathematician. The general conception of the rate of change of one variable magnitude with respect to another variable magnitude for any given value of the latter hardly existed at all; still less the conception of rates of change. No general method existed by which such rates of change could be calculated as soon as the functional relation between the two magnitudes was given. And it was not recognized that the problem of integration is the converse of the problem of determining rates of change. All this we owe to Newton; and independently, and in a rather different form to Leibniz.

It would be out of place here to enter into an elaborate discussion of a highly technical subject; so I must be brief and dogmatic. Newton, influenced no doubt by his dynamical interests, regarded all other variables as functions of time, and all variation as primarily the increase or decrease of a magnitude as time flows on. He invented a general method for determining the rate of change of any magnitude, given as a function of time, at any moment. These rates of change with respect to time he called *Fluxions*. When he had to consider the rate of change of a magnitude x with respect to another magnitude y, of which x is given as a function, he proceeded as follows. He imagined y to increase uniformly with time, so that its fluxion is constant. He imagined x to vary with time according to such a law as would make x the given function of y. The rate of change of x with respect to y is then the ratio of the fluxion of x to the fluxion of y.

The true state of the case as between Newton and Leibniz is roughly as follows. As regards priority, they made their discoveries quite independently. Newton's discovery was earlier than Leibniz's, and Leibniz's publication was earlier than Newton's. As regards the relative merits of their respective forms of the calculus, the following may be said. Leibniz avoided the needless dragging in of time where time is not concerned, and thus established the calculus on a much wider basis. But Newton's fluxional method has considerable advantages in providing the beginner with an intuitive and familiar illustration of the concepts of the calculus. Leibniz's notation was incomparably better than Newton's, and the subject could hardly have developed far without it. Neither Newton's nor Leibniz's exposition of the fundamental concepts and principles of the calculus is logically impeccable. But Newton, who tried to base the calculus on the notion of limits (though he never wholly succeeded in exorcising the ghost of infinitesimals), is far less open to objection than Leibniz, who unblushingly used infinitesimals, and neglected their squares and higher powers with a gay indifference which recalls Rousseau's treatment of his illegitimate children. Soon after Newton's death the logic of his exposition of Fluxions was severely and justly criticized by Berkeley in his *Analyst* and his *Defence of Freethinking in Mathematics*. A long controversy took place, in which Jurin, Robins, and Pemberton were the chief participants. In the course of this controversy the foundations of the fluxional method were thoroughly discussed, and the theory was purged of most of its logical defects. It reaches its high-water mark of logical rigour in the profound but unreadable *Treatise* of Maclaurin. The fluxional method achieved purity at the expense of fertility. 'Like a virgin dedicated to God', to quote Bacon, 'it produced nothing'. And it completely isolated English mathematicians from their Continental brethren. So, when Peacock, Herschell, and Babbage in 1812 founded their *Analytical Society* at Cambridge to introduce Leibniz's form of the calculus, or, as Babbage happily put it, 'To promote the principles of pure *D*-ism in opposition to the *Dot*-age of the University,' they were doing a most necessary work, though the immediate consequence was an orgy of logical licence.

I have now completed, so far as is possible in the time at our disposal, a survey of the life and the scientific work of Sir Isaac Newton. On the base of Roubiliac's statue in our ante-chapel at Trinity are the simple words:

NEWTON

Qui genus humanum ingenio superavit

Supreme intellectual achievement needs no more elaborate memorial than this bare record of fact.

JOHN LOCKE

JOHN LOCKE was born on 29th August 1632, in a small house adjoining the churchyard of the beautiful parish church of Wrington in Somerset, about a mile distant from the former home of the present writer. The house has now disappeared; but Locke is commemorated by a tablet in the porch of the church, close beside the memorial to Hannah More, who lived and laboured for many years at Barley Wood near Wrington, an estate now owned by a member of the prolific and beneficent family of Wills. His mother was Ann Keen or Ken, daughter of a tanner at Wrington. Locke had one younger brother, who became an attorney, and died childless of consumption during Locke's lifetime. Locke's paternal grandfather was Nicholas Locke of Sutton Wick, Chew Magna, a village in the Mendips. Nicholas was a younger brother of the Lockes of Charon Court, Dorsetshire. Locke's father, John Locke, senior, began his career as clerk to Francis Baber, Justice of the Peace, of Chew Magna. During the Civil War he was made a captain in the Parliamentary Army through the interest of Colonel Alexander Popham of Pensford, a village in north Somerset, some five miles from Bristol. After the Restoration he settled down at Pensford as an attorney and became a small landowner there. His house was called Beluton. Locke spent his early years at Pensford, and inherited his father's small property in the neighbourhood.

Through the interest of Colonel Popham, Locke was admitted as a scholar to Westminster School in 1646. The school was then a centre of extreme Puritanism. In 1652 he took the wrong one of the two turnings open to brilliant Westminster boys, and went to Christ Church, Oxford, as a junior student, instead of entering Trinity College, Cambridge—obviously his spiritual home—as a Westminster exhibitioner. Christ Church also was dominated by Puritanism during Locke's undergraduate days, and he saw enough of the intolerance of the Puritan sectaries at school and at college to disgust him with their theology and to make him a highly latitudinarian member of the Church of England.

Locke did not find the official curriculum of Oxford much to his taste, and he confesses that at first he spent much of his time in meeting, conversing, and corresponding with 'pleasant and witty men', which is no bad occupation for an intelligent undergraduate in his first two years. He took his B.A. degree in 1655 and his M.A. degree in 1658, and he was made a tutor of Christ Church in 1660, the year in which the Royal Society was founded; so, even from a purely academic standpoint, he cannot have wasted his time.

The question then arose of what he should do for a permanent career. His own health was poor, for he suffered from asthma and there was consumption in his family. He had, therefore, been led to study medicine, more with a view to treating his own ailments than to practising on others. He never, in fact, took an M.D. degree, though he made some attempts to do so, and was often referred to by his friends as 'Dr.' Locke. But he was recognized by so great an authority as Sydenham to be a first-class physician, and, as we shall presently see, his medical skill was an important factor in gaining for him an entry into the world of affairs. He did not take his M.B. degree until 1674, when he was forty-two years old. Very soon after this he was appointed to one of the two medical studentships at Christ Church.

Before his position in the medical world was thus regularized much had happened to Locke. In 1664 he made tentative advances towards a diplomatic career by taking a position as secretary to Sir Walter Vane, the English envoy to Brandenburgh. In the same year, however, he was back again at Oxford studying experimental natural philosophy, which had become highly fashionable. Locke's main scientific interests seem to have been in chemistry and meteorology. He kept a record of the temperature, pressure and hygrometric state of the atmosphere at Oxford between June 1666 and June 1683.

JOHN LOCKE

In 1666 a curious concatenation of circumstances initiated a friendship with a great man of affairs, which was destined to influence Locke's life profoundly. Anthony Ashley Cooper, then Lord Ashley and afterwards first Earl of Shaftesbury, had been injured by a fall from his horse which had caused an abscess in the breast. He had been advised to drink the waters of Astrop, and had commissioned Dr. Thomas, an Oxford physician, to procure him a quantity of this water. Thomas, who was obliged to be away from Oxford at the time, delegated this commission to his friend Locke. When Ashley reached Oxford the Astrop water had not yet arrived, owing to some mistake on the part of Locke's agent. Locke therefore called on Ashley in order to explain and apologize. Ashley received Locke with his usual courtesy, and was so taken with his conversation that he asked him to stay to supper that evening, to dine with him the next day, and to drink the waters with him.

The friendship so strangely begun very quickly ripened. In 1667 Locke stayed with Ashley at Sunning Hill. He now became Ashley's private physician, and performed a drainage operation with a silver tube on the abscess, which probably saved Ashley's life, though he was never completely cured. Ashley was deeply grateful; but, highly as he esteemed Locke as a physician, he saw that Locke had greater gifts, and encouraged him to study political, theological, and philosophical subjects.

Ashley is known to most of us mainly as an extremely unscrupulous and factious politician, the 'bloody bold Achitophel' of Dryden's poem, the idol of the Protestant underworld of London in which he professed to be able to raise 10,000 'brisk boys' to overawe the Government, and a prime mover in the abominable business of Titus Oates and the Popish Plot. Yet he was a man of great ability and charm, and was not without excellent points of character. In an extremely corrupt age he seems to have made no use of his innumerable opportunities to increase his private fortune by taking bribes or defrauding the public. And, when he was Lord Chancellor, he enjoyed a high reputation as a careful and upright judge. He had a genuine belief in religious toleration, though he was not prepared to extend it to Roman Catholics, on the one hand, or to extreme Protestant fanatics like the Fifth Monarchy Men, on the other.

BIOGRAPHY

Each of us has many different facets to his character, and, according to the company that we are keeping at the moment, one or another of them flashes out. Shaftesbury was no doubt at his best in the presence of a man like Locke. At his best he must have been a delightfully intelligent and witty companion, and Locke must have derived immense benefit from his friendship and from meeting the distinguished group of men of the world into which he was now introduced. One side of Shaftesbury's nature is illustrated by the following conversation between him and Charles II. 'I think you must be the wickedest man in England, Shaftesbury,' said the King to him. 'For a subject, sir, I believe I may be,' replied Shaftesbury. Whatever Shaftesbury's faults may have been, Locke always expressed the deepest admiration for his intellect, his resourceful courage, and his exquisite courtesy; and such a testimonial from such a man cannot lightly be set aside.

We have now to think of Locke as a don of about thirty-five years of age and of lower middle-class origin, launched into the society of some of the proudest and most brilliant English noblemen, at a period when all English noblemen were proud, and many were brilliant. In this difficult situation he behaved with perfect tact, avoiding both servility and the uneasy assertion of equality. Once, when a party assembled at Ashley's house sat down immediately to play cards instead of conversing, Locke was observed to take out a pocket-book and to be writing in it with great diligence. When someone asked him what he was doing, he replied that, as he was privileged to be in the company of some of the brightest wits in England, he had thought that it would profit him to record their remarks during the last two hours. He then read out the Caroline equivalents of 'Three no-trumps', 'Two spades doubled', and so on. The players had the good sense and the good feeling to appreciate the joke, and spent the rest of the evening in rational conversation.

In 1668 Locke went to France in attendance on the Earl and Countess of Northumberland, but he soon returned, owing to the sudden death of the earl. He again took up residence with Ashley, who was now Chancellor of the Exchequer, and was living in Exeter House, London. Ashley entrusted him with the education of his son, who was sixteen years old and very delicate. He also employed Locke to choose a suitable wife for the

32

young man, as he was afraid that he might die childless and that the family might become extinct. In this embarrassing task Locke was completely successful. The lady of his choice had seven children by her marriage with the young nobleman, and all of them were quite healthy, as they had every chance of being if they were brought up on the extremely sensible rules laid down by Locke in his *Thoughts on Education*. Locke acted as tutor to the eldest of them, who afterwards became the celebrated moralist Shaftesbury, author of the *Characteristics*, whose high-falutin style and exaggerated sentiments are parodied by Berkeley in the *Alciphron*.

In 1672 Ashley became Earl of Shaftesbury and Lord Chancellor. He at once appointed Locke his secretary for the presentation of benefices. In the following year Locke was made Secretary to the Board of Trade. In 1675 Shaftesbury fell from power, and Locke lost these offices. His health, never very strong, had been tried by living in London, so he took the opportunity to make a long stay in Montpelier, varied by occasional visits to Paris. There he met Guenellon, the Amsterdam physician; Römer, the Danish astronomer who first calculated the velocity of light from the eclipses of Jupiter's moons; Thevenot the traveller; and other distinguished men of letters and science.

In 1679 Shaftesbury was restored to favour for a short time. He became Lord President of the Council, and promptly sent for Locke. But Shaftesbury was now at the end of his tether. He was soon in trouble again, and was shut up in the Tower. On his release he fled to Holland and died soon after, an exile in the country to which, in the days of his power, he had applied the phrase *delenda est Carthago*. Locke had been so much associated with Shaftesbury that he deemed it wise to retire to Holland himself in August 1683, less than a year after his patron's flight and death.

During all this time Locke had been enjoying his Christ Church studentship. Charles II now caused Sunderland to write to Dr. Fell, the Dean of Christ Church, to inquire as to the best means of depriving Locke of this studentship. Fell had to admit regretfully that, although every attempt had been made to entrap Locke into seditious remarks by criticizing Shaftesbury and the Whigs in his presence, his self-control was so great that he could never be provoked to an injudicious word or an angry look. Moreover, the fact that Locke held one of the medical studentships freed him from the ordinary duty of residence, so that he could not be deprived on the ground of his long absence abroad. The situation was most perplexing, and the best that Fell could suggest was that he should exercise his right to summon Locke into residence by 1st January. If Locke failed to obey, he could then be deprived for contumacy. If he obeyed, Fell expressed the pious hope that he might be found to have been less cautious in his words or actions in London than he had been in Oxford, and that the law might be able to get hold of him. These methods were too slow and too uncertain for Charles and Sunderland. So, on 11th November 1684, a royal command was issued from Whitehall that Locke should be deprived of his studentship for 'factious and disloyal behaviour'. On 6th November Fell informed Sunderland that the order had been obeyed, and Sunderland replied by conveying to the college the King's satisfaction at this ready obedience to his commands.

On the death of Charles II William Penn, the Quaker, who was in favour with James II, offered to secure from the latter a pardon for Locke. Locke declined the offer on the ground that he needed no pardon since he had committed no crime.

Worse troubles soon followed. In 1685 the Duke of Monmouth and his followers were preparing in Holland for the expedition which ended so disastrously at Sedgemoor. Locke would have nothing to do with this foolhardy plan. He had no high opinion of Monmouth's brains or character, and he was by nature timid and a man of peace. Nevertheless, the English Government included Locke's name in a list of eighty-four persons whom they demanded to be given up by the Dutch Government. For some time Locke was in considerable danger, and he had to live in hiding in the houses of several Dutch friends. Fortunately, the Dutch Government remained polite but evasive, as when, on a later occasion, they were asked to hand over the Kaiser to be executed, condemned and tried, in order to fulfil Mr. Lloyd George's election pledges.

In Holland Locke made several very good friends, of whom the most distinguished was Limborch, a learned and liberal-minded professor of theology, with whom he carried on a long

34

and affectionate correspondence. He also met Le Clerc, in whose recently founded *Bibliothèque Universelle* the preliminary epitome of the *Essay on Human Understanding* was published.

The cup of James II's folly was now almost full. He had succeeded in alienating the Church of England without conciliating the Protestant dissenters, and in frightening every corporate institution in the country. Locke was called into council by Burnet, Mordaunt, and William of Orange himself about the proposed invasion of England. In November 1688 a Protestant wind wafted the Dutch deliverer to Torbay, and in February 1689 Locke followed in the same ship which bore Queen Mary and Lady Mordaunt to our shores.

Locke was now fifty-seven, and he had as yet published nothing. But he had been observing, reflecting, discussing, and writing all his life, and now he began to issue important works in quick succession. He had declined the offer of an embassy to Brandenburgh, and had accepted the almost sinecure office of Commissioner of Appeals, with a salary of £200 a year. So he had now a modest income and ample leisure.

In 1689 appeared his first *Letter on Toleration*. It was written in Latin to Limborch, and was first published at Gouda, but an English translation appeared in the same year. It led to controversies which caused him to publish a second and a third letter on the same subject in 1690 and 1692 respectively.

In February 1690 appeared Locke's main contribution to political theory: *Two Treatises on Civil Government*. In the first treatise Locke was concerned to refute the doctrine of Sir Robert Filmer, who had claimed to prove that the power of kings is absolute, from the two premises that Adam was given absolute sovereignty over all creatures and that kings are the heirs of Adam. Locke had no great difficulty in making this theory look very silly. Unfortunately he did not directly tackle the very much stronger arguments of the very much abler writer Hobbes, who had argued that in every State there must be *some* authority which is absolute, though this might be either a single individual or an assembly of individuals which was a single legal person.

Locke expounded his own positive theory in the *Second Treatise*. Like Hobbes, he makes use of the fiction of an original State of Nature and of the genesis of government from this by

D   35

means of an original Social Contract. In the state of nature, if it ever existed, men were subject only to the obligations of the moral law which God has instituted, and which he has enabled all men to discover by reflection. But this law, though binding, is often broken. In the state of nature each man has an equal right to punish anyone who transgresses the moral law. But what is everybody's business is nobody's business, and so this situation is found to be extremely unsatisfactory. Accordingly, men agreed among themselves to delegate the right of punishment to certain public officials, and to give to the latter such powers as may be necessary for the efficient exercise of this function. The Government, thus appointed, is under an obligation not to exceed the powers which have been granted to it for the specific purpose of keeping order and punishing evildoers. On Hobbes's view the purpose of instituting government is to enforce peace between individuals and to defend the community against other communities. Owing to the insatiable covetousness and mutual envy of men nothing less than unlimited power in the sovereign will enable it to perform these duties, so there is no question of a sovereign with powers limited by agreement with its subjects. So great are the miseries of the state of nature, and so impossible is it for any individual to defend himself and his possessions for long against all the rest, that this complete sacrifice of all one's rights to the sovereign is well worth while. On Locke's view the subjects can transfer the sovereignty from one man or assembly to another if the sovereign breaks the original contract, and they can modify the powers which they have granted to their sovereign if they are found to be excessive or defective for the end for which they were given. On Hobbes's view subjection to a sovereign, like marriage on the extreme Catholic view of that institution, is 'for better or for worse'. To pursue the metaphor, the obligation can be dissolved only on the plea of impotence, i.e. if the sovereign fails to keep peace within the community or to defend it against other communities.

According to Locke, men in the state of nature are born free and equal in rights. Property, in that state, depends on labour. Each man has a right to that, and only to that, on which he has worked. But, as population increases, it becomes necessary to have positive rules about the acquirement, possession, and transference of property. These are partly utilitarian, but they always contain a large mixture of arbitrariness and it is an important part of the duty of the Government in any old and settled community to see that they are kept.

It is obvious that Locke's theory, like all political theories, contains a good deal of fiction and nonsense. But it was plain wholesome nonsense, better suited to the needs of the time and place than the more highly seasoned fictions of Hobbes or of Filmer. The *Letters on Toleration* and the *Treatises on Civil Government* may be regarded as the theoretical statement of the practical principles in accordance with which the English revolutionary settlement was constructed. In the hands of logical Frenchmen and rhetorical Americans Locke's principles were developed by the latter part of the eighteenth century into what Jeremy Bentham called 'nonsense on stilts', and were embalmed in the constitution of the United States which survives like an ancient family ghost haunting a modern sky-scraper.

Locke himself is the author of a constitution, and a very curious document it is. Shaftesbury was one of the original proprietors to whom Charles II granted the territory of Carolina, and Locke, at Shaftesbury's request, prepared an elaborate constitution for it which was never put into execution. It is extremely aristocratic and oligarchical, and seems admirably designed, as the preamble states, 'to avoid erecting a numerous democracy'. The territory was first to be divided into counties. One fifth of each county was to be divided into eight equal signories, which were to be the inalienable possession of the eight proprietors. Another fifth was to be divided into eight equal baronies, which were to be the inalienable possession of the hereditary nobility. The remaining three-fiths was to be divided into twenty-four colonies, grouped into four precincts. The colonies were to be planted with the common people. There was to be an elaborate system of manors and courts-leet. More interesting than this attempt to supply the Americans with the last enchantments of the Middle Ages is the part of the constitution which deals with religion. Any seven or more persons who agreed in religion could form a church. The tenets of any church were to be written clearly in a book, which was to be kept by the public authorities and to be open to inspection. They $must$ include the following three propositions: (1) That God exist$_s$;

(2) That God ought to be publicly worshipped; and (3) That it is lawful to make an oath or solemn affirmation, in accordance with some recognized visible ritual, when giving evidence in a court of law, calling God to witness that one means to tell the truth. Besides these three fundamental doctrines any others, not inconsistent with them, might be included in the creed of any church. No person over the age of seventeen who had not entered his name as a member of some church could enjoy any of the rights of a citizen or own property. It will be observed that these rules would exclude atheists and certain very antinomian Protestants from citizenship, but no others. This was Locke's intention. Joining or withdrawing from any church was to be completely voluntary; no member of any church was permitted to speak ill of any other church or to molest any of its members; and any religious body which failed to submit to these rules was to be treated as an unlawful and riotous assembly. Slaves were to be admitted to church membership, but this was to make no difference to the legal authority of their masters over them.

In March 1690 Locke's main philosophical work, the *Essay concerning Human Understanding*, was published. The first beginnings of this, Locke tells us, took place at a conversation held in his rooms twenty years before with five or six friends, in the winter of 1670. They had been discussing theological and ethical questions, and the difficulties in which they had landed had led him to wonder whether they ought not first to enquire into the powers and limitations of the human mind. Would it not be wise to undertake a preliminary investigation in order to find out what subjects are susceptible of being understood by our minds and what subjects, if any, are altogether beyond our reach? Locke undertook to do this, and to communicate the results at the next meeting. He thought that a single sheet of paper would suffice to contain his answers to the question. But he had started on a quest which was to occupy him pretty continuously for the next twenty years, which was to fill a large volume divided into four long books, and was to develop into the scepticism of Hume and the critical philosophy of Kant. The journal which Locke kept while at Montpelier in 1675 shows that he was then busily engaged in reflecting on the subject. The *Essay* was completed, except for a few finishing touches, in

Holland in 1687. A preliminary epitome of it appeared in French in Le Clerc's *Bibliothèque Universelle* for January 1688. The first edition of the complete work was published in London in March 1690. It was promptly condemned at a meeting of Heads of Houses at Oxford, each of whom undertook to prevent it being read in his own college. Locke received £30 for the manuscript, which is about the same as Kant received for the manuscript of the *Critique of Pure Reason*. It went through many editions, and has probably been the most widely read philosophical work ever published in England. A good testimony to its popularity is the fact that a novelist like Fielding, writing for the entertainment of the general public, does not hesitate to quote in his novels characteristic doctrines from the *Essay* in Locke's own technical language.

The popularity which the *Essay* enjoyed cannot be attributed to any marked graces of style. Of the great English philosophers —Bacon, Hobbes, Locke, Berkeley, and Hume—Locke is the only one who is not, in his way, a master of English prose. At best he is pedestrian, and at worst he is verbose and tedious, though he does not employ a forbidding terminology, like Kant or Hegel or Whitehead. In reading the *Essay* one feels oneself to be in presence of a very intelligent, scrupulously honest, man, of no great intellectual subtlety or constructive ingenuity, who heartily desires to get at the truth for himself and to persuade others of it by fair means and by fair means only. Perhaps in the long run Locke gains in persuasiveness by his very limitations. In reading Hume we cannot help suspecting that he is 'too clever by half'; Berkeley, as Hume said, 'admits of no refutation, and produces no conviction'; Hobbes may be hitting us below the intellect by the irresistible appeal of his wit and his naughtiness; but Locke, we feel, is not so much cleverer than ourselves as to be capable of playing tricks with us even if he wanted to do so. He is the Mr. Baldwin of philosophy, and he derives from his literary style some of the advantages which that statesman owed to his pipe and his pigs.

I will now give a very brief sketch of Locke's main philosophical positions. He distinguishes sharply between knowledge and belief. By 'knowledge' he means exactly what Descartes meant by it, viz. seeing the necessity of necessary facts. Sometimes knowledge can be acquired by direct inspection of the relevant terms, as when we recognize that anything which had shape would necessarily be extended. More often it can be gained only indirectly through intermediate ideas and a chain of reasoning, as when we prove that the angles of a Euclidean triangle must be together equal to two right angles by producing one side and drawing a line through the external angle parallel to the other side. Locke thinks that our need to use intermediate ideas and chains of reasoning is a human defect, which is certainly absent in God and possibly in angels.

Belief differs in kind from knowledge. Unlike knowledge, it has degrees of certainty, reaching in some cases to complete conviction. Belief has causes, such as association, authority, etc., some of which are likely to produce true belief, and others to produce false belief. But it is never caused, as knowledge always is, by insight into the necessity of what we are asserting. It had commonly been held that certain abstract principles are recognized by all men as soon as they begin to reflect, without need for us to contemplate concrete instances of them. All other knowledge was supposed to be derived from these principles by syllogistic reasoning. Locke, like Bacon and Descartes, strongly opposed this view, and this is the essential point of his rather wearisome polemic against innate ideas and principles. According to him, we come to recognize general principles only by reflecting on particular instances of them which have been presented to our attention by sensation or introspection. We may then come to see that they are necessary and self-evident. But such general principles are usually too abstract and trivial to be of much use. Much of our reasoning consists in seeing the necessary connexions between various links in a chain of singular propositions, instead of arguing syllogistically from abstract major premises.

The question then arises: 'What sort of things can we know, and about what sort of things can we have only belief or opinion?' According to Locke, much the greatest part of our knowledge is about what he calls 'the agreements and disagreements of ideas'. Such knowledge consists in seeing that the presence of a certain attribute in anything would entail or exclude the presence of a certain other attribute either in that thing or in something else related to it in a certain specific way. Thus we can see that anything that had shape would have to be extended. And we can see that if anything were a husband something else would have to be a female. Some such knowledge is called 'trifling' by Locke, e.g. the knowledge that a negro must be black. But much of it is what he calls 'instructive', i.e. it is knowledge of facts which are not analytically contained in the definitions of their terms. Lastly, if the knowledge is to be what Locke calls 'real', we must know that it is about at least possible existents. The knowledge that a round square would be round is not only trifling, but also unreal. Arithmetic, algebra, and geometry are the great examples of knowledge which is at once instructive and real. Locke thought that ethics might be developed into such a science too.

About existent substances we have very little genuine knowledge. Each of us is directly acquainted with his own mind, and therefore has intuitive knowledge of the existence of one mental substance. And from the contingency of our own existence we can infer that we depend on an Existent whose existence is necessary. Thus we have demonstrative knowledge of the existence of God, and of certain facts about him.

We have not genuine knowledge about the existence of any particular material substance. We have ideas of sensation, including the experiences of dreams, imagery, and hallucination, as well as those of normal waking life. Locke does not doubt that these are caused by the action of material substances on our minds. But we are not acquainted with any material substance, as each of us is with his own mind; and we cannot infer with certainty from the occurrence of any sensation or group of sensations to the present existence of such and such a material substance in such and such a place, still less can we demonstrate the continued existence of a particular material substance when the sensations which led us to believe in its present existence are no longer occurring. There are, of course, various tests which we can and do use to distinguish between dreams or hallucinations and veridical sense-perceptions. But neither severally nor collectively are they demonstrative; though in some cases we may be justified in having so strong a conviction that, in ordinary loose phraseology, it would be called 'knowledge' of the present existence of a certain material substance.

We have a natural tendency to ascribe all the qualities of which we become aware by sensation to material substances.

This, on Locke's view, is partly justified and partly mistaken. Shape, size, motion, and solidity really do belong to the material causes of our sensations. But colour, taste, smell, etc., do not; though they are signs of certain powers or dispositions in material things. These powers are connected with the minute structure and the molecular movements of the parts of material substances.

Physics and all the natural sciences are doomed for ever to remain at the level of probable opinion. Certain perceptible qualities have been found invariably to accompany each other in our experience, e.g. a certain density, a certain colour, and a certain melting-point. The first and crudest stage of science is to take note of these hitherto unbroken conjunctions and to assert that they are instances of universal connexions. This is not knowledge, for we can see no trace of necessity, as we can in the connexion between shape and extension. At a more advanced stage the perceptible qualities are correlated with hypothetical minute structure and internal movements, their conjunctions with each other are explained, and hitherto unobserved conjunctions are inferred and verified. But we are still as far as ever from knowledge, in Locke's sense of the term. For it is an utterly unintelligible brute fact that such and such minute structure and motions should be correlated with such and such a perceptible quality, e.g. with a blue colour or an ammoniacal smell.

Locke finds it self-evident that every event must be a change in some substance, and that every change must be initiated by the active power of some agent. But he confesses that we have no very clear ideas of substance or of causation. The fundamental active power of a mind is the power of initiating changes in itself and in the material world by volition. The fundamental active power of matter is that of communicating motion to other matter by impact. Yet both transactions, when reflected upon, are found to be equally complete mysteries in which the mind cannot get that satisfaction which it finds in contemplating the luminous necessities of geometry or algebra.

Unlike Descartes, Locke can see no intrinsic impossibility in one and the same substance having both material and mental characteristics. He thinks he can show that God must be purely mental, but he leaves it an open question whether men may not be material substances which God has endowed with the mental powers of cognition and conation.

On the question of voluntary decision Locke was a determinist. He held a rather unusual form of the doctrine of Psychological Hedonism. Every decision is completely determined by 'the most pressing present uneasiness'. This uneasiness may be due to present pain, in which case its intensity will be proportional to that of the pain. But it may be due to the absence of some contemplated good, and in that case it may not be proportional to the admitted magnitude of the missing good. A drunkard may recognize that prosperity is a much better thing than a glass of brandy, but the present uneasiness due to the lack of the former may be less intense than that due to the lack of the latter. The only measure of the goodness of a contemplated state of affairs is the nett balance of pleasure which it would give to one if it were actualized; but we may feel more uneasiness at the absence of what we believe to be a less nett pleasure than at the absence of what we believe to be a greater one.

These are the main points in Locke's theory, as expounded in the *Essay on Human Understanding*. There are three comments to be made. (1) It seems plausible and modest to say that we ought to determine the powers and limitations of the human mind before embarking on metaphysical inquiries for which it is perhaps unfitted. But unless we start with *some* ontological premisses about the nature of our minds and of the rest of the world and about the relations between the two, the epistemological problem is quite indeterminate. And the kind of answer which can reasonably be given to it will vary with the ontological premisses which we assume. (2) In Locke's day it seemed reasonable to ask metaphysicians to desist from their labours until epistemology had completed its task and marked out the region in which they could profitably work. For metaphysics was old and disillusioned, whilst epistemology was young and hopeful. But, after the efforts of 250 years, we know that there is no better prospect of agreement in epistemology than there is in metaphysics. (3) Locke's philosophy held in solution many different and incompatible elements, which have since been separated by the labours of his successors. No one of them, when taken by itself and carried to its logical conclusion, is as plausible as the confused mixture of them all. And the original mixture is plausible only so long as we fail to distinguish its components and to notice their mutual incompatibility.

It is now time to return to the history of Locke's life. One of the most valuable and unpopular acts of the Whig Government was to recall the silver money then circulating in England, which had been greatly debased by clipping, and to issue new coins with milled edges in place of it. This was equivalent to a process of deflation, and it involved certain hardships which were unscrupulously exploited by the opposition. It was Locke who first pointed out the dangers of inflation due to debased coinage in tracts which he published in 1691 and 1695. These writings on currency exercised a considerable influence, and the government acted on Locke's advice about the practical details of the re-coinage.

In his later years Locke found that the smoke of London disagreed with him, and he lived mostly at a country house called Oates, near Harlow, in Essex, belonging to Sir Francis Masham. Lady Masham was a daughter of Cudworth, the Cambridge Platonist, and she was herself a theologian of some distinction. Locke had known her before he went to Holland, and she was a very kind friend to him in his later years. He became a member of the family, but insisted on paying a weekly sum for the board and lodging of himself and his servant. He lived at Oates from 1691 to the end of his life. He seems to have been very happy there, and to have received frequent visits from friends, such as his old pupil, Shaftesbury's grandson, Molyneux, Newton, and Anthony Collins, a neighbouring squire who acquired some reputation later as a Deist.

At Oates Locke was always busy writing and thinking. In 1693 he published his *Thoughts on the Education of Children*, which he had written down for his old Somersetshire friend, Edward Clarke of Chipley. This is an extremely sensible and delightful book. Locke, unlike most of his contemporaries, thought that beating should be used only as a last resort. And he is strongly of the opinion that, when the regrettable necessity for it has arisen, it should be administered by the tutor in presence of the father, and not by the father himself. By this means the child will continue to respect his father as the source of justice and authority without beginning to hate him as the inflicter of pain.

Any hatred that may be generated will be directed to the tutor, and it is part of his professional duty to bear it. Locke is very anxious that fathers should treat their sons as reasonable beings and as younger friends at the earliest possible moment. So soon as a boy grows out of his first childhood his father should consult him on small matters about which he is likely to have adequate knowledge, such as the state of the tennis lawn and the best way to cure the defects in the wireless set.

As might be expected, Locke's medical advice is extremely sensible. Children should early be accustomed to getting their feet wet. If we were properly brought up, wet feet would be no more harmful than wet hands are now. Nor is Locke too fastidious to treat the homeliest details of personal hygiene. The importance of acquiring regular habits in what he delicately terms 'paying court to Madam Cloacina' is insisted upon, and the reasons for fixing the hour after breakfast for this rite are discussed at considerable length. It will be seen then that, although Locke lived too early to share in our clean wholesome fun about the Œdipus complex and infantile anal-erotic fixations, he did not ignore the facts on which these amusing fantasies are founded.

One odd opinion remains to be noted. Locke deliberately concludes that it is on the whole better for a boy to be educated at home by a tutor, if his parents can afford it, than to be sent away to school. Whilst most of us would, I suppose, heartily disagree with this opinion, it is fair to remark that in Locke's day public schools were certainly much worse, and upper middle-class homes were probably much better, than they are now. As public schools have improved they have naturally grown more expensive. At the same time the upper middle-classes have become relatively poorer, and so this most desirable section of the English nation has been forced to limit its families to a most undesirable extent. Now many of the disadvantages of home education are mitigated if one is a member of a large family of brothers and sisters, living in a spacious house and grounds in the country, with parents who are wholesomely busy in the house and on the estate, and with other such families within easy walking or riding distance. If one could get anything like a decent tutor, I have little doubt that it would have been far better to be educated in such a home than to be pitched into the squalid brutality and semi-starvation of a seventeenth or eighteenth century public school.

I have illustrated the widespread popularity of Locke's *Essay* in eighteenth-century England by reference to Fielding's novels. I must now mention that the *Thoughts on Education* plays a prominent part in Richardson's novel *Pamela*. Most of my readers will remember how skilfully that humble and incorrigibly virtuous heroine piloted the magnificent but wayward Mr. B. past the shallows of seduction and the rapids of rape into the haven of holy matrimony, and how she settled down at the end of Volume II as a great lady of the county. If any of them have persevered to the fourth volume, they will have discovered that Mr. B., in the early years of their son Billy, gave Pamela a copy of Mr. Locke's book on education to read while he was away. Pamela took him at his word, and filled seven long and, it must be confessed, extremely boring letters to him with an elaborate exposition and criticism of Mr. Locke's views. The novel-readers of the eighteenth century seem to have swallowed this with the avidity with which their descendants devour the works of Mr. Edgar Wallace or Mr. P. G. Wodehouse. We can scarcely wonder that such men conquered India, lost America, and broke Napoleon.

In 1695 Locke published a treatise on the *Reasonableness of Christianity*. Locke was an absolutely sincere Protestant Christian. He held, as we have seen, that the existence of God can be demonstrated apart from revelation, and he had no doubt that the Bible contains a revelation of God's nature and intentions and about our duties to him and to each other which we could not have learnt in any other way. But he realized that the Bible has to be interpreted by men to the best of their ability, and he denied that the interpretation put upon difficult passages by any man or institution could be accepted as infallible. There is a kernel of doctrine which is quite plain and is accepted by practically all Christians. This is sufficient for salvation. All further elaborations are matters of more or less probable opinion, on which men will always differ and on which they had better agree to differ. Locke and his master, William III, both wished to make the Church of England as comprehensive as possible, and to bring into it all English Christians but Roman Catholics and the wildest kind of Protant dissenters. Unfortunately most men are not Lockes and are not Williams; they cannot be happy, and perhaps they cannot be spiritually healthy, without believing nonsense with a degree of passionate conviction proportional to the lack of evidence for it. And they cannot be content without persecuting other people who disagree with them.

Experience seems to show that, in the prolonged absence of such passionate superstitions, mankind tends to stagnate. The scheme of comprehension failed at the time, through the opposition of high-flying Anglicans and high-flying Puritans. And when in practice it seemed to be almost realized in England by the middle of the eighteenth century, the result was a kind of spiritual deadness which, though we might perhaps welcome it as a temporary respite from our present dangers and excitements, is not a satisfactory permanent condition for the human spirit.

Much of Locke's energies at Oates were occupied in writing answers to controversialists who had attacked his published works. His most elaborate controversy was with Stillingfleet, Bishop of Worcester. Stillingfleet was primarily concerned to defend the doctrine of the Trinity against certain Unitarian writers who had claimed Locke as a supporter, and this led him to attack many of Locke's philosophical doctrines. The discussion was ended by Stillingfleet's death. Locke was much the abler controversialist of the two, but it may be doubted whether the bishop had not a stronger case than appears from his writings.

In 1695 Locke was appointed a Commissioner of Trade and Plantations at a salary of £1,000 a year. He performed his duties with great skill and conscientiousness, but they necessitated frequent and prolonged visits to London, which became more and more trying to him, and so he resigned in 1700. King William was very loth to accept his resignation, and pressed him to continue to hold the office without personally attending the meetings of the Board. But Locke felt that he could not honestly continue to draw a large salary after he had ceased to be able to perform his duties, a sentiment which the King must have found highly surprising in one of his English servants.

Locke now lived almost continuously at Oates. He was an active man, so far as his health would permit. He liked gardening and walking, but latterly he could not walk very far because of his asthma. He could still occasionally ride a horse, and, when this was too much for him, he would go for a drive after dinner in a chaise. He was very fond of company, and particularly liked talking to intelligent children. Locke had the happy gift of conversing easily and naturally with men of very different levels of intellect and culture. He would encourage people to talk about their own trades or professions, thus putting them at their ease and acquiring for himself a wealth of information about the details of practical life. In his earlier years his temper had been somewhat choleric, but, as he grew older he had it in almost perfect control. In an intemperate age he was very temperate in his habits, and he ascribed to this the preservation of his eyesight which he kept intact to the end.

In the summer of 1704 his strength began to fail, and he prepared himself to quit this life in a spirit of calm thankfulness for the blessings which he had enjoyed and in the firm hope of a happy immortality. He died in his study, where Lady Masham had been reading the Psalms to him, on 28th October 1704, in the seventy-third year of his age. He is buried in the churchyard of High Lever in Essex, and a characteristically modest Latin inscription, composed by himself, was placed against the church wall. He had lived to see the triumph of most of the causes for which he had fought; he had combined with singular success the active and the contemplative life, winning the respect of the learned world and the gratitude of a great king whose favours were never lightly granted; his latter years had been spent in peace, prosperity, and domestic happiness; and his influence was destined to spread in ever-widening circles throughout the century which was just beginning.

HENRY SIDGWICK

HENRY SIDGWICK was born on 31st May 1838, at Skipton. He was the third son and fourth child of Rev. William Sidgwick and Mary Crofts. There is a family tradition that the Sidgwicks came originally from Dent on the borders of Yorkshire, Lancashire, and Westmorland. Certainly there is a hamlet in Westmorland called 'Sedgwick'. The *Dictionary of English Place Names* derives this name from 'Siggis Wick', i.e. the dairy farm of a Norse settler called 'Siggi'. It is also certain that there have been 'Sedgwicks' or 'Sidgwicks' living and farming around Dent for at least four centuries. This branch of the family changed the 'i' into an 'e' about 1745. It happened that their most distinguished representative, Adam Sedgwick, was a Fellow of Trinity and Professor of Geology in Cambridge when Henry Sidgwick entered the college and for many years afterwards. He was a famous Cambridge character and died in January 1873 at the age of eighty-seven, being then as Henry Sidgwick remarks, 'by nearly *thirty* years the oldest man in College'. Beyond these two facts nothing is known for certain on this matter. Henry Sidgwick's uncle, Raikes of Skipton, who was interested in the family tree, could not trace the Skipton Sidgwicks with any confidence beyond Henry's great-great-grandfather, a Leeds tobacconist known as 'Honest James'. Henry bore this genealogical cross with equanimity, saying 'So we must *begin* with Tobacco. One might start from a worse thing.' With Henry's grandfather, William Sidgwick, we are on firm ground. He came from Leeds to Skipton in 1784 and owned a cotton-spinning mill worked by water-power in the grounds behind the castle. In winter he dwelled in the gatehouse of the castle, but he also had a house called *Stone Gappe* in the country a few miles away. Four of his five sons stayed at Skipton in the business; but the other son, William, destined to become a clergyman and the father of Henry, was sent to Trinity College, Cambridge, where he graduated in 1829.

Henry Sidgwick's mother, Mary Crofts, came from the East Riding of Yorkshire. She had been left an orphan with her three brothers and two sisters at an early age, and they were brought up by their uncle, Rev. William Carr, who was the fourth in succession of his family to hold the living of Bolton Abbey.

William Sidgwick and Mary Crofts were married in 1833. After holding cures at Rampside and Barnborough, William was appointed headmaster of Skipton grammar-school in 1836. He died in that office in 1841 when Henry was three years old. His widow survived him by thirty-eight years, dying on 11th January 1879. It is evident from her portrait, her correspondence with Henry, and the efficient way in which she brought up her young family, that she was a woman of strong character, keen intelligence, and considerable culture. She taught Henry Latin from the age of six to that of ten, when he began to go to school. About this time he developed the slight stammer which he never quite lost.

Mrs. Sidgwick had settled at Redland, now a suburb of Bristol, in 1844, and Henry's first school was one at Bristol called 'Bishop's College'. In 1850 he joined his elder brother at a school at Blackheath, near London, kept by Rev. H. Dale. At that time and for many years afterwards Blackheath was the only place in England at which the game of golf was regularly played. Though Henry did not become a devotee of it, he came near to being a martyr to it; for he was almost killed by an accidental blow from a golf-club with which another boy was driving.

The next scene in Sidgwick's education introduces on the stage a character who was to play an important part in his early life. This is Edward White Benson, who married Sidgwick's sister in 1859 and became successively headmaster of Wellington, Bishop of Truro, and eventually Archbishop of Canterbury. He was a cousin of Sidgwick's father, and had been left suddenly and unexpectedly in 1850 with a number of younger brothers and sisters to support. His relatives helped him, and in this connexion he got to know Mrs. Sidgwick. Her husband had been strongly prejudiced against public schools on moral grounds; but Benson, who became a master at Rugby in 1852, persuaded Mrs. Sidgwick that the moral tone of that school at least, with the influence of Dr. Arnold still fresh upon it, was above reproach. Accordingly Henry was sent to Rugby in September 1852. He was at first in Evans's House, but in 1853 Mrs. Sidgwick moved to Rugby and both Henry and Benson lived in her house. During this period Benson exercised a considerable influence over Sidgwick, and this lasted until his second year at Cambridge. It was largely on Benson's advice that Sidgwick followed his father to Trinity College, Cambridge, instead of taking a scholarship at Balliol.

At this time Rugby was producing an extraordinary number of brilliant scholars, who distinguished themselves at Oxford or Cambridge. It was also pervaded by that spirit of high-mindedness and anxious conscientiousness which we now associate rather with college at Winchester. Among Sidgwick's school friends were T. H. Green, Charles Bowen, and H. G. Dakyns. He was destined to criticize severely the philosophy of the first of these. With the last of them he carried on an intimate correspondence throughout his life. His school career was brilliant and happy. Though not specially good at games, he had no dislike for them. He was already an omnivorous reader, and was at that time a very keen amateur dramatist and actor.

In October 1855 Sidgwick entered Trinity College, Cambridge. He combined, as was then inevitable, the study of mathematics and classics. He was a competent mathematician, being classed as thirty-third Wrangler in the tripos of 1859; but his career in classics was highly distinguished. His successive undergraduate years were marked by the Second Bell Prize in 1856, the Craven Scholarship in 1857, and the Sir William Browne's Prize for Greek and Latin Epigrams in 1858. They culminated in a first class in the classical tripos and the First Chancellor's Medal in 1859. In the same year he was elected to a fellowship at Trinity.

At Oxford and Cambridge the friends whom a man makes as an undergraduate and the intimate talks that he has with them are at least as important a factor in his education as the studies which he pursues for his degree. Sidgwick considered that his election, in his second year, to the society called *The Apostles* had more effect on his intellectual life than any one thing that happened to him afterwards. The society used to meet in the rooms of one or other of its members at 8.30 on Saturdays, and, after consuming anchovies on toast, it would discuss some subject introduced by the host for the evening. The period from 1855 to 1875 was one of immense activity in the realms of ideas and of practice. The traditional view of the Jewish and Christian scriptures was being undermined by the writings of Strauss and Baur and Renan; and the doctrine of evolution was being established in biology by experts like Darwin and Huxley, and was being exploited by enthusiastic amateurs like Herbert Spencer as the key which was to unlock all the problems of the universe. So intelligent, sensitive, and cultivated young men, such as the Cambridge Apostles, breathed an atmosphere of intellectual oxygen which has seldom existed before or since.

In a fragment of autobiography which Sidgwick dictated in the last fortnight of his life he describes the decade from 1859 to 1869 as 'years of storm and stress as regards my religious convictions and ecclesiastical relations'. Outwardly he was leading the normal life of a conscientious young don, spending his Long Vacations either reading in Cambridge or staying in Germany learning the language and studying under certain German professors. He had not yet decided to remain at Cambridge. In 1861 Temple, then headmaster of Rugby, offered him a mastership at that school. He accepted this at first, but then altered his mind and declined on the ground that his real vocation was study and not teaching. In 1862 he tells his friend Dakyns that he is still hesitating between the Bar and Cambridge.

From 1862 to 1865 he made a very serious study of Hebrew and Arabic, culminating during the Long Vacation of 1864, which he spent at Göttingen in the house of Professor Benfey, a Sanscrit scholar who had held a post at Rugby in Arnold's time. He placed himself under the tuition of Ewald and Wüstenfeld, and records the extreme generosity of these scholars, who gave him much of their time and refused to take any payment. I think it is fairly plain, from his letters to Dakyns at the time, that Sidgwick, like other young English dons who have spent Long Vacations in German families, formed a mild romantic attachment for one of the daughters of his host. However this may be, he acquired and ever afterwards retained a great love and admiration for the German people and for the life which was lived in Germany university circles before the war of 1870. He says in 1864, 'If anything were to drive me away from England, it would only be a half-banishment so long as I had Germany to fall back upon.' And again, 'The Germans seem to have attained the *end* of civilization, i.e. intellectual and æsthetic development, without the usual concomitant disadvantages of civilization, viz. luxury and ceremony.'

Sidgwick's reason for making this intensive study of Semitic languages was undoubtedly in order to fit himself to understand the religion and criticize the literature of the Old Testament. By 1865 the evolution of his religious opinions had reached a point at which this had ceased to seem very important to him. He once more took private pupils in classics, and he tried to make himself so far as possible financially independent of his fellowship and his assistant tutorship at Trinity, foreseeing that he was likely soon to find himself obliged on conscientious grounds to resign these offices.

In 1865 he began his official connexion with what in Cambridge is called 'Moral Science' and in other places 'Philosophy'. He examined in the Moral Sciences Tripos in November 1865 and again in 1866, and he spent the whole of the Long Vacation of the former year in reading philosophical works to prepare himself for the task. In 1867 it was arranged that he should lecture in Moral Science for Trinity College.

By 1869 the difficulty of conscience with which he had been wrestling for some years past came to a head. In those days fellows of colleges had to declare themselves to be members of the Church of England. Sidgwick had decided that he no longer fulfilled this condition literally enough to allow him to hold his fellowship with honesty. He therefore resigned it and his assistant tutorship in June 1869. He records with appreciation the kindness and understanding with which the Master and Fellows of the College treated him at this crisis of his career. They appointed him College Lecturer in Moral Science at a salary of £200 a year. He was therefore able to continue his teaching work, but the step which he had felt bound to take had very seriously diminished his income. In 1864 he had told his mother that he had already saved £1,700 and that he expected to put by £400 a year so long as he stayed in Cambridge. But as late as 1873 he tells his friend Tawney that he is earning only about £300 a year from all sources.

When Sidgwick first came to Cambridge the Knightbridge Professorship of Moral Philosophy was held by John Grote, a very able and original thinker whose writings have received less attention than they deserve. Grote died in 1866, and at that time Sidgwick was only twenty-nine. He was then much more interested in classics and Semitic languages than in moral philosophy, and he did not think of putting in for the chair. Frederic Dennison Maurice was appointed, and he held the office until his death in 1872. This time Sidgwick, after a good deal of hesitation, decided to stand for the chair on finding that Hutchison Stirling, who first introduced Hegelianism into England, was not, as he had expected, a candidate for it. The electors chose neither Sidgwick nor any of the other competitors whom he had thought to be strong rivals. The sound evangelical reputation of Rev. T. R. Birks, whose name had not then and has not since occupied an outstanding position in the roll of philosophers, won their suffrages. Sidgwick, in writing to his mother, consoled her and himself with the reflexions which sons usually make to their mothers on such occasions. But it is plain from his letters to other persons that he was not unreasonably annoyed. At first he thought that the electors had deliberately intended to express their contempt for Moral Science and their conviction that it should be subordinated to Theology. Later inquiries showed him that he had over-rated their malice and underrated their stupidity, and that they had really been under the impression that they were choosing the best moral philosopher available. Sidgwick finally dismissed the incident in a letter to Frederick Myers with the charitable remark, 'Birks is a man of ability and has a work on Ethics on his desk.' So far as I am aware it remained there.

The year 1875 was an important one for Sidgwick, and marked the end of this period of storm and stress. In October Trinity College appointed him Prælector in Moral Philosophy. This gave him once more a fixed position; it increased his income by £250 a year; and it was an unmistakable sign that his work and his character were appreciated by his colleagues.

For some time now Sidgwick had been actively investigating the phenomena of Spiritualism. I shall consider his work in in Psychical Research in more detail later; at present the important fact about it is that it led to his marriage. Arthur Balfour, who had been a pupil and friend of Sidgwick at Trinity, and Lord Rayleigh, who had married one of Balfour's sisters, were associated with Sidgwick in these investigations. Sidgwick met his future wife, Eleanor Mildred Balfour, at the houses of her brother and her brother-in-law, and they collaborated in experiments with mediums. They were both of them also keenly interested in the higher education of women, and they had worked together in connexion with Newnham Hall, the institution from which Newnham College developed. They became engaged in December 1875 and they were married on 4th April 1876. Mrs. Sidgwick appears to me to have been, not only the ablest *woman*, but one of the ablest *persons*, in England during her lifetime. I did not have the privilege of meeting her until she was over eighty, when I became a fellow member with her of the Council of the Society for Psychical Research. Even then she seemed to me to stand head and shoulders above the rest of us. I am not competent to speak with any authority of the great work which she did, in collaboration with her husband, for Newnham College. But I say without hesitation that her work in psychical research was of absolutely first-rate importance. The numerous and elaborate papers which she contributed to the S.P.R. *Proceedings* are masterpieces of clear statement, sound reasoning, and balanced judgment, which must be regarded as classics in this most difficult field of inquiry. She survived her husband for many years, dying in February 1936 shortly before her ninety-first birthday. It would be hard to conceive of two people more ideally fitted to each other than Henry Sidgwick and Nora Balfour.

The Sidgwicks built a house in Cambridge, called Hillside; and the early years of their marriage were rendered particularly happy by the presence in Trinity of three of Mrs. Sidgwick's brothers and, somewhat later, of her brother-in-law, Lord Rayleigh, who succeeded Clerk Maxwell as Cavendish Professor of Physics.

During the early eighteen-seventies Sidgwick was busy thinking out and writing down the great work on Ethics which is his most important contribution to philosophy. It was accepted, under the title of *The Methods of Ethics*, by Macmillan in the summer of 1874 and published in December. The proof-sheets were sent by the publishers to John Morley, and his favourable comments greatly consoled Sidgwick, who had become very depressed and diffident over the work before he completed it for the press. He suspected that he was robbing Macmillan, who had consented to publish it on a half-profit basis. Actually it has run into six editions. It has been translated into Japanese and widely read in Japan, without producing any markedly chastening effect on the moral tone of that exuberant country.

In 1877 Sidgwick wrote an elaborate article for the *Encyclopædia Britannica*, which afterwards appeared in book-form as *Outlines of the History of Ethics for English Readers*. It soon became a standard work, and has run into five editions. During this year his mother's health broke down. She took a turn for the worse in the latter part of 1878 and died early in the following year. She had left Rugby some years before and had been living at Oxford where her son William was a don.

For many years past Sidgwick had been labouring to further the higher education of women at Cambridge, and in this task his wife joined him with enthusiasm. In October 1875 such progress had been made that a Hall of Residence, called *Newnham Hall*, had been built and opened for thirty students. The number of women students increased so much that in 1880 a second Hall, now called *Sidgwick Hall*, was built close to the first. Sidgwick and his wife let their house Hillside and temporarily took up residence in this new Hall in October 1880.

In 1881, to his great joy, Sidgwick was made an honorary fellow of Trinity, thus becoming once more and without conditions a member of the foundation from which he had felt obliged to resign in 1869. About this time Birks, the Knightbridge Professor, became paralysed, and the Vice-Chancellor had to appoint a deputy. He very strangely ignored Sidgwick and appointed the latter's pupil Cunningham. This seemed to be a deliberate slight, and Sidgwick inferred that he would again be passed over when the chair should become vacant. However, in 1882 and 1883 he did act as deputy for Birks; and, when the latter died in July 1883, Sidgwick stood, though with no great enthusiasm, and was elected to the Knightbridge

Professorship. He held this office until within a few months of his death. In those days politics and economics formed part of the curriculum for the Moral Sciences Tripos; and Sidgwick was hard at work during the early eighties writing his treatise on *Political Economy* which was first published in 1883 and ran into three editions in the course of the next twenty years.

From about 1870 onwards there had been a strong movement, both in Oxford and Cambridge, towards making radical changes in the University, the individual colleges, and the relations of former to the latter. Sidgwick held strong and definite views on the alterations which were desirable, and he played a very prominent part in this agitation. Eventually in 1876 Lord Salisbury's government set up a statutory commission for the two universities on the lines desired by Sidgwick and his friends. In the summer of 1877 Sidgwick travelled in Germany in order to study the merits and defects of the German university system. By the end of that year he had written a very elaborate memorial in answer to the questions put by the commissioners. The new statutes came into force in 1882, and a body called the *General Board of Studies* was constituted and entrusted with the duty of carrying out in detail the policy laid down by the commission. Sidgwick joined this board in November 1882 as representative of the Special Board of Moral Science, and served on it until the end of 1889.

The General Board had the extremely difficult and delicate task of extending and reorganizing the teaching of the University out of moneys to be raised by taxing the revenues of the individual colleges. It happened that the scheme came into force just at the time when the colleges were most deeply submerged under the wave of agricultural depression which engulfed England in the last quarter of the nineteenth century. The problem of allocating money to competing subjects, which would in any case have been an embarrassing one, was enormously complicated by the consequent deficiency in the total sum available for division. Sidgwick wrestled with the financial question and devised a very complex and ingenious scheme of monetary concessions to the more hardly hit colleges. It had to be dropped, however, because ten out of the seventeen colleges affected by it declined to make the alterations in their statutes which it would have entailed.

Sidgwick did not confine himself to giving his time and thought to the financial troubles of the university. He contributed most liberally out of his own pocket. From 1884 to 1888 he paid £300 a year out of his professorial stipend in order to establish a Readership in Law for F. W. Maitland. During the same period he provided £200 a year towards the expenses of teaching Indian Civil Service students at Cambridge. In 1889 to 1890 he gave £1,500 towards buildings for the department of Physiology. And from 1897 until his death he supplied £200 a year from his stipend towards the new professorship of Mental Philosophy and Logic to which James Ward had been appointed.

The general educational policy which Sidgwick advocated for the university was as follows. In the first place, he was anxious to open it to as many different kinds of student as possible. For this reason he contended, not only for the admission of women, but also for the abolition of compulsory Greek in the entrance examination, for the development of technical subjects, such as engineering, and for undertaking the professional training of young men who had passed into the Civil Service and were preparing to go out to India. Secondly, he wanted university and college teaching to be much more elaborately organized and co-ordinated than they had ever been before.

On the whole Sidgwick's work on the General Board seems to have given little satisfaction either to himself or to others. Few of his colleagues whole-heartedly shared his views; he led them into controversies in which they engaged with reluctance and were defeated with relief; and the general impression seems to have been that the Board was meddlesome without being effective. The last straw was the candid criticism to which he was subjected by Alfred Marshall, who was appointed Professor of Political Economy in 1884, and thus automatically became a member of the Special Board of Moral Science. The story is amusing and characteristic enough of both parties to be worth relating here.

Marshall was elected on 13th December 1884. He lost no time in tactical manœuvres; for, on 17th December, having heard Sidgwick's views, as Chairman of the Special Board, on the nature of the lectures required in Economics, he called on the latter and delivered a terrific denunciation. In this he expressed the opinion that Sidgwick was a petty tyrant who wished to regulate, trammel, and hamper a man who knew more about the subject than himself. It was evidently one of those occasions on which plain speaking ceases to be a duty and becomes a positive pleasure. Sidgwick tried to explain his position, and the two men parted friends. But on 23rd December Marshall returned to the attack in a long and impressive letter in which he analysed Sidgwick's academic career; pronounced it to have been a failure; ascribed this to Sidgwick's mania for over-regulation; and amiably contrasted T. H. Green's lectures, crowded with enthusiastic listeners from all departments of Oxford life, with Sidgwick's handful of specialist undergraduates assiduously taking down notes for the Moral Sciences Tripos. Finally, when Marshall gave his inaugural lecture in February 1885 he courteously but definitely pronounced against the Sidgwickian policy of university organization.

Marshall was an old friend, and Sidgwick respected his opinions. In his *Journal* for 24th February 1885, he wrote: 'I must abandon my efforts. Too many forces are against me—Westcott, Seeley and now Marshall.' Sidgwick's personal response to the home-thrusts of this very candid friend is interesting. He proceeded to write down for himself his own reflections on Marshall's strictures. Referring to the unfavourable comparison with T. H. Green, he writes: 'I would not if I could, and I could not if I would, make philosophy—my philosophy—popular.' Regarding his alleged mania for over-regulation, he writes: 'I don't desire to have my own way or to coerce others. But I have a great desire in all social relations for definite understandings. Not knowing what road is best for humanity, I want all roads that claim to be roads to be well made and hedged in.' This incident illustrates vividly the old Cambridge story that, when it was proposed to separate Economics from Moral Science and to establish a Special Board of Economics, one moral scientist declared that he would certainly vote for the proposal on the ground that 'it would be nice to let Marshall have a little Hell of his own'.

In 1885 Sidgwick was invited, and declined, to stand as Liberal candidate for one of the Cambridgeshire divisions. He disliked intensely the Liberal practice of truckling to agrarian disorder in Ireland, though he had no confidence that the English electorate would support a firmer policy for an adequate period. He broke off his holiday in Davos in 1886 to come back and vote for the Conservatives in the General Election of that year.

In October 1886 W. H. Thompson, the Master of Trinity, died. Certain members of the college were anxious that Sidgwick should be made Master. The appointment is in the gift of the Crown. Sidgwick was not at all keen on the office, which is mainly honorific and ceremonial. The Crown appointed his old friend and contemporary, Dr. H. M. Butler, who held the mastership for many years after Sidgwick's death.

In November 1890 Sidgwick was elected to what is called in Cambridge the *Council of the Senate*. This committee had a very great influence in moulding university policy and embodying general principles in concrete proposals. Here Sidgwick soon came to occupy an outstanding position. He had a remarkable power of seeing the good points in opposed suggestions and in drafting compromises which combined and synthesized them.

In March 1892 Mrs. Sidgwick accepted the principalship of Newnham College on the death of Miss Clough. A new wing had been added to the building, and, when it was completed in December 1893, the Sidgwicks finally left their house Hillside and moved into it. They had pleasant rooms overlooking the college garden. In his later years Sidgwick had grown very fond of gardens and flowers, in particular he loved masses of yellow blossoms. He used to walk about meditating in this garden, stroking his beard on the underside and holding it up against his mouth, which was a characteristic gesture of his.

During the eighteen-nineties Sidgwick lost many of his old and intimate friends by death. John Addington Symonds, whom he first met in 1867 and with whom he had constantly corresponded and exchanged visits, died at Rome in April 1893. Roden Noel, with whom he corresponded on literature and metaphysics, and whose poetry he highly appreciated, died suddenly in May 1894 while on a journey. In January 1895 his friend and Cambridge colleague, J. R. Seeley died. And in October 1896 he lost his brother-in-law and lifelong friend Benson, the Archbishop of Canterbury.

Sidgwick himself had been remarkably free from serious illness throughout his life, though he had never been a robust man and had suffered from minor ailments which taken together must have caused him much discomfort. In the summer months he was a martyr to hay-fever. In his second year at Cambridge he had had a prolonged and serious attack of dyspepsia, and this left him liable to recurrent bouts of indigestion. During the rest of his life he had suffered from severe attacks of depression accompanied by sleeplessness. In later years he made strenuous efforts to conceal his depression from others; and he found that this effort, in which he largely succeeded, was beneficial to himself. But the sleeplessness remained, and, in a letter to Sully, the psychologist, in 1896, he says that he is liable to get as little as five and a half, four and a half, or even three and a half hours of sleep in a night. He would never take drugs to relieve sleeplessness, nor would he sit up and read. He found it best to lie still and meditate, thus getting rest if he could not get sleep.

In February 1900 he began to be seriously unwell. In May he consulted Mr. Allingham, an eminent London surgeon, and learned that he was suffering from an internal cancer which must be operated on without delay and could not be permanently cured. For the first fortnight he told no one but his wife. He still felt full of intellectual vigour, and he began to arrange his unpublished papers. He directed that James Ward should take charge of those on philosophy and Miss Constance Jones of those on ethics, that Dr. J. N. Keynes should bring out the third edition of his *Political Economy*, and that Mrs. Sidgwick should get expert advice about his *Development of European Polity* and publish it if thought fit. Ward published a collection of his philosophical papers in 1905 under the title *The Philosophy of Kant and other Philosophical Lectures and Essays*. Miss Jones published his *Lectures on the Ethics of Green, Spencer, and Martineau* in 1902. And Mrs. Sidgwick published his *Development of European Polity* in 1903.

On 19th May he went to Oxford and read a paper to the Oxford Philosophical Society criticizing the metaphysics of T. H. Green. He was in brilliant form at the subsequent discussion; and no one but his brother Arthur, to whom he had told the facts in the morning, suspected that they were listening to a man under sentence of death. During the next week he informed his most intimate friends, such as Dakyns, G. O. Trevelyan, and Frederick Myers. On the 25th he presided at a meeting of the Synthetic Society in London at which his brother-in-law, Arthur Balfour, read a paper on *Prayer*. On the 27th he was the life and soul of a luncheon-party at Frederic Myers's house, collected to meet Myers's brother, Ernest, who had been intending to stay with the Sidgwicks. After lunch conversation turned on the metre of Swinburne's *Super Flumina Babylonis*; and Sidgwick, who was an exquisite reader and reciter of English verse, repeated the poem, which ends with the lines:

> Where the light of the life of him is on all past things
> Death only dies.

A fellow-guest, who knew that the speaker was a doomed man, wrote to Myers afterwards, saying: 'I think that the sound of his voice and the light on his face will be before me when the call comes for me; and I shall be grateful for his death as well as for his life.'

On 29th May he resigned his professorship and said good-bye to his friends at Cambridge. On the following day he went to London and spent the night at Arthur Balfour's official residence, 10 Downing Street, where he talked brilliantly at a family dinner with Arthur and Alice Balfour, and Mrs. Sidgwick. The next day he was operated upon by Allingham and he remained in the nursing-home until 3rd July. After a short rest by the sea he went to stay with the Rayleighs at Terling in Essex. There he grew steadily weaker. On 13th August there was a decisive change for the worse and on 28th August he died in his sixty-third year. He left no instructions about his funeral, and he was buried in the village churchyard of Terling in accordance with the rites of the Church of England. Some years earlier, when he had felt that a specifically Christian ceremony would be unsuitable for him, he told his wife that the words most fit to be pronounced over his grave were these: 'Let us commend to the love of God with silent prayer the soul of a sinful man who partly tried to do his duty.'

Having completed my account of the main events in Sidgwick's life, I will now make some remarks, which must necessarily be brief and inadequate, about his religious, ethical, and philosophical perplexities, and about the work in psychical research which these led him to undertake.

HENRY SIDGWICK

It will have been plain from the history of Sidgwick's life that he was a man with a very strong and very efficacious sense of duty. Doubtless sloth, sensual pleasure, and self-indulgence had little attraction for him, and he found no theoretical problem and no great practical difficulty in sacrificing that side of life to the ideals of self-culture and self-development with the associated pleasures of literature, art, travel, and intelligent social intercourse. The real moral problem for him, both in theory and in practice, was the conflict between these latter ideals and certain *prima facie* duties. For the present purpose these may be divided into two classes. In the first class there is the general obligation to do one's utmost to increase the happiness and further the development of other men, even though this be possible only at the expense of one's own culture and development. In the second class there are a number of more special obligations, such as that of strict intellectual honesty, duties to one's parents, to one's country, and so on. The duties in the second class are liable to conflict with each other and with the duty of impartial beneficence, and both are liable to conflict with the ideals of maximum self-culture and self-development.

In the earlier part of Sidgwick's life the main conflict was over the duty of intellectual honesty. In deference to it he felt morally obliged to throw up his fellowship and assistant tutorship. Yet it was certain that this would diminish his opportunities for self-culture and distress his mother, it was quite likely that it would reduce his usefulness to his own generation as a teacher, and it was doubtful whether its remote and collateral effects on himself and on others would outweigh these certain and probable evils. In the later part of his life the main conflict must have been between the obligation to spend time and energy in university politics and administration, in order to further educational and financial policies which he believed to be beneficial to humanity, and the obligation to study and reflect on philosophy, to develop his personality, and to maintain and increase his general culture.

Now we are all, of course, faced with conflicts of this kind. And most of us arrive, by middle life, at some practical compromise, which may be more on the side of self-culture and self-development or more on that of impartial beneficence or more in the direction of certain special obligations, according to our various temperaments and circumstances. But Sidgwick was not only a highly conscientious man. He was also a man with an exceptionally clear head and an intense desire for intellectual precision and coherence. If he had to make a compromise between various conflicting obligations, he wanted to see precisely why this rather than that compromise was the right one for a person of his nature placed in his situation. In order to do this he needed to find a general principle by which the relative moral urgency of conflicting obligations could be estimated, and he required that this principle should be such that any rational being would accept it as self-evident on careful and honest reflection. I think it is fair to say that this was the central philosophical problem for Sidgwick throughout the whole of his adult life.

Now he was dissatisfied with all the solutions of this problem which others had suggested, and he never solved it to his own satisfaction. What he did towards elucidating it may be stated very roughly as follows. (1) He discussed with extreme thoroughness and subtlety what he calls 'The Morality of Common Sense', i.e. the various *prima facie* obligations, such as truth-telling, just-dealing, chastity, etc., which fall into our second class. A decent plain man, if he considers each of these duties separately and in the abstract, will be inclined to feel that each of them is unconditionally binding, from its own nature and without reference to the goodness or badness of its consequences, whether immediate or remote, direct or collateral. But it is easy to put concrete cases to him in which it is impossible to obey some of these obligations without infringing others. Sidgwick tried to see whether the principle of each could be formulated clearly, so as to be a self-evident and unexceptionable axiom, and whether collectively they would form a coherent system. He showed conclusively, I think, that this is impossible. His discussion of the Morality of Common Sense seems to me to be the best work of the kind since Aristotle's.

(2) Sidgwick held that there *are* certain principles of moral obligation which answer these two conditions. But they are all extremely abstract negative axioms, which merely rule out certain obviously unfair ways of distributing such goods as are distributable. Individually they are little more than tautologies

and collectively they do not suffice as premisses from which a concrete system of rights and duties could be deduced.

(3) Subject to these limiting conditions about distribution, it seemed evident to Sidgwick that the duty of beneficence is fundamental and unexceptionable. Each of us, when called upon to act, ought to do that one among the alternatives then open to him which will produce the greatest nett balance of good or the least nett balance of evil in the aggregate of conscious beings throughout all future time and including himself. This may be called the 'Optimific Act'.

(4) Sidgwick held, further, that nothing is intrinsically good or bad except actual experiences, and that the only good-making or bad-making characteristic of an experience is its pleasantness or unpleasantness respectively. He tried to make his readers see this for themselves by analysing carefully the most plausible *prima facie* exceptions to it. We may sum this up by saying that the optimific act for a given agent in a given situation is the 'Most Felicific Act' open to him at the time.

(5) Sidgwick claimed to show in detail that all the special obligations, such as truth-telling, patriotism, etc., which common-sense morality recognizes, can be rationally justified, in so far as they are binding, by reference to the duty of universal beneficence, the negative axioms about distribution, and the special nature, circumstances, and limitations of human beings. Each such duty is a *secondary* principle, commonly but not unconditionally binding. In exceptional circumstances each may break down, and cases are not uncommon in which several of them are relevant and conflict with each other. In all such cases appeal must be made to the *primary* and unconditional duty of impartial beneficence, hedonistically interpreted. This principle, which provides a rational ground for the secondary rules, also accounts for the occasional exceptions to them and supplies a method of solution when two or more of them conflict.

(6) So far, then, Sidgwick has succeeded, to his own satisfaction, in reducing morality to an intellectually coherent system. But he is left with a final conflict for which he can find no solution, viz. between the principle of completely impartial beneficence and that of rational egoism. Each of the two following principles seemed to him to be thoroughly self-evident when he

considered it in isolation. (i) Each man's primary and unconditional duty is to try to maximize the *general* happiness; he ought
to seek his own happiness so far and only so far as it is a part or
a condition of the general happiness. (ii) Each man's primary
and unconditional duty is to try to maximize *his own* happiness;
he ought to seek the happiness of others so far and only so far as
it will contribute in the long run to his own. Now it was perfectly plain to Sidgwick that these two equally self-evident principles would in many cases dictate different courses of action,
even when we make the utmost allowance for the pleasures and
pains of sympathy, of an approving or a guilty conscience, of
public opinion, and of legal rewards and punishments. He
could discover no more ultimate principle from which to deduce
these two and by which to adjudicate between them in cases of
conflict.

The connexion between this crux in Sidgwick's ethical theory
and his interests in psychical research and theology is as follows.
A necessary, though not a sufficient, condition for ensuring that
the course of conduct dictated by the universalistic principle
should coincide with that dictated by the egoistic principle is
that the individual should survive the death of his body. This
would make it at least possible that the happiness which he
sacrifices in this life under the guidance of the former will be so
made up to him in the life to come that he will not in fact have
infringed the latter. But survival alone will not suffice to ensure
this. It will not be ensured unless further the universe (including
this world and the world to come in a single system) is ordered
as a good man of superhuman wisdom and power would have
ordered it. In the West, at any rate, this hypothesis has generally
taken the concrete form that the world has been created and is
governed by an actual person of this kind, viz. God.

In his purely philosophical works Sidgwick treated the survival of the human individual and the existence of God simply
as postulates. If they are false, there is an ineradicable incoherence in a very important department of human thought; if they
are true, this incoherence is removed. Sidgwick declines to say
whether this is a valid reason for holding these propositions to
be true. He contents himself with the following cautious and
conditional statement. Certain universally accepted principles
of scientific method are, he thinks, in a precisely similar position

to these two postulates as regards the evidence for them. If so, it is inconsistent of those who accept the former to reject the latter, unless they can produce some positive reason for doing so.

It would be out of place for me to embark on an elaborate criticism of this argument here, so I will confine myself to two *obiter dicta*. In the first place, I do not find either of Sidgwick's ethical principles self-evident. Secondly, if they both were so, I cannot see that the fulfilment of his two postulates would have the least tendency to remove a radical incoherence in human cognition. Whether the postulates be fulfilled or not, one at least of the ethical principles must be false. So, if both appear equally self-evident, there must be at least one ethical proposition which is false and yet seems self-evidently true.

As regards the existence of God Sidgwick saw no prospect of going beyond the position which I have described. But, as regards the human individual's survival of bodily death, he thought that it was at least conceivable that empirical evidence might be found which would convert the mere methodological postulate into a fairly probable scientific hypothesis. All over the world and throughout all human history there had been an immense mass of alleged facts which we may roughly describe as 'ghost-stories'. And recently, in England and America especially, there had been a great output of phenomena, genuine or fraudulent, in connexion with spiritualistic mediums. It was certain that most of these tales would collapse on investigation, and quite likely that they would all do so. But it was possible that a nucleus of them might have to be accepted, and that the most plausible explanation of these might be to ascribe them to the posthumous agency of human beings who had survived the death of their bodies. This is the connexion between Sidgwick's philosophy and his concern with psychical research.

In 1881 Sir William Barrett was making experiments of Thought-Transference at Trinity College, Dublin. On Barrett's suggestion a conference of those interested was called on 6th January 1882, and at this the Society for Psychical Research was first planned. It was definitely constituted in the February of that year with Sidgwick as first president, and he gave the inaugural address on 16th July. He had not consented readily or without deep consideration and much hesitation; but, once he had decided, he gave his time, thought, labour, and money unsparingly to the Society. In its earlier years he presided at all the Council meetings and he took an active part in experiments, in examining witnesses, and in collecting and appraising evidence. His almost unique combination of scrupulous intellectual honesty with unquenchable hope and dogged persistence in face of disappointment made him an ideal psychical researcher. He started the S.P.R. on the right lines and kept it in them until good habits had become automatic. And the prestige of his name and character and position compelled the indifferent and the hostile to respect the Society and its work on pain of writing themselves down as crassly ignorant or grossly biased.

The position which Sidgwick reached as a result of his long travail with psychical research was the following. He considered that telepathy, both spontaneous and experimental, between the minds of living persons had been established to his own satisfaction, and he had good hopes that it might become a generally accepted fact. But he did not think that adequate empirical evidence had been produced for human survival of bodily death, and he seems to have grown more and more doubtful as to whether it ever would be produced. Since his death the available facts have become far more complex and still more queer, and it is difficult to suggest any hypothesis which will fit them all.

More than any man of whom I know Sidgwick did succeed in 'seeing life steadily and seeing it whole'. The strong desire for unity and symmetry, which he shared with all philosophers, never led him to over-simplify the facts. His high ethical and religious ideals never caused him to whitewash unregenerate humanity or to view through rose-coloured spectacles the frantic struggle to feed and breed and kill and escape which makes up the life of most men and of all animals save domestic pets. His whole-hearted acceptance of the methods and achievements of natural science never hid from him, as it does from so many, the standing miracle of man as thinker, artist, organizer and moral agent. This perfect balance, which Sidgwick so conspicuously possessed, does not make for exciting and spectacular systems of philosophy or of politics. These are the work of men who seldom hear and never heed what Clifford called 'that still small voice which whispers "Bosh!"' How numerous and how rancorous they are to-day, and what a relief it is to escape for an occasional hour from them and their new and nasty Jerusalems into the golden afternoon of Victorian civilization and the Sidgwickian atmosphere of good sense and sweet reasonableness!

JOHN McTAGGART ELLIS McTAGGART

JOHN McTAGGART ELLIS McTAGGART was born in 1866, and educated at Clifton and Trinity College, Cambridge. In 1888 he was placed alone in the first class of the Moral Science Tripos. In 1890 he became President of the Union Society. He was elected to a prize-fellowship at Trinity in 1891. Soon after this he paid a long visit to New Zealand, where, in 1894, he married Miss Margaret Elizabeth Bird of Taranaki. In 1897 he was made College Lecturer in the Moral Sciences, an office which he held until 1923. He then retired, after completing his twenty-five years' service, apparently in perfect health and certainly at the height of his intellectual powers. He still continued to give some of his former courses of lectures, but his main philosophical work after his retirement was the preparation of the third draft of the second volume of his *Nature of Existence*. Besides these professional labours he gave valuable help to Trinity by his active membership of the committee which drew up the new college statutes rendered necessary by the changes which the Royal Commission had imposed on the university and the colleges.

In January 1925 McTaggart and his wife were taking a holiday in London. He was seeing many of his old friends, and was to all appearance in the best of health and spirits, when he was suddenly stricken down. After a short but painful illness, borne with admirable courage and patience, he died on 18th January 1925, in a nursing home in London at the age of fifty-eight; passing, as he firmly believed, to the next stage in the long but finite journey from the illusion of time to the reality of eternal life. He must, it seems, have been suffering for some years from a

70

weakness of the heart, unsuspected by himself or his friends. It was characteristic of him that he left minute instructions for his funeral and for the disposition of his letters, papers, and manuscripts. In accordance with his wishes, his body was cremated; and, instead of the customary religious service, a favourite passage from Spinoza's *Ethics* was read by one of his oldest friends. This passage—*Homo liber de nulla re minus quam de morte cogitat; et eius sapientia non mortis, sed vitae meditatio est*—is engraved on his memorial brass in the ante-chapel of Trinity, which has been fitly placed beside those of his teachers, Sidgwick and Ward. On this brass is an admirable Latin inscription, composed by an old friend who was an eminent classical scholar. At McTaggart's request no specifically Christian symbol or sentiment appears.

McTaggart's life was spent in the service of philosophy, and it is fitting to begin with an account of his philosophical works. While he lived he published the following books: *Studies in Hegelian Dialectic, Studies in Hegelian Cosmology, Some Dogmas of Religion, A Commentary to Hegel's Logic*, and the first volume of *The Nature of Existence*. At the time of his death he had completed the second draft of the remaining volume of *The Nature of Existence* and was engaged in writing the third draft. This volume has been published recently; from the third draft, so far as that goes, and thenceforward from the second.

McTaggart was an extremely careful and conscientious writer and thinker. All his published works had been completely rewritten several times before being sent to the press, and the earlier drafts were submitted to his friends for criticism in respect of logical rigour and literary form. It might have been feared that so much elaboration would lead to a heavy and lifeless production. This is certainly not so with McTaggart, who must plainly be ranked with Hobbes, Berkeley, and Hume among the masters of English philosophical prose. His style is pellucidly clear, yet he never ignores a qualification or over-simplifies a subject for the sake of literary elegance. When he asserts a proposition he generally foresees, emphasizes, and tries to answer the objections which can reasonably be made to it. In this respect he resembles Sidgwick. But Sidgwick's writing, though always clear and dignified, is somewhat heavy; the reader of his works is always enlightened, often elevated, seldom excited, and hardly ever amused. There are, e.g. few abler or more conspicuously honest books than Sidgwick's *Methods of Ethics*; yet, after several careful readings of it, one is ashamed to find how little one has remembered of the details. McTaggart, though he never strained after humour or strewed his writings with epigrams, achieved both often enough to lighten the burden of a difficult argument, to fix a doctrine in the reader's mind by an apt illustration, and to deflate a pretentious fallacy by a pointed thrust. The abstractedness and complexity of the subjects with which he dealt, and the thoroughness with which he treated them, prevent his books from being easy reading. But, unlike his master Hegel and too many of Hegel's followers, he never added to the intrinsic difficulties of a subject by confused thinking or cloudy metaphorical writing. To McTaggart Hegel played the part of the drunken Helot, whose awful literary example helped to preserve and refine the crystalline clearness of his own style. At times McTaggart's writing rises to heights of intense emotion and great beauty, which are all the more impressive from their rarity and their restraint.

McTaggart's publications fall into three quite distinct, but closely connected groups. The first consists of his three books about Hegelianism. The second contains one work only, viz. *Some Dogmas of Religion*. This is the only book which McTaggart wrote for the educated amateur, as distinct from the trained philosophical specialist. The third comprises the two volumes on the *Nature of Existence*, in which he expounds his own system of constructive metaphysics by his own methods. Something will now be said about each of these three groups in turn.

McTaggart's character combined, as will appear in more detail later in this sketch, many apparently inconsistent features. Perhaps there is nothing at first sight more paradoxical about him than the fact that so much of his life should have been devoted to the study and exposition of Hegel's philosophy. If the style be the man, no two men could have had less in common than Hegel, with his vile technical jargon and his constant abuse of metaphor and verbal ambiguity, and McTaggart, with his short, clear, direct sentences, and his lawyer-like determination to make every clause completely 'water-tight'. If Hegel be the inspired, and too often incoherent, prophet of the Absolute; and if Bradley be its chivalrous knight, ready to challenge any one who dares to question its pre-eminence; McTaggart is its devoted and extremely astute family solicitor.

Moreover, Hegel was unlike McTaggart in his merits as well as in his defects. Hegel's strongest point is the comprehensive and intimate acquaintance with science, mathematics, history, law, art, social institutions, and religion, which forms the background of his writings. This gives them a solidity which is impressive even to readers who detest his style and can see nothing but verbal jugglery in his arguments. Such a background is lacking in McTaggart's works. It is of course obvious that he has a wide knowledge and a discriminating appreciation of English literature, and that he felt the interest of a cultured amateur in certain small sections of English history. But he knew little or nothing of science or mathematics and no more of the classics than he had acquired with pain and disgust at Clifton, whilst he viewed the claims of history to be a serious subject with an amused contempt which some of his colleagues found hard to bear.

Again, McTaggart, in theory at least, was a strong individualist. According to him, social institutions are simply means to the welfare of their members; church and state and family are no more to be regarded as ends than the drainage system or the underground railways. Nothing could be less like Hegel's view. It may, however, fairly be doubted whether the intense emotions of loyalty and patriotism which McTaggart felt towards certain societies, e.g. towards Clifton, Trinity, and England, could possibly have been justified on his own theory, or could have existed unless he had unwittingly thought, felt, and acted in accordance with a view not very different from Hegel's. Closely connected with the difference of emphasis which has just been mentioned is another difference, of profound importance, which was recognized by McTaggart. It is plain that McTaggart's two fundamental convictions were that man is immortal, and that the love of one man for another is of infinite value and profound metaphysical significance. Now he admits that Hegel took so little interest in immortality as hardly to mention it in the course of his voluminous writings. And he admits that there is only one passage, viz. in the account of the *Kingdom of the Holy Ghost* in the *Philosophy of Religion*, in which Hegel seems to ascribe any deep metaphysical importance to love; and, even then, it is doubtful whether he means by 'love' what McTaggart meant by it.

Nor do the differences between the two philosophers end even here. Hegel often makes it an objection to other forms of philosophy that they move at the level of Understanding; e.g. that they enunciate a number of alternatives, which are assumed to be severally self-contained, mutually exclusive, and collectively exhaustive, and that they then proceed to knock down all but one of these and to embrace the sole survivor. As against this he holds that philosophy should use Reason, which shows how a number of alternatives that seem to be exclusive and self-subsistent are really but so many different aspects of a single more concrete category. Now, although McTaggart, in discussing Hegel's method, accepts this doctrine, it must be confessed that he paid but little heed to it in his own philosophizing. He is rather conspicuously a devotee of the method of the Understanding, with its characteristic merits and defects; and, if he has a fault, it is a tendency to withdraw his eye from the facts themselves, and to indulge in extremely clever forensic 'logic-chopping' with verbal expressions and uncriticized categories.

Had McTaggart anything in common with Hegel? In temperament they shared one fundamental characteristic. Each consisted of a mystic, kept in perfect control by a sound common-sense citizen of great practical ability who loved order and decency and hated sentimentality and high-flown nonsense of every kind. It is safe to say that McTaggart would have disliked the German romantics of Hegel's time as much as Hegel himself did, and that Hegel would have shared McTaggart's contempt for teetotallers, Nonconformists, pacifists, Irish and Indian Nationalists, and the Labour Party. Now a kind of sentimental and muddle-headed admiration for 'rebels' and 'rebellion', as such, was common form among the comfortably placed bourgeois intellectuals who formed the societies in which Hegel and McTaggart lived. It is natural that both men should have reacted against it. And it is natural that both should often have carried the outward expression of this reaction to extremes which they might have found it hard to justify. Beyond this resemblance the master and the disciple seem to have almost nothing in common except the conviction that the universe is at bottom a spiritual system, and that human reason is competent to discover and prove many important and paradoxical conclusions about it without the aid of special empirical investigation.

Suppose the following problem in psychology had been propounded: 'Take an eighteenth-century English Whig. Let him be a mystic. Endow him with the logical subtlety of the great schoolmen and their belief in the powers of human reason, with the business capacity of a successful lawyer, and with the lucidity of the best type of French mathematician. Inspire him (Heaven knows how) in early youth with a passion for Hegel. Then subject him to the teaching of Sidgwick and the continual influence of Moore and Russell. Set him to expound Hegel. What will be the result?' Hegel himself could not have answered this question *a priori*, but the course of world history has solved it *ambulando* by producing McTaggart. It is natural then that McTaggart's interpretation of Hegel should differ greatly from that of other commentators, and that it should often be hard to believe that Hegel had ever imagined, or would have accepted, the doctrines which McTaggart ascribed to him. If McTaggart be challenged on any particular detail he can generally quote one or more almost unintelligible sentences from Hegel, and can triumphantly show that they are capable of bearing the surprising and ingenious interpretation which he has put upon them. And, against critics or rival interpreters of Hegel, he can generally quote passages which are immune to their criticisms and inconsistent with their interpretations. And yet, if McTaggart's account of Hegelianism be taken as a whole and compared with Hegel's writings as a whole, the impression produced is one of profound unlikeness. 'Whatever Hegel may have meant', the reader says to himself, 'it surely cannot have been this.' 'And', he hastens to add, 'it was probably nothing nearly so sensible or plausible as this.' If we compare McTaggart with the other commentators on Hegel we must admit that he has at least produced an extremely lively and fascinating rabbit from the Hegelian hat, whilst they have produced nothing but consumptive and gibbering chimeras. And we shall admire his resource and dexterity all the more when we reflect that the rabbit was, in all probability, never inside the hat, whilst the chimeras perhaps were.

BIOGRAPHY

McTaggart's first book, *Studies in Hegelian Dialectic*, is an enlargement of the dissertation on which he was awarded his fellowship at Trinity. In it he tries to explain, and to defend against critics, the Dialectical Method, as used in passing from category to category within the *Logic*, and also the transition from the *Logic* as a whole, through *Nature*, to *Spirit*. His account of the Dialectical Method within the *Logic* is, in essence, the following. There is one and only one complete and self-subsisting category, viz. that which Hegel calls the *Absolute Idea*. All other categories are partial factors in the Absolute Idea. Every rational being has an implicit knowledge of the Absolute Idea; but no human being starts with an explicit knowledge of it, or reaches such knowledge except by the Dialectical Method. If any category, other than the Absolute Idea, be supposed to express adequately the formal nature of Reality, our implicit knowledge of the Absolute Idea forces a certain complementary and opposed aspect of Reality on our attention. On further reflection a more concrete category is presented to our notice, in which these two complementary and opposed aspects are seen to be combined and reconciled with each other. We now try to regard this new category as adequately expressing the formal nature of Reality. The same process takes place as before. Thus we work gradually upward; our still implicit knowledge of the Absolute Idea reacting at every step with the knowledge of it which has so far been made explicit, until at last all our knowledge of it is dragged into the light of clear consciousness.

McTaggart pointed out in this book that the nature of the relations between the successive categories gradually changes as we pass from those of *Being* to those of the *Notion*. The opposition between thesis and antithesis, which is very marked at the beginning of the *Logic*, becomes less and less intense as the series nears the Absolute Idea. In the categories of *Being* the difficulty is to see how thesis can lead to antithesis and how the two can ever be reconciled; in those of the *Notion* the difficulty is to see that there is any real opposition between thesis and antithesis or distinction between antithesis and synthesis.

In defending Hegel's method against its critics McTaggart had to deal with three main objections, viz. (1) that, within the *Logic*, the transitions from category to category are made possible only by the surreptitious use of empirical knowledge; (2)

that, in the transition from *Logic* to *Nature* and *Spirit*, Hegel
made an unjustifiable leap from essence to existence; and (3)
that, throughout his system, Hegel constantly claimed to
deduce concrete empirical details in physics, psychology, and
politics by pure thought from *a priori* premisses. McTaggart's
answer to the first objection is his theory of the Dialectical
Method, outlined above. His answer to the second is that Hegel
did in fact use an existential premiss, but that it is so obvious
that he never explicitly stated it. The existential premiss is:
'Something exists' or 'There is something'. If this be granted—
and no one can consistently reject it—it is granted that Hegel's
category of Being has application. If the validity of the arguments in the *Logic* be admitted it then follows that the category
of the Absolute Idea must have application. And it is evident,
from the nature of the Absolute Idea and of the categories
which immediately precede it, that, if it applies to anything, it
applies to the universe as a single collective whole.

McTaggart meets the third line of attack by denying the
allegation, and explaining how Hegel laid himself open to this
misunderstanding even by friendly and intelligent critics. The
celebrated transition from Logic to Nature, as interpreted by
McTaggart, like the Beatitudes, as interpreted by the late Dr.
Rashdall, proves to be a mere storm in a teacup which need
disturb nobody. It may be stated as follows: 'We know *a priori*
that anything that exists must have some characteristics which
cannot be known *a priori*, and that these must be consistent with
those characteristics which can be known *a priori*.' Or, to put it
in a different but equivalent way: 'Everything must be characterized by the categories, but nothing can be characterized
merely by the categories.' The reasons why this innocent proposition was so much misunderstood and why so much needless
scandal arose were the following. In the first place, Hegel, having to find names for some hundreds of categories, called some
of them after certain concrete processes, such as *Mechanism*,
Chemism, *Life*, etc., which, he thought, approximately illustrated these categories. His readers were then liable to think
that he was claiming to deduce concrete empirical facts. Moreover, by this practice he unfortunately confused himself besides
raising false hopes in his readers. For he often went on to make
subdivisions and to indulge in elaborate discussions about

points of detail, which were suggested to him by the associations of the name that he had given to a category and were
neither entailed by the earlier stages of the *Logic* nor relevant
to its later stages. In fact, as my Lord Chesterfield said of the
Garter King-at-Arms, 'the foolish fellow didn't know even his
own foolish business'. These explanations apply mainly within
the *Logic*. Within *Nature* and *Spirit*, on McTaggart's view, Hegel
never pretended that the various subdivisions, or the transitions from one subdivision to another, were discoverable or
justifiable *a priori* by pure thought.

Assuming that McTaggart's explanation, qualifications, and
admissions suffice to remove antecedent objections to the very
possibility of Hegelianism, the question still remains whether *in
fact* Hegel succeeded in passing dialectically from Pure Being
to the Absolute Idea. This can be answered only by a detailed
investigation into the *Logic* category by category. This McTaggart undertook in his *Commentary to Hegel's Logic*, a work of
amazing patience and ingenuity for which all English students of
Hegel are deeply indebted to him. The conclusions which he
reached may be summed up as follows. Many of the transitions
are valid, but several are invalid. Not only are there isolated
failures; there are whole sets of categories such that the transitions into, within, and out of the set must be rejected. In the
case of isolated failures, McTaggart often suggested an alternative of his own, which he thought would be valid and adequate;
in the other cases he did not attempt this. But he records his
conviction that Hegel's final result comes nearer to the truth
than any other philosopher has reached, and that it could almost certainly be proved from Hegel's starting-point by the
Dialectical Method, provided that suitable modifications were
made at certain crucial points. The admitted breakdown of
Hegel's argument at certain points seemed the less serious to
McTaggart because he had come to the conclusion, which he
admits that Hegel had never contemplated and would probably have rejected, that there might be a number of alternative
and equally valid dialectical paths from one category to another.

Studies in Hegelian Cosmology, which was published between the
two works which have now been considered, is a series of essays
in applied Hegelianism. To the general reader it is far the most

entertaining of McTaggart's books on Hegel. Most of Hegel's English followers were interested mainly in his philosophical conclusions and his applications of them to politics, ethics, and religion. These they considered true and important, whilst they abandoned, with a smile or a sigh, the Dialectical Method by which he had claimed to establish his conclusions. McTaggart used to call this 'Hegelianism with the proofs left out'. And, for his part, he took exactly the opposite view of Hegel's achievements. He thought that the Dialectical Method and the purely metaphysical results of it were valid and important, whilst he regarded all the concrete applications which had been made of Hegelianism as unjustified and most of them as positively false. Most of the essays in the *Hegelian Cosmology* fall into one or another of two classes, viz. those in which McTaggart tries to show that Hegelianism supports the doctrines that he wished to believe, and those in which he tries to show that it does not support the doctrines which other Hegelians wished to believe. In the positive part of the book McTaggart argued that, whatever Hegel himself may have held, his general principles, when fully worked out, imply that the Absolute is not a person but a perfect society of perfect and eternal persons each of whom is in love with one or more of the rest. Moreover, it is probable that each human mind, as it really is, is identical with one of these persons. If so, each of us in reality is eternal, and, *sub specie temporis*, our eternity will probably appear as persistence throughout the whole of time.

In reading the negative part of the book it is worth while to remember that the school of English Hegelianism which flourished during the latter part of the nineteenth century had, as a whole, certain characteristics which filled McTaggart, and would probably have filled Hegel, with an amused annoyance that was quite compatible with genuine respect for and friendship with many of its members. With a very few exceptions, of whom far the most notable was Bradley, it was (if we may say so with becoming submission) a paradise of pompous prigs. 'The sort of people', McTaggart would say, 'who wanted to believe that they ate a good dinner only in order to strengthen themselves to appreciate Dante.' The destructive part of *Hegelian Cosmology* is certainly written with this school and its special foibles in view; and, if a naughty desire to shock Bosanquet never led McTaggart to assert what he did not believe, it almost certainly did influence his choice of subjects, of examples, and of expressions. Thus McTaggart maintains that the state is a means and not an end; that the fact that the Kingdom of Heaven is a perfect society of intimately related persons gives us no guidance whatever in politics or ethics here and now; and that, although neither ethical nor psychological hedonism is true, the hedonic calculus is an adequate guide to conduct and is the only one available to us. He also stresses every passage in which Hegel minimizes the importance of sin and treats it as a necessary stage in the advance from innocence to virtue. It was indeed his considered opinion that boys and undergraduates should be given ample opportunities to sin and be punished for it. There was no short cut to virtue, and the sins that they were tempted to commit, unlike those of older men, were seldom socially dangerous. Provided they were punished—and this was of course essential—society could afford to treat them as salutary and slightly amusing episodes like mumps or measles. It was in this connexion that McTaggart once formulated the principle that 'every undergraduate should be compelled to satisfy his tutor that he had been drunk at least once a year as a guarantee of good faith that he was not a teetotaller'.

The book ends with a very interesting expository essay in which McTaggart discusses the relations of Hegelianism to Christianity. He points out that, in spite of certain superficial likenesses, the differences are fundamental. And he concludes that, whilst Hegelianism is a most useful ally of Christianity against popular materialism and against Deism or Unitarianism, it is in the end the most dangerous rival that Christianity has ever had. For Hegelianism contains in a purified form, without mythology and without compromising historical associations, all that is true in the highest religion. The Hegelian comprehends, appreciates, and assigns its true place to Christianity among the manifestations of the human spirit, and, in so doing, sees through it and passes beyond it.

This essay forms a natural transition from McTaggart's books about Hegelianism to his *Dogmas of Religion*. It is strange that this work failed to secure a high degree of popular success. It presupposes no knowledge of philosophy; it is written with admirable clarity and abounds with wit; and it deals with problems which have interested almost all intelligent men in all ages. It opens with an attempt to prove that dogmas, i.e. metaphysical propositions about the universe, are essential to religion; and that they can be satisfactorily established only by metaphysical reasoning. Probably the most important chapter in it is that on *Human Immortality and Pre-existence*. McTaggart had this reprinted separately; and, during the war of 1914 to 1918, he sent copies of it to some who had lost friends and relations, in the hope that it might help them in their bereavement. Here he does not attempt to *prove* human survival of bodily death. He held that positive arguments for immortality must come from metaphysics; and he claimed to supply such a proof, on Hegelian lines in the *Cosmology*, and in another and quite original way in the *Nature of Existence*. He took little interest in Psychical Research; holding that, even if the alleged results were certain and were incapable of a normal explanation, they would still be susceptible of so many alternative supernormal explanations as to add very little force to the probability of survival and none at all to that of immortality. What McTaggart claims to show here is simply that the antecedent objections to human survival, drawn from common sense and natural science, are quite baseless. In this connexion he takes an extremely Berkeleian view of matter, going so far as to say that the independent existence of matter is 'a bare possibility to which it would be foolish to attach the slightest importance'. It follows from McTaggart's arguments in his other works that the existence of each of us, *sub specie temporis*, occupies the whole of time. He held it to be most likely that this existence is split up into a series of many successive lives, each beginning with a birth and ending with a death. Here he takes this as an hypothesis; defends it against the more obvious difficulties; and claims that it would explain many well-known facts, such as love at first sight, and some men's innate capacity for activities which others acquire, if at all, late in life and with great pains. He tries to show that loss of memory of our previous lives would not make this kind of survival worthless, and would be, in some respects, a positive advantage.

The remaining chapters in the book deal with more hackneyed subjects, such as Determinism and Divine Omnipotence. Though always acute, and often extremely entertaining, they do not show McTaggart at his best, for the subjects tempt him to indulge a taste for setting up and knocking down men of straw, which he shared with most highly skilled dialecticians. E.g. omnipotence is taken to include the power of doing what is *logically*, and not merely what is *causally* impossible; and free will is taken to mean indeterminism in its extremest form. No theologian of repute accepts omnipotence in this sense, and no philosopher or moralist of repute accepts free will in this sense. And the elaborate sapping and mining of these two lath-and-plaster fortresses by all the engines in McTaggart's dialectical armoury begins by being amusing but soon becomes wearisome. McTaggart ends by rejecting the notions of an omnipotent God, and of a creative but non-omnipotent God; but he allows the bare possibility of a non-omnipotent non-creative God. 'The only reason against the existence of such a being is that there is no reason for it.' McTaggart's atheism becomes still more definite in the *Nature of Existence*, where he shows that the structure of reality, as determined by him, is incompatible with the existence of either a creative or a controlling self, though it is compatible with the existence of a self which *appears* to control the rest of the universe.

There can be no doubt that McTaggart's greatest achievement is his last book, *The Nature of Existence*. It is the less necessary to give a detailed account of it as McTaggart himself has given an admirable synopsis in his contribution to *Contemporary British Philosophy*, vol. i. The work forms a complete deductive system of *a priori* metaphysics on the grand scale, and may quite fairly be compared with the *Enneads* of Plotinus, the *Ethics* of Spinoza, and the *Encyclopaedia* of Hegel. In English philosophical literature it occupies a unique position. One other Englishman, Professor Alexander, has indeed thought out and written down a highly comprehensive and original theory of the universe; but the distinguished author of *Space, Time, and Deity* would not count his work, nor wish it to be counted, as a deductive system with the smallest possible number of empirical premisses.

McTaggart at one time had meant to write a new dialectic, and the original title of the book was *The Dialectic of Existence*. But, although he continued to hold that the dialectical method of argument is valid, he wisely decided in the end to use straightforward deduction in building up his own system. It will be worth while to indicate the logical peculiarities of McTaggart's general method, and the degree of certainty which he attached to his various conclusions. The premisses of the first volume fall into three classes; viz. (1) axioms, i.e. propositions which are, and can be seen to be, intrinsically necessary; (2) contingent propositions which are rendered completely certain by perception; and (3) a peculiar class of propositions, the description of which may be deferred for the moment. Only two premisses of the second class are used, viz. that something exists, and that there is more than one substance. And the latter of these is not really needed, for it is entailed by the former together with one of the axioms. The argument now proceeds, using only premisses of the first two classes, and therefore reaching conclusions which are absolutely certain if no mistake has been made, until it reaches the crucial point of the whole system. The crucial point is the following. McTaggart regards it as self-evident that every substance must consist of parts which are themselves substances. Now this axiom, when combined with certain propositions about substance which he has deduced from other axioms, threatens to lead to a complete contradiction. The deadlock can be avoided on one and only one condition. The proposition which asserts that this condition is fulfilled must therefore be accepted, though it is neither a self-evidently necessary proposition nor a contingent proposition which is guaranteed by perception. It is called the *Principle of Determining Correspondence*, and it is the only member of the third class of premisses. The remaining conclusions of the first volume are certain, provided that no mistake has been made, except for the possibility that the Principle of Determining Correspondence may not be the only way of avoiding the conflict between the axiom of endless divisibility of substance and the deductions from the other axioms.

In the second volume the world as it appears to us here and now is viewed in the light of the conclusions of the first volume. The results are partly negative and partly positive. The negative conclusions are certain, for any apparent feature of the existent which would be incompatible with its nature, as determined in Volume I, must necessarily be delusive. Tried by these tests the characteristics of being spatial, being material, being a sensum, being a judgment, being a supposition, and many other apparent characteristics physical and psychical, are found wanting and are rejected as delusive. The delusiveness of temporal characteristics is supposed to be established independently by an argument of great ingenuity which McTaggart had published some years before in *Mind*. It will be seen that the negative aspects of McTaggart's system are much more startling than those of most idealists. On his view, not only do we radically misperceive all that we perceive by our senses, we also radically misperceive ourselves and our mental processes when we introspect. Nevertheless, McTaggart holds, and tries to prove, that, although introspection is thus largely misleading, it is an act of direct acquaintance with *oneself* and not merely with certain mental events or processes which belong to oneself.

The positive results of the second volume are admittedly only probable, though McTaggart thinks that their probability is very high indeed. The general line of argument is as follows. It has been proved in Volume I that the universe must consist of a certain set of substances called *Primary Parts*, each of which is divisible into parts within parts without end. These must be interrelated in certain complicated ways in order to answer the requirements of the Principle of Determining Correspondence. Does our everyday experience present us with any things that might reasonably be identified with these Primary Parts? McTaggart's answer is that the required conditions could be fulfilled if each Primary Part were a mind whose whole content was its perceptions of itself, of certain other minds, of its own perceptions, and of their perceptions.

In addition it must be assumed that a perception of any part of a whole is *ipso facto* a part of a perception of that whole. A system composed of such minds would fulfil the necessary conditions, and we cannot imagine any other kind of system that would fulfil them. Now it must be admitted that our minds, as they appear to us in introspection, do not appear to have all these characteristics, and do appear to have some which are incompatible with these. But we already know that introspection must largely misrepresent the nature of our minds and their processes to us. So it is quite likely that each human mind, as it really is, is one of the Primary Parts of the universe. It is from this that McTaggart infers that each human mind is really

84

eternal, and must appear, *sub specie temporis*, as persisting throughout the whole of time. And it is from the intimate cognitive relations which must subsist between the Primary Parts of the universe, if these be minds, that he infers that every mind, as it really is, must be in love with one or more others to a degree which we can at present only dimly imagine.

Love, according to McTaggart, is the fundamental emotion; and by 'love' he means, not philanthropy or benevolence, but that passionate personal affection which none of us in this life can feel towards more than a very few persons. No philosopher but Plato has treated love so seriously, has analysed it so carefully, or has written about it so eloquently as McTaggart. Yet there is a profound difference between the two philosophers on this point. For Plato the love of a man for his friend is only a stepping-stone by which the soul rises to the contemplation and love of the Idea of the Good. For McTaggart it is the one supremely valuable thing in the universe; it cannot be a step towards something higher, for there is nothing above it.

Now, when McTaggart seeks to combine the positive and the negative parts of his doctrine, he is brought face to face with the ghost which haunts every system of Absolute Idealism. This is the seemingly hopeless conflict between the error which must exist if the negative results be accepted and the perfection which must exist if the positive results be accepted. Perhaps the finest part of the whole work is the transparent honesty with which McTaggart states and emphasizes this problem, and the heroic effort which he makes to solve it in detail. Hegel brushes it aside with the magnificent epigram: '*Die Vollführung des unendlichen Zwecks ist so nur die Täuschung aufzuheben als ob er noch nicht vollführt sei*'; McTaggart accepted the spirit of this epigram and tried to show how it could be realized without contradiction. It is impossible here to do more than mention that, on McTaggart's view, all other misperception is bound up with the misperception of the world as being in time. His solution, if valid, would provide an answer to the two fundamental problems which all other systems of Absolute Idealism have shirked: 'How can a timeless and changeless reality appear to endure and to change?' and 'How can the perfect parts of a perfect whole misperceive it and themselves as imperfect?'

The reputation of books and their writers with posterity depends on so many unforeseeable conditions that no prudent person will risk a prophecy on such a subject. Deductive systems of speculative philosophy are at present out of fashion, and it may be that the human intellect has been so disheartened by past failures and is now so preoccupied with the methods and results of the natural sciences that it will never again take much interests in attempts to solve the riddles of the universe by deductive reasoning from *a priori* premisses. But this at least may be said. The system expounded in the *Nature of Existence* is equal in scope and originality to any of the great historical systems of European philosophy, whilst in clearness of statement and cogency of argument it far surpasses them all. If subtle analysis, rigid reasoning, and constructive fertility, applied with tireless patience to the hardest and deepest problems of metaphysics, and expressed in language which always enlightens the intellect and sometimes touches the emotions, be a title to philosophical immortality, then McTaggart has fully earned his place among the immortals by his *Nature of Existence*.

It remains to say something of McTaggart as a teacher and as a man. His teaching work in Trinity consisted mainly of lecturing. It has happily never been the custom of Cambridge to exhaust and sterilize its dons by sacrificing the best part of their lives to the drudgery of hearing and criticizing undergraduates' essays, and in McTaggart's time the duties of a college lecturer included even less of such work than they do at present. McTaggart was an admirable lecturer; he loved the work, and he gave many courses. His normal stint consisted of three courses of lectures for the Tripos, each of which went on throughout the three terms of the academic year. Each course consisted of two hours a week of actual lecturing, and a third hour of discussion. In addition he usually gave an advanced course of an hour a week, called *Problems of Philosophy*. In this he would generally take some important philosophical book that had lately appeared and would discuss it with the class. Moreover, for many years he gave a course of introductory lectures, one on each Friday evening of term, to members of the University and of the women's colleges who were not studying philosophy. It is a grave defect in the curriculum of Cambridge that the study of philosophy is confined to a few specialists, and that the vast majority of undergraduates go through their whole university career without suspecting the existence of such a subject. McTaggart's popular lectures were meant to do something towards meeting this defect. They were brilliantly successful, and it is quite certain that they implanted in a fair proportion of his listeners a lifelong interest in philosophy. So fond was McTaggart of lecturing that, even after he retired, he continued, by agreement with his successor, to deliver his courses on the *General History of Modern Philosophy* and the *Problems of Philosophy* as well as the popular lectures.

McTaggart was a highly peripatetic philosopher, and must have walked many miles in his lecture-room whilst conducting his pupils from Descartes to Hegel and from Pure Begin to the Absolute Idea. The smaller lecture-rooms at Trinity, now gay with green paint and brightened by the portraits of eminent Victorians which the fastidious taste of a later age has rejected from Hall, resembled in McTaggart's time the more neglected kind of family vault. Here he lectured to small but select classes, consuming at each lecture in successive sips a tumbler of cold water provided by the college. At intervals a representative of the College Office, known as a 'marker', would appear for a moment silently and suddenly at the door, armed with a list, and, after looking severely round at the audience and the lecturer, would as suddenly and silently vanish. It was never known what he suspected, or whether his suspicions were confirmed or allayed. These gloomy and even sinister surroundings were enlivened by McTaggart's verbal wit and the happy oddity of his illustrations. Phoenixes, dragons, griffins, rocs, and unicorns, indeed most of the fauna of heraldry and mythology, formed the staple subjects of his examples, and were imagined in situations in which one would have been greatly surprised to meet them.

McTaggart was better as a formal lecturer than as the conductor of a conversation-class, and he was better in lecturing on metaphysics than on the history of philosophy. In a conversation-class he was too apt to confute a questioner with a few pungent phrases and there leave the matter, instead of trying to draw him out and discover what, if anything, lay behind his question. Thus the conversation-classes were liable to dwindle into an uncomfortable silence after the first twenty minutes or so. Much the same criticism must be made on McTaggart's treatment of the great historical thinkers up to Hegel. Their fallacies and confusions were remorselessly exposed, as by an extremely able public prosecutor, and they left the witness-box with their reputations apparently ruined for ever. Yet the audience was left with the impression that they had hardly had a fair run for their money, and that, if they had been lucky enough to secure McTaggart as counsel for the defence, they might at worst have been dismissed with a caution. This impression was confirmed by the very different fate which befell Hegel when his turn came. In his case McTaggart lavished incredible patience and ingenuity to find a sensible meaning for the seemingly unintelligible and a plausible reconciliation for the seemingly inconsistent.

Though these were real defects, the undergraduates who attended McTaggart's lectures or wrote essays for him could not fail to be interested, instructed, and immensely impressed. Perhaps McTaggart never made a disciple, and certainly he never tried to. But on those undergraduates who worked with him he exercised the powerful formative influence of good example, the only kind of influence which can be exerted without impertinence and accepted without indignity. They learnt from a master of rigid reasoning and lucid writing how difficult it is to avoid, and how important it is to detect, logical fallacies and verbal ambiguities. They learnt how hard it is to *prove* or to *disprove* anything, by seeing that most of the arguments by which great philosophers have claimed to establish or refute propositions in fact do little more than slightly to raise or slightly to lower their probabilities. Insensibly their intellectual standards were exalted and refined, until slovenly thinking and loose rhetorical writing in themselves or in others began to evoke the same reaction of disgust as dirty finger-nails or bad table manners or a Cockney accent. It must be added that the tendency to 'score off' a questioner, which was liable to manifest itself in the publicity of a conversation-class, was completely in abeyance when McTaggart dealt individually with his pupils in the privacy of his own rooms. Under the latter conditions, not only they, but many strangers who had no claim on his time or attention except an interest in the problems of philosophy, found him sympathetic, helpful, and wonderfully patient.

McTaggart's character was original and very strongly

marked. Perhaps his fundamental emotions were loyalty to his friends and devotion to certain societies of which he was a member. He could forgive any fault in a beloved individual except lukewarmness or opposition to the purposes of a beloved society. This made the war of 1914 to 1918 a particularly tragic event in McTaggart's life. He was passionately patriotic; and he fully accepted at the time, and continued to accept to the day of his death, the view that the Allies were wholly right and the Central Powers wholly wrong. To some of his most intimate friends this view seemed both antecedently incredible and in conflict with known facts; and they felt just as passionately that it was their duty, at a time when calm reason seemed likely to succumb to blind passion, to incur unpopularity by publicly stating and reiterating the other side of the case. Feelings were too deeply moved for either side to display that tact and forbearance which both would have shown under happier circumstances. The clash that ensued was a true tragedy in Hegel's sense, 'a conflict of right with right'; and, in it, wounds were given and received which, in some cases, never healed. It would be impertinent to pursue this matter farther; but this at least may be said. McTaggart's love of England was no armchair patriotism. Anyone who knew him must acknowledge that he would willingly have died for his country; and he served it during the war in such ways as were open to a man of his age and physique, up to and beyond the limit of his powers.

The three societies to which McTaggart felt the strongest emotions of loyalty were Clifton, Trinity, and England. It would not be unfair to say that he regarded the Absolute as the heavenly pattern of which these were the least imperfect earthly copies. It was never his lot to take any public part in the affairs of England, but he was an assiduous and valuable member of the governing body of Clifton, and he played an active role on the College Council of Trinity. The popular conception of a philosopher as a child in practical affairs has never gained much support from the facts of real life; the examples of Mill, Hume, Locke, Leibniz, and Plato are enough to refute it, and to them McTaggart must certainly be added. He was an admirable man of business, cool, cautious, and methodical, both in his own affairs and in those of the societies of which he was a member. Any one who had to make a difficult practical decision, and needed advice, could hardly do better than to state his case to McTaggart and be guided by him.

McTaggart combined a number of opinions which, though logically consistent with each other, are seldom held by the same person. In the case of most of his contemporaries at Cambridge a knowledge of a small number of their principles or prejudices enabled one to infer all the rest with a fair degree of certainty. This was far from being so with McTaggart, who unwittingly exemplified Bergsonian principles by performing actions and expressing opinions which were incalculable before the event but rationally explicable after it. He added greatly to the gaiety of college meetings; for he was always liable either to use arguments which every one accepted to support conclusions which no one else had thought of, or to support conclusions that every one accepted by arguments which had occurred to no one else.

As an illustration of an unusual combination of opinions one may mention the fact that he was an atheist, a firm believer in immortality, and a strong supporter of the Church of England against both popish and protestant dissent. Most of his views on church and state are explicable by the fact that he was in the main an admirable example of that most admirable, but now unhappily rare thing, an Erastian Whig. His defence of church establishment was stated in his early years in a famous speech at the Union, which caused acute embarrassment to most of its supporters; and this remained his view up to the end. An established church is desirable for two reasons. In the first place, it makes for freedom of thought *within* the church, for the limits of permissible theological divergence are ultimately settled by lay lawyers on purely secular grounds. And, secondly, it makes for freedom *outside* the church, for the jealousy which dissenting Christians feel towards the Establishment prevents them from uniting with it to persecute non-Christian opinions. McTaggart supported this deductive conclusion by examples drawn from the United States and the Colonies.

His Whiggism was shown again in his extreme constitutionalism. Antecedently it might have been supposed that he would have sympathized with the Fascist revolution in Italy. But actually he held that Fascism and Bolshevism are two sides of the same medal (a medal which, it would have been unkind to remind him, was struck by Hegel) and that he could not consistently bless the former whilst cursing, as he very heartily did, the latter. Again, he was an extremely strong free-trader; and this both caused him to vote Liberal in 1906 and enabled him to avoid doing so in 1910. For, soon after the Government of 1906 came into power, it introduced a patent bill in which it was enacted that any foreign firm which was granted an English patent must set up a factory in England. This was interpreted by McTaggart as a betrayal of the free-trade citadel; and, as all parties were now faithless to his Dulcinea, he was able to return with an easy conscience to the one which did not outrage all his other convictions and sentiments.

Perhaps the only political opinion of McTaggart's which is, at first sight, hard to reconcile with Whig principles is his belief in compulsory military service. This he had held strongly many years before the war, when it was highly unpopular with most Englishmen. But was not this really 'an appeal from the new to the old Whigs'? For did not the Whigs of Charles II's time object to mercenary standing armies, and extol in their place the old national militia?

Another apparent paradox in McTaggart's opinions was that he was as strongly 'liberal' in university politics as he was 'conservative' in national politics. He was, e.g. a strong feminist in the matter of the admission of women to full membership of the university. This paradox, however, depends largely on the usage of words. There is no essential connexion between liberalism and the view that men and women should be educated together, or between conservatism and the view that they should be educated separately. Nor is there any essential connexion between liberalism and the view that the colleges should be subordinated to the university, or between conservatism and the view that the university should be subordinated to the colleges. Yet those who hold the first alternative on these two subjects are called 'academic liberals', whilst those who hold the second are called 'academic conservatives'. There is thus no kind of inconsistency between academic liberalism and political conservatism, or between academic conservatism and political liberalism. If there were more men like McTaggart, who considered each question on its merits instead of dressing himself in a complete suit of ready-made opinions, such combinations would be much more frequent than they are, to the great benefit of both academic and national politics.

It remains to mention a few of McTaggart's more personal tastes and interests. He had a passion for ritual, which showed itself in his love of wearing his scarlet doctor's gown and taking part in university and college ceremonies. His knowledge of the history of university offices and rituals, of the minute details of procedure, and of the true order of the academic hierarchy, was extensive and accurate; and he was punctilious in insisting that no mistakes should be made in such matters. Perhaps this caused him to look with a slightly more lenient eye on popish than on protestant dissent; though it did not make him any less firm against the pretensions of the Bishop of Rome, or prevent him from referring to his church as 'the Roman schism'.

He loved good living, and he set an example to other married fellows by the great part which he played in the social and corporate life of the college. He dined regularly in Hall; attended all college feasts; and was a faithful supporter of the old custom of drinking wine nightly in the Combination Room after dinner, a custom which had fallen into such decay in Trinity that McTaggart sometimes found himself on a week-night in the lonely, if splendid, situation of the Seraph Abdiel. Once a year he played at cards. The game, which was 'Beggar-my-Neighbour', used to be played after the Christmas Feast with another distinguished fellow of the College. McTaggart would start the game with sixpence in his pocket, and would play until he had lost it or until it was time to gather up his winnings and go home to bed; a system of limited liability which was highly characteristic of him. It was his custom after a feast to write down any story about a past or present member of the university which he had heard and had thought good. These stories, recorded each on a separate slip of paper, with the name of the teller, the date and occasion of the telling, and sometimes a few notes of his own, were kept in four file-boxes labelled 'College Stories'. He bequeathed them to an old friend; and we may perhaps venture to hope that, when a suitable time has gone by, they may be edited and printed.

McTaggart was an omnivorous reader of novels, good and bad. His memory for their plots and characters was extraordinary; he could, without apparent effort, give to an inquirer a full and accurate account of stories which he had read once years before. He was also devoted to those diaries, collections of letters, biographies, and memoirs which make the chief personalities of eighteenth-century England such living figures to ourselves. Few even of professional students of the eighteenth century can know their *Boswell*, their *Horace Walpole*, or their *Lord Hervey* better than McTaggart did. Certain Victorian poets had a great attraction for McTaggart; to judge from the frequency with which quotations from them occur in his works, his favourites were Browning and Swinburne. Such tastes and such knowledge made McTaggart a most valuable member of the library committee of the Union. His long and distinguished connexion with that society has been appropriately commemorated by setting apart a bookcase in the library, filling it with a collection of eighteenth-century memoirs bought by subscription, and affixing to it a brass memorial plate.

A biography, at best, is a series of photographs, taken from a limited number of positions, on a selectively sensitive plate, by a photographer whose presence affects the expression of the sitter in a characteristic way. There will certainly be omission and selection, and it is only too likely that there will be positive distortion. This sketch represents McTaggart as he appeared to one much younger than himself; whose relation to him was first that of pupil to teacher, and then, after a long interval and for too short a time, that of colleague. Those who knew him in his earlier years and in other relations would find much to add to this account, and perhaps something to alter in it. But no memoir of McTaggart which approximated to the truth could fail to convey the impression of a thinker of the very first rank, and of a rich, original, and lovable personality.

WILLIAM ERNEST JOHNSON

WILLIAM ERNEST JOHNSON was born at Llandaff House, Cambridge, on 23rd June 1858. He was the fifth child and second son of William Henry Farthing Johnson and Harriet Brimley. His father was proprietor and head master of Llandaff House school, a famous Cambridge academy which was owned and conducted by members of the Johnson family from 1823 to 1925.

The Johnsons came from Huntingdonshire, and were strong dissenters (Baptists) in religion and ardent Liberals in politics. The first of them to own the school was W. E. Johnson's paternal grandfather, William, born at Ramsey in 1793, son of Henry, a baker in that town. Grandfather William as a boy had delivered bread to his father's customers. He was taught Latin by a kindly clergyman who sympathized with his aspirations for learning, and he is said to have carried his first Latin grammar with him in the basket with the bread and to have conned it during his rounds. After acting as usher at a private school kept by Mr. Newton Bosworth at Merton Hall, Cambridge, he went back to Ramsey in 1814 and there set up a school of his own. In 1816 he married Miss Eliza Barker, a Ramsey schoolmistress. Meanwhile Mr. Bosworth had removed his school to Llandaff House. In 1823 Grandfather William returned to Cambridge with his wife, and took over the Llandaff House school from Mr. Bosworth. In 1851 he handed over the school to his son, William Henry Farthing Johnson, and retired to Ramsey, where he died at the age of seventy. All those of his eight children who lived to grow up became schoolmasters or schoolmistresses.

W. E. Johnson's ancestors on his mother's side lived in Bedfordshire. His maternal grandfather, Augustine Gutteridge Brimley, was a Bedfordshire farmer who set up as a grocer in Cambridge and throve so well at his trade that he became Mayor of the town. He married in turn two daughters of James Gotobed, landlord of the Bull Hotel, Cambridge. His son, George Brimley, became librarian of Trinity College, Cambridge. His daughter, Harriet Brimley, married W. H. F. Johnson in 1851 and became the mother of W. E. Johnson.

W. E. Johnson's father was born in 1825. He was sent at the age of sixteen to be usher at a private school in Brixton, where he showed himself under difficult circumstances to have in him the makings of a great schoolmaster. He was a large and vigorous youth, who managed to be a strict disciplinarian without losing popularity with the boys. The latter were wont to refer to him as 'Mr. Elephant'. He was at Corpus Christi, Cambridge, from February 1843 to the end of 1846. After that he helped his father at Llandaff House till his own marriage with Harriet Brimley in 1851, when, as already stated, he took over the school.

Harriet Brimley, W. E. Johnson's mother, was a great lover of poetry, and a beautiful reader of her favourite poets, Wordsworth, Tennyson, and Clough. Sympathizing as a matter of course with anti-slavery views, she would read, too, with fervour and expression the *Biglow Papers* of Russell Lowell. For some time after her marriage she taught in the school and acted as matron, but eventually the cares of a growing family of young children made her relinquish these duties, though she continued for many years to take occasional pupils in French and German.

W. E. Johnson was one of a numerous and very closely united band of brothers and sisters. His elder brother, George William, after a distinguished academic career at Cambridge, entered the Colonial Office and became an eminent civil servant and an indefatigable worker in the cause of the oppressed. His sister Harriet carried on the school after her father's retirement in 1893 till 1925 when she relinquished it to a former pupil. His sister Alice was for long Editor and Research Officer to the Society for Psychical Research, and in that capacity initiated the series of experiments on cross-correspondences in automatic writing, which, whatever may be the right interpretation of them, are among the most interesting and important phenomena with which the

Society had to deal. His sister Fanny kept house for him after the death of his wife, and it was owing to her unceasing and devoted care of him in health and in sickness that he was able to accomplish so much, in spite of constant delicacy and frequent serious illness.

Llandaff House was a building of historical interest and dignity, and it had a deep influence on Johnson and his brothers and sisters. The oldest part of it had a beautiful wide staircase and gallery and panelled rooms, and dated back probably to the time of Queen Anne. It took its name from Richard Watson, Bishop of Llandaff and Professor of Chemistry in the University in the latter part of the eighteenth century. Watson had lived in it and partly rebuilt it, adding two rooms called 'the Parlour' and 'the Great Room' by the Johnson family. Between Llandaff House and the as yet unspoiled fields belonging to Downing College was a shady walk, called 'The Grove'. The authorities of Downing allowed the Johnsons and some neighbours to use this walk, and it was the favourite playground of the children. The Grove was made all the dearer to the family by the fact that it was held on a precarious tenure and might have to be surrendered at any moment.

It would be impossible to depict Johnson's early life and surroundings better than by quoting from a memoir in manuscript which Miss Fanny Johnson has kindly written and lent to me.

Life indoors for the children was a succession of lessons with a strict governess or still stricter father. Breakfast and midday dinner were taken in silence in the company of the boarders (yclept 'Rough-'uns', a corruption probably of 'Ruffians'). There were family prayers morning and evening, chapel twice on Sunday, and serious occupation in the intermediate hours, or the writing of sermons and other religious exercises. Willie was an adept at the latter, and sometimes composed hymn-verses to his favourite tunes. It was borne in upon us from our cradles that we were not quite as other men socially or religiously, that we were in fact 'Dissenters'. Theological and politico-religious talk was the staple of conversation when guests were present. The guests, indeed, apart from family connexions, were chiefly ministers who came to 'supply' the pulpit in the occasional absences of our own pastor. Our parents were of the Baptist persuasion, though, as we discovered later, of broader views than the bulk of their co-religion-

ists. Such topics were mooted in table-talk as the importance of
immersion as against sprinkling in baptism, the proper forms of
church-government, or the more exciting problems of the nature
of Hell, of Eternity, or the Atonement, and whether the Resurrection would be universal or partial, i.e. only for the elect. There is
a legend that Willie at the age of eight or ten once stood in the
middle of Parker's Piece and remarked to all and sundry: 'I am
a sturdy little Dissenter.' The occasion was probably an election
when open-air speeches were made on Parker's Piece, and party-
feeling (in our case Liberal feeling) ran high.

It is interesting to remark at this point how much the Cambridge school of moral science in the nineteenth and early
twentieth centuries owed to cultivated Liberal Nonconformist
homes, such as Johnson's, with their tradition of plain living
and high thinking, and their passion for freedom of thought.
Professor James Ward and Dr. J. N. Keynes were both nurtured in similar surroundings to Johnson's; and, although Sidgwick was of Anglican origin, he was a protagonist in the fight
for the abolition of religious tests in the University. As Johnson
grew older he no doubt moved away from the precise theological tenets of his ancestors. In a letter to his sister Fanny, dated
18th September 1883, he writes as follows: 'I agree with you
about not calling oneself an Atheist. But I'm blessed if I should
call myself an Agnostic either. I should not call myself anything.
One's troubles force one to cry out vaguely to some unknown
something very often, and sometimes one fancies it has its effects
in the best way possible. And, if one can't get on without that,
one can't call oneself names of that sort.' He went with his
children regularly to church on Sunday mornings, and played
hymns to them in the evening. Until they were of an age to
judge for themselves he never made them aware of his own
doubts, though his dislike of *extempore* prayers, which had been
the bane of himself and his brothers and sisters in childhood,
was sometimes referred to. I do not know what position he
finally reached about such matters, but I always had the impression that he continued to accept some form of theism. And
of course the distinction between the Nonconformist and the
Anglican type of mind cuts right across the distinction between
Theism and Atheism. McTaggart, though an atheist, could
never have been anything but an Anglican; and Johnson could

never have been anything but a Nonconformist, whatever his final views about theism might have been.

Johnson's political views, like his religious opinions, developed with time and experience but underwent no essential modification. He remained a strongly convinced free-trader to the end of his life, and could give very impressive arguments for the faith that was in him. He would almost certainly have regarded the return of England to protection, not only as economically futile, but as a kind of moral and intellectual lapse on the part of a nation which had seen and chosen the better part while the rest of the world remained sunk in the folly and wickedness of economic nationalism. His attitude towards the present régime in Russia was highly characteristic. He had, of course, nothing but contempt for the constant nagging at all things Russian practised by the stupider members of the Conservative party in England, and no form of religion could be much more alien to him than that of the Russian Church. But he was horrified at the persecution of Russian Christians by the Soviet government, and he had no patience with the disingenuous attempts of many members of the English Labour Party to minimize, to condone, and to suppress the facts. It was far better, he held, to sacrifice trade with Russia than to make ourselves accomplices in the crimes of her government against freedom of thought and worship.

In a letter to his sister Fanny of 17th March 1877 there is a passage about his reading *Friendship's Garland*, which is worth quoting in connexion with the development of his early political views. 'Do you know Matthew Arnold's *Friendship's Garland*? That is the staple of my reading—or rather being read aloud to. . . . It is a most brilliantly sarcastic hit on the political ideas of Englishmen from *Miall*ism to *Mill*ism—those two *isms* that you and I, I fear, are steeped in. 'Liberty' and 'Publicity', 'Church-disestablishment' and 'to enable a man to marry his deceased wife's sister'—have *we* not been guilty of calling this the all in all to be aimed at, the great Politico-Economical desideratum? If so, let us now submit to the government of the Wisest—after Carlyle—to receive Governmental Education—after Matthew—and perhaps even Military Subordination—after Bismarck.' The earlier part of Johnson's life coincided with the high noontide of Liberalism in England. Gross and palpable abuses were yearly being removed; the country was well and cheaply governed and was abundantly prosperous; and the gloomy forebodings of opponents of free trade and democracy —almost all of which we now see being fulfilled to the letter— were so plainly belied by experience at the time that they could be comfortably dismissed as the ravings of stupid and selfish reactionaries.

By the beginning of this century the shadows of Liberalism were lengthening, and it was never to enjoy glad confident morning again. At last came the disaster of 1914, a crisis which, as his sister says, 'shook Johnson's whole being'. I will quote again from her memoir. 'Sensitive to pain in an extreme degree himself, the infliction of suffering or the sight of suffering in others was unendurable. Yet his mental make-up prevented his becoming a whole-hearted pacifist, and he was denied the consolation of taking definite *sides* with the minority. Of this, as of many other problems, he looked for a logical solution and found none.'

At the age of eight Johnson was attacked by a severe illness which was the beginning of lifelong ill-health. He became subject to severe attacks of asthma which developed into chronic bronchial trouble. There were few winters in which he was not incapacitated for weeks at a time. In consequence of this his course at school and at the university was much interrupted and hampered. He studied at first under his father, and then for a few years at the Perse School, where he had the advantage of being taught the classics by Heppenstall, one of its most distinguished head masters. For a short time he went as a boarder to the Liverpool Royal Institution School, of which his uncle, Henry Isaac Johnson, was head master from 1874 to 1889. Here he was attacked by so severe an illness that the doctors advised him to winter in the south of France. He spent the winter of 1877 at Hyères. The affliction of bodily sickness was not without its compensations on the side of family affection and personal friendships. It created a specially intimate and lifelong tie with his sister Fanny. In childhood she would play at 'architecture' with him, using a splendid box of bricks which was the chief family toy, and constructing under his direction while he lay in bed models of the Fitzwilliam Museum or Addenbrooke's Hospital. Later, when he became passionately interested in music, they would play duets together in such harmony as to seem almost one. At Hyères he formed a close friendship with the Hon. Mrs. O. N. Knox, daughter of the first Lord Monteagle, who was herself staying there in search of health. Mrs. Knox was musical, and would have been a fine singer but for the consumptive trouble which ended her life some ten years later. Johnson's letters at this time are full of music and the Knoxes. In one of them he remarks: 'My letters, you have observed, are very redolent of Knox. Knox in fact is the order of the day. I am half afraid it "knocks" you up, if you'll excuse the pun.' Mrs. Knox was a cultivated woman and something of a poet, and she brought Johnson into touch with a different social and artistic tradition from that in which he had been nurtured. Her tact and sympathy were of immense help to him at the critical period of young manhood. For several successive years he spent the winter with this family at whatever place Mrs. Knox's health required her to visit.

Music played a most important part in Johnson's life from first to last. His sister writes: 'There is no doubt that his deepest emotions were uttered through the medium of music. While he interpreted the fugues and preludes of Bach, the sonatas of Beethoven, or the Carnival of Schumann in his own exquisite and inimitable manner he was giving voice to his real innermost self, and listeners felt themselves in touch with a great soul.' He began to play the piano soon after his first illness. He was almost self-taught, save for occasional lessons by means of piano duets with his sister Fanny. She writes of these early days: 'His taste and exquisite touch on the piano were already admired when he stayed as a young boy at the house of his uncle, Alexander Macmillan, the publisher, where some excellent musicians were *habitués*. He became a perfect accompanist to singers whose taste for good things coincided with his own. More rarely he would accompany players of the violin or other instruments who came from time to time within his orbit.' A common love of music was partly the basis of nearly all his strongest and most lasting friendships, including his marriage. Towards the end of his life, as weakness grew upon him, piano-playing became his main solace.

A letter written on 28th November 1874, to Fanny on her birthday, is full of his practising the violin to play in the *Messiah* at a forthcoming amateur concert. 'I suppose', he writes, 'you know that I am going to add my iota to the desert of sound (if there is such an expression) in the next Amateur concert? Is not it splendid? I have had one practice, in which I first felt as if I was playing every note out of tune; but when we came to the very loud parts I drew my bow boldly and imagined I was doing it all right. And then the Hallelujah Chorus! Was not that splendid? I played that, I think, better than anything else.' In another letter of 27th June 1874 there is a most elaborate discussion of the nature of 'bars' in music. The young musician and logician yet-to-be evolves a theory of 'periods', states his view as to the relation of these 'periods' to 'bars', candidly admits that there are facts which will not square with his theory, and suggests that fact and theory might be reconciled by assuming 'the same kind of licence that is allowed in having *pauses* in bars'. He characteristically ends by saying: 'I don't think that's satisfactory; but I think there must be some truth in it, don't you? And I shall try to get further to the bottom of it.'

One youthful experience of Johnson links him with an eminent professional singer. Staying at an hotel in the Black Forest he met a lively family of boys, one of whom had a glorious voice which Johnson accompanied on the derelict hotel piano. This boy became known to the public a few years later as the famous singer Plunket Greene.

Johnson's lifelong delicacy prevented him from pursuing any active form of sport to great lengths. Cricket played a large part in the thoughts and conversation of the children at Llandaff House. Their father was a good amateur cricketer, and a favourite game of pretence among the children was to assume the names and personalities of famous local cricketers who played on Parker's Piece. But Johnson himself cared more for football, in the rather informal way in which it was then played. He was also devoted to mountain climbing in the Lake district or Switzerland, though his unorthodox costume—trousers and low shoes, without nails—would have shocked the professional climbers of to-day.

It is time to speak of Johnson's academic career. He approached moral science by way of mathematics. He won a mathematical scholarship at King's College, Cambridge, in

1879. In 1882 his name appeared in the mathematical tripos list as 11th Wrangler, bracketed with Ropes of King's and Sanderson who afterwards became the famous head master of Oundle. For some years he made his living as a mathematical coach, taking over Sanderson's pupils when the latter left Cambridge. He wrote a textbook on *Trigonometry* which was published by Messrs. Macmillan in 1888. The judgment of the publisher's reader, a very eminent mathematician, was as follows:

> This is a very fresh and unhackneyed presentation of the subject and does not take the ground of any English book that I know. When I say that it is like Homersham Cox's *Arithmetic*, or Clifford's *Dynamic*, or Chrystal's *Algebra*, you will understand at once its merit and defect. It is sure to be welcome to the thoughtful teacher, and give him a great deal to reflect upon, and some few in the Universities would find their account in reading it; but the ordinary student would find it an impossible text-book. . . . The book is in fact a good treatise but by no means a manual.

The reader remarks that the publication of the book would be likely to end in financial loss. The publishers took the risk with their eyes open, and the gloomy forebodings of their reader were fulfilled.

From quite early days Johnson had begun to be interested in moral science, and particularly in logic. In a letter of 16th July 1882 to his sister Fanny he mentions that he is studying logic every day before breakfast. In the same letter he embarks on a long and most characteristic discussion on grammar and its relations to psychology, on the one hand, and to logic, on the other. This was occasioned by some suggestions which Fanny had made in an earlier letter for reforms in the teaching of grammar. The passion for neat and accurate divisions, and for inventing new technical terms, which is so noticeable in his later work, here begins to show itself.

In 1883 he was placed in the First Class of the Moral Sciences Tripos, distinguished in Psychology, along with G. F. Stout of St. John's, the eminent psychologist and philosopher. The two shared the actual seniority of the year, though names had then begun to be placed in alphabetical order.

In those days Economics was included in the Moral Sciences Tripos, and it was a subject in which Johnson's mathematical logical, and psychological interests could combine with the happiest results. For a great many years he lectured in the University on the mathematical theory of Economics. His principal published contribution to this subject was an article which appeared in the *Economic Journal* for 1913 (vol. xxiii, p. 483). It is entitled *The Pure Theory of Utility Curves*. It ran to thirty-one pages, and has been described by the late Lord Keynes as 'substantial'. Professor Edgeworth contributed a review of it to the *Economic Journal*, vol. xxv, p. 36.

Johnson competed for a prize-fellowship at King's, but at his second and final attempt the electors preferred the claims of Ropes, his 'bracket' in the Mathematical Tripos. This was naturally a great disappointment, and it was of financial importance since Johnson was not well off and had to set about earning his living. Lack of means had forced him to live at home while an undergraduate at King's. The atmosphere of the college was at that time predominantly Etonian; and poverty, ill-health, and difference of social outlook made him unduly bashful. He tended to shrink into his shell and to make few friends in his own college. In a letter to Fanny, dated 29th November 1877, he writes: 'How is it that I always get on better with women than with men? I fear me there is something decidedly womanish in my character. I hardly get beyond monosyllables with any man here. They seem to talk so much upon subjects where my ignorance of the world becomes painful, or at least prevents my joining them.' This letter is written from Hyères, and refers no doubt primarily to the men whom he was meeting there; but it would probably have been true of his relations with contemporary undergraduates also. His Cambridge friendships were formed mainly with men in other colleges. The most permanent of them was with William Bateson of St. John's. The two had in common an ardent love of truth, in spite of divergent interests and temperaments. Had Johnson gained a prize-fellowship he would have been relieved of financial anxiety, and his self-confidence would have received a much needed encouragement. But he was destined to have to wait many years for adequate recognition and comparative freedom from financial worries.

Johnson's first teaching post was that of lecturer on Psychology and Education to the Cambridge Women's Training College. This office he held for many years, during which he also for some time lectured and examined for the College of Preceptors. Henry Sidgwick early recognized Johnson's worth, and quietly but persistently brought him forward, helping him with practical advice and moral support until he began to be appreciated within the University as an outstanding figure. From 1893 to 1898 he was University Teacher in the Theory of Education. In 1896 he succeeded Stout as University Lecturer in Moral Science. This post he held until 1901. In 1902 he was appointed Sidgwick Lecturer in Moral Science in the University, an office which he continued to hold until his death. For many years he lectured on psychology for Part I of the Moral Sciences Tripos, whilst Dr. Keynes lectured on logic for Part I. When Dr. Keynes became Registrar, Johnson took over the logic lecturing and handed over the psychology to Dr. Moore who now returned to Cambridge as University lecturer. Henceforth Johnson's formal lecturing was confined to logic. But, throughout most of the period, he coached pupils in all subjects connected with Moral Science.

One of the sections in Part II of the Tripos is Advanced Logic. It is not often that a candidate chooses this section, but, whenever one did, Johnson provided the whole of the necessary teaching. In 1909, when the present writer was preparing for another section of Part II of the Tripos, Johnson had not been called upon to lecture on Advanced Logic for many years. But he had rashly advertised in the lecture-list that he would lecture on this subject 'by arrangement' if pupils presented themselves. The chance was too good to be missed, and three undergraduates, one of whom was afterwards Professor Laird of Aberdeen and another Professor L. J. Russell of Birmingham, appeared. The result was that we had the most valuable and exciting course of lectures that could be imagined. Johnson had been reflecting for years on logic, probability, and theory of knowlege, and had written down roughly many of his thoughts. Also he had been engaged for years in reviewing for *Mind*, vol. i of Russell's *Principles of Mathematics*. The review never appeared; it would indeed have filled several numbers of *Mind*. But we had the benefit of it and of much else. A great deal of the matter of these lectures was afterwards incorporated in his *Logic*; certain theorems on probability are published, with due acknowledgment, in the formal part of Lord Keynes's *Treatise on Probability*; but all was new at the time and much has never been published. In those days Johnson was still able to go out to lecture. He used to do so in a classroom in King's. In the winter he would often wear a large red shawl. Latterly for many years he lectured in his own house, to which he was often confined by bronchitis for the whole winter.

Johnson's manner of lecturing was not ideal. He had a tendency to spend a great amount of time on certain points, to let himself be diverted from the main issue, and thus to be forced by lack of time to leave out important slices of the subject. These defects naturally grew on him with age and increasing bodily weakness. The candidates for Part I of the Tripos generally found it expedient to take his lectures twice over in successive years, in the hope that the gaps of one year would not coincide with those of the next. As an examiner in the Tripos or the Intercollegiate Examinations he seemed to the present writer to have the same kind of failing. If one were trying to set a paper with him he would often single out one of the proposed questions and devote so much time and energy to explaining exactly how he would have put it, and what he thought to be the right answer to it, that other and equally important questions had to be hurriedly settled at the end. In judging a candidate's paper he was very liable at first to concentrate on some small weakness or silliness in one answer, to lose sight of the merits of the rest of his paper, and to mark him down with Draconic severity. But he was always fundamentally just and, provided that his co-examiner was patient and tactful and had a good case, he could always be brought to judge the candidate's work fairly as a whole. He set extremely good questions, particularly in formal logic and in ethics. Any one who takes the trouble to look through the examples at the ends of chapters in Dr. Keynes's *Studies and Exercises in Formal Logic* will find that the hardest, neatest, and most ingenious problems are marked 'J', which means that they were devised by Johnson. His fertility in producing problems on the syllogism seemed inexhaustible; year after year he supplied them for the Logic papers in Part I of the Tripos or the Intercollegiate Examination.

Whatever may have been Johnson's defects as a teacher for the practical purpose of getting through the Tripos, the many generations of undergraduates who attended his lectures or were coached by him realized that they were in contact with a very great thinker and a personality which was rendered all the more lovable by its occasional oddities and petulancies. On the whole young men form a very accurate estimate of their teachers, and the letters which I have read and the conversations which I have heard show clearly how high this estimate was. Not only was he esteemed by those who became distinguished philosophers themselves and were thus able to view him from approximately his own level; many who had no pretensions to philosophic eminence and engaged in other activities when they went down have acknowledged how much they owed to his teaching and example.

In 1895 Johnson married Barbara Keymer Heaton. Her father was a lecturer in chemistry, her mother the author of a life of Albert Dürer, and many members of her family circle were writers or artists by profession. It is characteristic of him that, as soon as he became engaged, and before ever the date of the wedding or the means of livelihood were secured, he went forthwith and bought a large grand piano as the most essential ingredient of housekeeping. It was a joke in the family that he must now proceed to have a house built round the piano. The first Long Vacation after his marriage was spent in his beloved Switzerland. His vigour was renewed and his mental activity quickened by his wife's sympathetic understanding. She had the rare gift of comprehending through the affections, and could enter into his interest in 'curves' and other abstruse problems without any formal knowledge of the subject. The aesthetic part of him, already developed musically, responded to her superior acquaintance with the colours and forms of nature. She was well trained by teachers who had studied under Ruskin, and she made charming sketches full of the feeling of that tradition. With her, too, he first began the study of botany, and afterwards handed on to his sons what he had acquired of the elements of a subject which specially appealed to his love of classification. Johnson's married life was ideally happy, but all too short. Two sons were born to him; and in 1902 his wife had the joy of seeing him honoured by his own college, which elected him to a fellowship. But she died suddenly two years later, leaving him with the two young children. He bore this heavy blow with the strength and courage which might have been expected from his character and upbringing, and his sister Fanny henceforth devoted her life to him and his sons.

Even after Johnson was elected to a fellowship he remained almost unknown outside Cambridge, and his financial anxieties were not at an end. Ill-health, diffidence, and a very high standard of achievement had prevented him from publishing any book since his *Trigonometry* 'fell stillborn from the press'. His only philosophical publications had been a series of three articles in *Mind*, N.S., vols. i, ii, and iii, entitled 'The Logical Calculus', and a contribution in French on 'The Theory of Logical Equations' to the International Congress of Philosophy in 1900. The King's fellowship was only for a term of years, and at that time the *modulus* was very small. Whenever the question of continuance came up, the college naturally and rightly required evidence that Johnson was doing work of such merit as to justify the prolongation of his fellowship. In the absence of any publications the only available evidence was the reports of his colleagues and pupils, and it was difficult for workers in other subjects to estimate the value of such reports. There were therefore recurrent periods of acute anxiety as to whether the fellowship would be continued. Happily it always was.

We owe the publication of Johnson's great work on Logic very largely to his pupil Miss Naomi Bentwich. It is unlikely that he would ever have brought himself to undergo the drudgery of preparing his scattered manuscripts for the press had not she relieved him of the labour and almost driven him to face the task. Johnson first broke his long silence in 1918, in two articles in *Mind*, N.S., vol. xxvii, entitled 'Analysis of Thinking'. In 1921 appeared the first volume of his *Logic*, in 1922 the second, and in 1924 the third. In preparing the third volume for the press he received help, particularly in connexion with the analytical table of contents, from his pupil Mr. J. A. Chadwick, afterwards Fellow of Trinity. There should have been a fourth volume, dealing with Probability. Unfortunately the physical and mental strain involved in preparing the first three volumes were greater than his friends realized at the time, and he was never able to accomplish the preparation of the fourth, though his friend and former pupil, Mr. R. B. Braithwaite of King's, worked hard and patiently with him to this end. Lord Keynes's important *Treatise on Probability* had appeared in 1921, with generous acknowledgments of the help and inspiration which the author had received from Johnson. The latter seems to have felt that he could not publish his own work on the same subject without elaborately noticing and criticizing the theories of Lord Keynes. Yet he lacked the strength and power of concentration which this would have demanded. Thus in the end he neither criticized Lord Keynes nor got his own theories clearly stated on paper, but fretted himself in his attempts to combine two tasks, either of which separately was now almost beyond his powers. Some four chapters in typescript taken down by Miss Bentwich remain.

Johnson's *Logic* was at once recognized as a book of the first importance, and its publication won him a long overdue recognition in the academic world outside Cambridge. In 1922 he was honoured by the University of Manchester with a doctorate in letters; in 1923 he was elected a Fellow of the British Academy; and in 1926 the University of Aberdeen conferred on him the degree of doctor of laws.

It would be out of place here to attempt to give an elaborate account of a difficult book on a highly technical subject. It will suffice to say that Johnson's *Logic* is very much more than a treatise on deductive and inductive logic as ordinarily understood. It contains most valuable and original chapters on fundamental problems of epistemology, metaphysics, and even psychology. The notions of Cause and Substance are elaborately treated; and there are chapters on the nature of magnitude, on the application of the notion of cause to mental events and processes, on the relation of causation to space and time, and so on. Often Johnson will throw out a suggestion of the utmost importance in an incidental sentence, as, e.g. where he distinguishes between the adjectival and the substantival form of the absolute theory of space and time. The third volume contains a mathematical appendix on the application of probability to induction which makes one regret more than ever that the projected fourth volume never saw the light.

The volumes as they appeared were elaborately reviewed in *Mind,* and have formed the subject of discussion in philosophical circles ever since. Johnson was not a particularly lucid writer, and the conditions under which the work was written and published were not favourable to clearness of exposition. Mr. Joseph, in two articles in *Mind*, vols. xxxvi and xxxvii, entitled 'What does Mr. Johnson mean by a Proposition?', claims to distinguish no less than twenty different senses in which Johnson uses this fundamental term; and even a more charitable or less acute critic than Mr. Joseph must admit that he can discover no one consistent theory on this point in Johnson's book. There was much in Johnson to remind one of Kant, a philosopher whom he greatly admired. There was the same love of making elaborate divisions and constructing technical terminology to name them. There was in both the defect which the late Lord Balfour happily described as 'contriving to be technical without being precise'. But, speaking for myself, I should say without hesitation that the frequent obscurities and pedantries in the writings of the two men never lead one to doubt for a moment that they were great intellects and great characters. The impression that one gets is that of a richness and depth of thought which the verbal medium is at times inadequate to convey. Many of Johnson's technical terms are, however, very happily chosen; they crystallize distinctions which have constantly to be borne in mind, and they are likely to find a permanent place in English philosophy. Among them I may mention the terms *continuant* and *occurrent* as contrasted with *substantive* and *adjective*, *determinable* and *determinate* as contrasted with *genus* and *species*, *logical ties* as contrasted with *relations, epistemic* and *constitutive* conditions for the validity of an argument, *problematic* and *demonstrative* induction, and so on.

It seems to be believed outside Cambridge that there is something called 'the Cambridge school' of philosophy, and deserving candidates for the degree of doctor of philosophy spend time and ingenuity in discovering, stating, and criticizing its supposed tenets. It is difficult to know where Johnson would find his niche in this temple. Though extremely well versed in the works of the great philosophers and in the classical physics, he read hardly any contemporary books on either physics or philosophy. I should doubt whether he had looked into any work by one of his colleagues since the first edition of Mr. Russell's *Principia Mathematica* except Lord Keynes's *Treatise on Probability*. The chapters in which he discusses physical and psychical substances and causation, and their relations to space and time, were of course written before the post-war excitements of relativity, the quantum theory, and psycho-analysis. But it is doubtful whether he would have wished to alter them, for he seemed to be almost wholly unmoved by these developments. It is difficult at present to say how far this limitation of outlook affects the permanent value of his treatment of these subjects. It may well be that, when the dust of recent physical and psychological theories and discoveries has settled, we shall find that no fundamental change in our old concepts of substance and cause is needed. It has often been the case that revolutionary scientific discoveries seemed to be of profound philosophical importance only so long as the scientists themselves were still groping in the dark. On the other hand, it does seem much more likely that many of our most fundamental concepts will have to be thoroughly overhauled and perhaps replaced by new ones. If so, much of the third volume in particular of Johnson's *Logic* will become of merely historical interest. Again, in matters of pure logic Johnson remained completely unaffected by the work of Dr. Wittgenstein or of recent German theorists on the foundations of mathematics, such as Weyl, Hilbert, etc. Whatever may be the outcome of these later developments much of Johnson's work will remain untouched, and we shall often return with relief and profit to his solid English sanity from the wilder flights of Teutonic speculation; but it may well be that his treatment of the laws of thought and the foundations of mathematics will become out of date. We can neither hope nor expect that all his work in a subject which is intensely alive and continually advancing will survive the test of time. He was the disciple of no 'school', and he had no ambition to be the master of one.

In 1927 Johnson was affected by a kind of stroke which impaired his speech though not his intellectual powers. He was still able to play at chess and patience, two favourite games of his. By 1928 his speech was almost completely restored and he was able to lecture again, but it was obvious that he was beginning to fail. The last year of his life was one of long and patiently borne suffering, which came to a sudden and merciful end on 14th January 1931.

The main features in Johnson's character will have become clear in the course of the above sketch of his life and work, but it will be worth while to add a few more personal details. His constant ill-health and the long struggle which he waged with *res angustae domi* made it impossible for him to play an active part in the life of King's or the University, but never embittered him or made him a hermit. The following extract from a letter from Lord Keynes is of interest in this connexion.

In my time he seldom or never dined in Hall except perhaps at a feast, but he was a very regular attendant at college meetings, and used particularly to enjoy talking and sipping sherry at the lunches which follow our more important Congregations. It would not be true to say that he was a recluse in the sense in which many Fellows of Colleges are. He was always intensely sociable, and loved conversation and society as much as any one in the world, though too much would soon tire him. It was simply that for some time past he had got into the habit of seeing people in his own house rather than elsewhere. As time went on his asthma confirmed this habit. But for many years he was a familiar figure entering the college to go to his rooms, where he spent a good deal of the day and saw all his pupils. . . . My main point is perhaps that it would be quite wrong to think of him as a recluse. In his early bachelor days the collective Johnson family had been one of the greatest centres of talk and social life in Cambridge, and the little tea-parties that went on at Ramsey House down to quite recent times were in continuous tradition with those at Llandaff House as far back as the '70's.

To these tea-parties, which Lord Keynes mentions, were invited all the undergraduates who were working with Johnson. There was generally a sprinkling of old pupils, and often one or two dons in other subjects than Moral Science would drop in. Miss Fanny Johnson would dispense tea, and Johnson would sit by the fire wrapped in the old red shawl which was so characteristic of him. He was an extremely good conversationalist, though he never talked for effect. Conversation was generally on 'serious' subjects, literature, philosophy, politics, etc., Johnson always had something original to say and very good reasons for saying it, and this reacted on his guests, who were inspired to follow suit and maintain a high level of thinking and sincerity. After tea there would be music, and Johnson would play one favourite after another on the piano or would induce such of his guests as were competent to do so to play to him.

Apart from subjects which were instinctively congenial, he studied seriously at various periods Hebrew, for which he even won a school prize; German, mainly from the point of view of philosophy; and, as already mentioned, botany. His interest in architecture was constant. Ancient churches and other buildings in various neighbourhoods were thoroughly explored with his children during holidays. The last time that he went out of doors (November 1930) he took a drive through Cambridge to get a glimpse of the many new buildings in the town which had reached or were approaching completion.

He had a good knowledge of the English classics, his favourite among the English poets being Wordsworth. His interest in character, whether in real life or in fiction, was keen and penetrating. He always maintained that psychologists were 'born not trained'. He shared with the late Dr. McTaggart a cult for Charlotte M. Yonge, and would discuss her characters, and those of George Eliot, Thackeray, and Trollope, as eagerly as if they were living acquaintances. He was a Puritan to the core, and passed by with dislike those novels in which the main interest is centred upon the physiological details or the psychological concomitants of sexual intercourse. Detective novels attracted him as 'problems', and he found relief in their remoteness from the horrors of actuality.

He had a profound special knowledge of Dickens and Jane Austen. Of each of these he would find something fresh and illuminating to say after each new reading. I should think that he could have rewritten a considerable part of the *Pickwick Papers* if all copies had been destroyed; and, in this connexion, I cannot do better than quote the inscription which a great personal friend wrote in the copy of his own book on *Charles Dickens* when he presented it to Johnson: 'To Will. Johnson, who ought to have written this book, from G. K. Chesterton, who did.' He modestly professed 'not to understand' poetry, but he could throw light on a difficult passage in Shakespeare if he chose. In a letter dated 9th October 1881 he remarks that he has been reading some novels by Henry James, and he tries to sum up his impression of the author in a sentence. 'Morally a stranger to human emotions, yet without a grain of cynicism; intellectually completely conversant with them, yet without a spark of apprehension.' He admits, however, that this 'won't do', and concludes as follows: 'At any rate his all-round and shrewd knowledge of human nature seems strangely combined with an apathetic coldness. The characters interest me without exciting any emotion . . .'

Biography, especially Boswell, was another source of keen interest. Again, when his elder son became a lecturer and wrote on art, he entered into everything that pertained to that subject with the same zest and critical acumen that he displayed in other directions.

It remains to mention the extremely generosity with which Johnson helped by advice and criticism those who were working at the same subjects as himself. In each successive edition of his *Studies and Exercises in Formal Logic*, Dr. Keynes mentions with gratitude the assistance which he had derived from Johnson; and Lord Keynes remarks: 'He was of course extraordinarily helpful and generous to me when I was at work on Probability.' I cannot resist quoting here another passage from Lord Keynes's letter. 'He used, when I was a child, regularly to lunch at Harvey Road with my father; I should think almost once a week. My father was then writing his book on logic, which would infrequently be a matter of conversation and discussion. They seemed to me in those days to sit endlessly over the meal, and I would be in a fidget to be allowed to get up and go. His voice and manner were quite invariable and unchanged in my memory from those days, more than forty years ago, up to the end of his life.'

The generation of Radical Nonconformists to which Johnson belonged was the finest and, it is to be feared, the last, flower of a very sound and very typically English stock. It had inherited a tradition of hard work, high seriousness, and solid good sense from a long line of ancestors who had 'learned and laboured truly to get their own living, and to do their duty in that state of life to which it should please God to call them'. It had emancipated itself from the narrowness of its older theological outlook without losing its faith in the higher spiritual values, and it had assimilated the best culture available at the time. Above all it really believed in reason and in reasonableness, and strove according to its lights to apply them to the solution of philosophic, political, and international problems. The motto which Johnson prefixed to his *Logic* was the old definition: 'Man is a *rational* animal.' He was fated to survive into one of those unhappy periods of human history in which theory and practice unite to exalt the generic characteristics and to minimize the specific differences of man. To those of us who have henceforth to steer our way as best we can through the cynical disillusionment of the cultured and the sentimental credulity of the mob the memory of such men as Johnson shines like a beacon, diffusing a clear steady light over angry seas of passion and nonsense. Of him and his generation we may say a little enviously:

> Vobis parta quies; nullum maris aequor arandum;
> Arva neque Ausoniae, semper cedentia retro,
> Quaerenda.

SECTION II

PHILOSOPHY OF SCIENCE

THE PHILOSOPHY OF
FRANCIS BACON

THE great man whose memory we are honouring to-day was so universal a genius, his speculative and practical activities were so various, that we must be content either with a superficial glance at his achievements as a whole or with the contemplation, at the risk of onesidedness, of a single aspect of his work. Faced with these unsatisfactory alternatives I choose the second. Others, better fitted than I, must appraise Bacon's merits as lawyer, statesman, and stylist; I shall consider only his claims to be the Father of Inductive Philosophy. It is fitting that Bacon should be viewed in that light in this country and this University. Inductive Logic is almost wholly the work of Englishmen; and in the short list of great Englishmen who have contributed to this branch of philosophy Cambridge is proud to number Bacon, Whewell, and Venn in the past, and Mr. Johnson and Mr. Keynes in the present. Even the restricted subject which I have chosen is of vast extent, so without further preface I will enter on it.

Bacon's grounds for dissatisfaction with the past and present state of human knowledge and his hopes for the future were stated in many forms; but they reduce in essence to the following. Our present Natural Philosophy amounts to very little. It consists of portions of Greek philosophy tricked out in various ways, so that the apparent plenty is like a number of dishes made of the same meat disguised with different sauces. Nor does it include the whole even of Greek philosophy; for Aristotle, like the Turk, would brook no rivals near his throne, and the Bar-

barian invasions extinguished what he and his followers had
failed to suppress. The current philosophy, derived from Aristotle, is difficult to criticize; partly because its technical terms
and fundamental concepts have passed into theology, law, and
common discourse; and partly because its premisses and modes
of reasoning are questionable, so that there is no common basis
for argument. But we can at least point out certain facts which
are very ill omens of its truth or usefulness. The Greeks were the
Peter Pans of the ancient world, and their philosophy has the
boyish characteristics of being 'apt to chatter and unable to
generate'. It started at a time when there was little knowledge of
geography or history compared with that which we now possess.
Plato and Aristotle, though men of the highest intellectual
power, could not make bricks without straw; their method of
teaching, which involved a school, an audience, and a sect, was
singularly unfavourable to disinterested observation of Nature
or free speculation on observed facts. The triumph of Aristotle's philosophy over its rivals is not to be ascribed to its intrinsic superiority. In philosophical matters general consent is
of ill omen, for a popular philosophy is usually one which in-
dulges human laziness by using loose superficial notions and by
substituting an appeal to a few high-sounding generalities for
the patient investigations of details. Two of the worst signs of
the current philosophy are that it does not progress and that it
does not lead to practical results. It stands still and wrangles
about old questions instead of settling them and passing on to
new ones. And in practical affairs we owe more to the sagacity
of animals and the blind instincts of ignorant men than to all
the theories of Natural Philosophy. The mechanical arts do
slowly progress through the growth of technical skill and the
co-operation of many hands. But Philosophy is like the statues
of the gods 'which are worshipped and celebrated but cannot
move'. The very perfection of systematic form which the traditional philosophy has acquired is a defect, for it diverts men's
minds from the narrowness of its foundations and the flimsiness
of its superstructure. Indeed the exponents of this philosophy
admit its barrenness by their constant complaints about the
obscurity and subtlety of Nature and the weakness of the human
mind. This appearance of modesty cloaks the pride which assumes that what cannot be known by their methods cannot be

known at all. And so progress is hampered equally by an unwarranted satisfaction with what has been done and by an unwarranted despair of accomplishing what remains to do.

If we now consider the empiricists, e.g. the alchemists and the magicians, we find the opposite defects. Each has laboriously tilled a very narrow field of phenomena, using no scientific method of culture, and snatching greedily at immediate practical results. Although they have by chance discovered some useful facts, they have failed both as theorists and as practicians. Their philosophical theories are crazy attempts to interpret the whole of Nature in terms of the small fragment of it with which each happens to be familiar. Nature can never be controlled except on the basis of a wide and deep knowledge of its inner structure and fundamental laws, and this can be won only by disinterested scientific investigation. Though no one has asserted more strongly than Bacon that ability to produce practical results is the ultimate test of scientific theories and the ultimate end of scientific research, no one has protested more vigorously against a narrow and short-sighted pragmatism. He compares it to the golden apple of Atalanta which diverted the runners from their course. And he compares those who are obsessed by it to harvesters who cannot wait till the crop has grown up, but trample on the young shoots in order to mow down moss.

If the old methods are still to be used the prospect is dark indeed. Our intellectual powers are no greater than those of the ancients; our only advantage over them is in the additional experience which has accumulated in two thousand years. And we cannot be more diligent than the alchemists and magicians who devoted their lives to the furnace and the crucible. Our only hope is to devise a new method which shall be to the mind as rulers and compasses are to the hand. The mere rationalists are like spiders who spin wonderful but flimsy webs out of their own bodies; the mere empiricists are like ants who collect raw materials without selection and store them up without modification. True and fruitful science must combine rationalism with empiricism, and be like the bee who gathers materials from every flower and then works them up by her own activities into honey. This marriage between rationalism and empiricism, and this discovery of a new method, are the tasks which Bacon set before himself. The times are peculiarly favourable, and he feels that he has the necessary qualifications. He will bring about the Great Instauration and will show men how to win back that dominion over Nature which was lost at the Fall.

Bacon has left us a detailed plan of the Great Instauration as he conceived it. It was to consist of six parts. The first was to be a complete encyclopaedia of the existing sciences, classified according to general principles which would make the gaps obvious. These gaps were not merely to be indicated. In each case suggestions were to be made as to the nature of the missing science and the best way of building it up. This portion of the plan is adequately fulfilled by the *De Augmentis*. The second part was to contain the principles of the new Art of Interpreting Nature, which is to put all human minds on a level and to provide them with an infallible mechanism for the discovery and invention, not of new arguments, but of new arts and sciences. Bacon's latest exposition of this is found in the *Novum Organum*. But it is admittedly incomplete in vitally important respects. This incompleteness it shares with the treatises on scientific method of Descartes, Spinoza, and Leibniz, all of which start with the same magnificent pretensions and end like noble rivers which never reach the sea but lose themselves in the sands of the desert. Bacon constantly said that he would return to the subject and that he knew how to complete it; but, in view of the failure of all similar attempts and the intractable nature of the problem, we may venture to believe that he was mistaken. The third part was to consist of a collection of particular data of experiment and observation specially chosen and arranged in accordance with principles laid down in Part II so as to form the empirical basis of Natural Philosophy. It is extremely fragmentary, consisting of three natural histories, prefaces to three others, a general preface, and the curious rag-bag of facts and fables called *Sylva Sylvarum*. Part IV, called the *Ladder of the Intellect*, was to consist of a number of fully worked-out examples of the application of the method. They were to be so chosen that the subject-matter of each should be intrinsically important, and that between them they should illustrate the use of the method in very varied media. Of this nothing is extant but a short preface. It is important to remember that we have no complete example of Bacon's method. The fifth part was to be called the *Forerunners, or Anticipations of the New Philosophy*. It was to contain interesting generalizations which Bacon had reached from his Natural History without using his special method of interpretation. These results are not guaranteed, and their importance is only temporary. The preface to this part exists; and it may reasonably be held that the admittedly imperfect investigation of the nature of heat which occupies so large a space in the Second Book of the *Novum Organum* is a sample of what Bacon meant to include in Part V. The sixth part was to be called *The New Philosophy or Active Science*. It was to consist of the complete science of Nature, theoretical and practical, firmly built on the facts of Part III by the methods of Part II. The preface is extant, but the work is naturally left to posterity.

Taking the Great Instauration as a whole, we may compare Part II to a factory full of ingenious machinery, Part III to a store house of selected materials for this machinery to work upon, Part IV to a showroom in which typical samples of the finished products are exposed to public view, and Part VI to a warehouse in which all the finished products are to be stored. Part V is a collection of goods made by inferior methods or only half finished, but useful enough for many purposes. Part I is a list in which the directors have noted what goods the public already have and what further needs remain as yet unrecognized or unsatisfied. Unfortunately the machinery is incomplete; and the engineer, instead of drawing the plans for completing it, has to spend his time in collecting raw materials and in penning eloquent prospectuses.

We will now consider Bacon's classification of actual and possible human knowledge. The first division is made by reference to the source from which the materials of knowledge flow into the mind. They may come either from the direct action of the Creator on his creatures, or from the action of the created world including ourselves. Thus human knowledge is first dichotomized into that which is acquired supernaturally and that which is acquired naturally. Each of these great divisions is then trichotomized on a psychological principle, viz. with reference to the cognitive faculty which the mind mainly uses in the work of knowing. Bacon recognizes three such faculties, viz. Memory (which for the present purpose includes Sense-perception), Imagination, and Reason. Memory and Imagination are concerned with particular things, events, and facts; Reason with general concepts, facts, and laws. Memory deals with real particulars and Imagination with feigned particulars. Thus human knowledge, whether of natural or of supernatural origin, is divided into History, Poesy, and Philosophy (or Science).

Before considering further subdivisions we must explain Bacon's views about supernaturally acquired knowledge; we shall then be able to confine ourselves to the knowledge which originates naturally. According to Bacon there are three subjects which need for their complete treatment data that spring from a supernatural source. These are Theology, Ethics, and Psychology. Each of these sciences can, however, be carried to a certain length without appeal to revelation. Each of them therefore divides into a natural and a revealed part. Theology is the most fundamental of the three, since the parts of Ethics and of Psychology which depend on revelation are branches of Revealed Theology.

Bacon holds that the existence of teleology in Nature is an obvious fact, and that the investigation of final causes is a perfectly legitimate branch of Natural Philosophy. It has, however, been misplaced; for it belongs to the division of Natural Philosophy which Bacon calls *Metaphysics* and not to that which he calls *Physics*. Bacon's epigram that 'the research into Final Causes, like a virgin dedicated to God, is barren and produces nothing' has been taken by careless or biased readers to be a condemnation of such research. It is nothing of the kind. It is simply a statement of the obvious fact that there is no art of Applied Teleology as there is an art of Applied Physics. Now Bacon holds that the existence and some of the attributes of God can be established conclusively by reflexion on the teleology of Nature. But this does not give determinate enough information about God to form an adequate basis for religion. The further details must be supplied by God himself in revelation. God, says Bacon, did not need to work miracles to convince atheists but to convert heathens.

His view about Ethics is very similar. We have a partial and inadequate knowledge of right and wrong by the light of Nature. But it does little more than show us that certain types of action are wrong; it gives no very determinate information about our positive duties. Divine revelation is needed to provide an adequate basis for a detailed morality.

The division of Psychology into a natural and a revealed part follows a different principle. There are not two Gods, one of whom is the subject of Natural and the other of Revealed Theology. But in man there are two souls, the rational and the animal. The former is immaterial, peculiar to man, and directly created by God at the moment of conception. The latter is shared with animals; it is material, and due to one's parents. It is described as 'a corporeal substance, attenuated and made invisible by heat', which resides mainly in the head, runs along the nerves, and is refreshed by the arterial blood. It is in fact our old friend 'the animal spirits' which are as material as methylated spirits. In man the rational soul uses the animal soul as its immediate instrument. Now the science of the rational soul, its origin, nature, and destiny, must 'be drawn from the same divine inspiration from which that substance first proceeded'. The science of the animal soul belongs to Natural Philosophy. Bacon's theory of the animal soul owes much to Telesius, while his sharp distinction between it and the rational soul is closely analogous to the theory which Descartes worked out in greater detail a little later.

It remains to consider Bacon's views as to the relations of reason and revelation. It is legitimate to exercise our reason on the data of revelation in two ways. In the first place we may try to understand them. But we have no more ground for expecting God's revealed nature to be agreeable to our reason than for expecting his revealed commands to be agreeable to our wishes. On the whole Bacon thinks that there is a strong presumption that the contents of divine revelation will be repugnant to our reason; and that, the more preposterous God's revealed nature and commands appear to be, the greater is our merit in believing in the former and obeying the latter. The position which Bacon here adopts has been most forcibly stated by Hobbes: 'The doctrines of religion are like the pills prescribed by physicians, which if swallowed whole do us good, but if chewed up make us sick.' The second legitimate use of reason in matters of revelation is the following. We may take the revealed nature and commands of God as fixed, and to us arbitrary, premisses like the rules of chess. We may then use reasoning to deduce remote consequences from them, just as we may use it in solving a chess problem. Each use of reason has its characteristic dangers. In trying to understand the contents of divine revelation we may distort them by forcing them into the mould of the human intellect. And in drawing consequences from revealed truths we may ascribe to the conclusions of our fallible reasoning that certainty which the premises derive from their Divine Author.

It is evident then that religion and morality have little to hope and nothing to fear from the advance of Natural Philosophy. Bacon has been acclaimed by the French Encyclopaedists, and abused by Joseph de Maistre, as an *esprit fort* who concealed his real atheism and materialism under a thin disguise of orthodoxy which sufficed to deceive the Wisest Fool in Christendom. Neither acclamation nor abuse is justified. It is evident that he was a sincere if unenthusiastic Christian of that sensible school which regards the Church of England as a branch of the Civil Service, and the Archbishop of Canterbury as the British Minister for Divine Affairs. Having seen fanatical superstition in action, and knowing of atheism only as a rare speculative doctrine, he naturally preferred the latter to the former. Actively fanatical atheism was not yet a practical possibility. It was reserved for a later age, which had reaped the fruits of the Great Instauration in poison gas and high-explosive shells, to witness the Barbarians of the East persecuting Christians in the name of Darwin, whilst the Barbarians of the West persecuted Darwinians in the name of Christ.

We can now deal with History, Poesy, and Philosophy, regarded henceforth as of purely natural origin. History is divided into Natural and Civil, according to whether it treats the particular facts of non-human Nature or the actions of men. As we have seen, a complete and properly chosen Natural History was to form the third part of the Great Instauration. The best account of what Bacon meant by such a History is contained in the tract called *Parasceve*, which he published along with the *Novum Organum*. He feels that some excuse is needed for publishing something which is mainly concerned with Part III when Part II is admittedly incomplete. His explanation is as follows. A complete Natural History will be an immense work, needing the co-operation of many men for long periods. It will be expensive, needing the help of royal, noble, and wealthy benefactors. It can, however, be carried on by men without special training or eminent intellectual qualifications, provided they are told what to look for, whereas Bacon himself and he only can complete the second part of the Great Instauration. He can provide others with the necessary methodological instructions without which the works of would-be Natural Historians will be as futile as those of their predecessors. Finally, Bacon says that the most perfect method of interpretation can accomplish nothing without an adequate and accurate Natural History to work upon, whilst even the existing methods of interpretation (bad as he believes them to be) could accomplish a great deal were such a Natural History provided. So the *Parasceve* is published to inspire the great to give their money and lend their authority, and to instruct plain men who are willing to offer their services how to collect that complete Natural History which is to restore to humanity its lost dominion over the material world. In the meanwhile Bacon is to be left in peace to his proper task of completing the method of Interpretation. Unfortunately the British Solomon, in partial reesmblance to his Jewish namesake, was too easily diverted from the austere beauties of science by others of a less ideal kind. And the plain men cared more for the eternal war of Church and Chapel than for winning the kingdom of Nature for humanity. Like the deaf adder they stopped their ears; and the architect of the Great Instauration was forced to dig his own clay and bake his own bricks.

The gist of Bacon's directions for forming a complete Natural History is as follows. Nature may act either freely and normally, or freely but abnormally, or under the deliberate constraint of man. Corresponding to these three possibilities there will be a History of the Normal, a History of Abnormalities, and a History of Experimental Results and Processes. Bacon rightly attaches very great importance to abnormal variations from the ordinary course of Nature, though he recognizes that all reports about them must be severely scrutinized before being accepted. The importance of abnormalities is twofold. They overthrow prejudices in favour of received theories, and they suggests practical means of making new artificial products. Bacon insists, and in this he is much ahead of his age, that there is no essential difference between the natural and the artificial. Again, he continually stresses the extreme importance of deliberate experiment as contrasted with mere passive observation. Experiment 'takes off the mask and veil from natural objects', and 'the vexations of art are . . . as the bonds of Proteus which betray the ultimate struggles and efforts of matter'. In the History of the Normal we need not enter into extremely minute varieties of species, as botanists and zoologists are wont to do; but we must not be too proud to include what is homely and familiar or too fastidious to record what is filthy and disgusting. The rays of the sun, says Bacon, illuminate the sewer as well as the palace and take no corruption; and 'if the money obtained from Vespasian's tax smelled well, much more do light and information from whatever source derived'.

So much for the contents of the Natural History. The principle of selection is that facts are to be chosen and recorded, not for their immediate use or intrinsic interest, but simply for their aptness to give rise to important inductions. Bacon gives some indication of the kind of facts which are likely to have this property in the account of Prerogative Instances at the end of the *Novum Organum*.

Finally, Bacon gives the following directions for recording the data. There are to be no controversies with other authors and no graces of style. The History is a storehouse to be entered only as occasion requires, and not a dwelling-house or an art gallery. If the facts to be recorded are certain they are simply to be stated without evidence. If they are doubtful and not very important the authority should be mentioned for reference but no arguments should be given. If they are both doubtful and important all information should be given about the authority which bears on his value as a witness. Commonly accepted fictions should not be passed over in silence. They should be explicitly mentioned and denied, and, if possible, the causes of the illusion should be stated. All data that are capable of accurate measurement should be measured, and where exact measures are impossible upper and lower limits should be stated. All difficult experiments must be fully and accurately described so that others may be able to criticize and repeat them. We cannot expect that all the alleged facts which will at first be included in the Natural History will be genuine. But so long as most of the observations are sound the presence of a small number of mistakes will not be disastrous. For the large mass of genuine facts will suffice to establish the general laws and structure of Nature, and in their light the few mistakes will stand out clearly and can be corrected at leisure. To sum up in Bacon's words: When we have this comprehensive Natural History, and not till then, we shall 'no longer be kept dancing in rings, like persons bewitched, but our range and circuit will be as wide as the compass of the world'.

I now leave History and pass to Philosophy, stopping for a moment by the way at Poesy in order to indicate a curious crotchet of Bacon's. He held that the stories of Greek mythology were deliberately composed to conceal from the vulgar and reveal to the elect profound philosophical truths; and he wasted much time and ingenuity in showing that some mute inglorious Newton has hidden the true principles of Natural Philosophy in the story of *Pan*, and that some prehistoric Clausewitz has embedded the rules of military strategy in that of *Perseus and Medusa*.

Bacon divides Philosophy according to its subject-matter into Natural Theology, the Science of Non-human Nature, and the Science of Man. But he holds that philosophy begins as an undivided stem which rises to some height before these branches emerge. The undivided stem he calls *First Philosophy* or *Wisdom*. First Philosophy consists of two parts, between which there seems to be very little connexion. The first consists of those general principles which are common to several different sciences. Bacon gives a number of examples, and among them the principle that the quantum of Nature is neither increased nor diminished by any natural process. He says that these common principles are not mere analogies but are the common impress of the Creator on diverse materials, so that this part of Philosophy displays the essential unity of Nature. It must be confessed, however, that some of his examples rest on mere metaphors and that his collection of common principles seems arbitrary and internally incoherent. The second part of First Philosophy treats of what he calls the *Adventitious Conditions of Essences*. From his examples it is clear that it was to ask and answer such questions as: 'Why does the world contain so much of some substances and so little of others?' 'Why is the arrangement of the stars and planets such as it is?' 'Why is pentadic sym-

metry so common among flowers and unknown among crystals?'
Bacon fully recognizes that there is a point at which we reach
ultimate principles and brute facts, and he insists that a philosopher may show as great folly in professing to explain the
simple and the ultimate as in stopping short in his analysis of
what is complex and causally explicable. Nevertheless the kind
of question which he relegates to the second part of First
Philosophy is obviously legitimate, though we must eventually
come to proportions and configurations which have simply to be
accepted as ultimate facts about the constitution of Nature.

Having already said what is necessary about Natural Theology we can now consider the two remaining branches which
spring from the common stem of First Philosophy. The Science
of Non-human Nature or Natural Philosophy is divided into
a theoretical part which seeks to explain given facts by discovering their causes, and a correlated practical part which seeks to
produce desired effects by applying this knowledge of causes.
Theoretical Natural Philosophy is subdivided into Metaphysics
and Physics. Metaphysics, in Bacon's sense, has two parts: the
study of Final Causes and that of Formal Causes. Physics is
concerned with Material and Efficient Causes. We have already
seen that Bacon regards the study of Final Causes as a legitimate
enquiry which is the basis of Natural Theology but gives rise to
no practical art. The art which corresponds, not to Metaphysics
as a whole, but to the Metaphysics of Forms, is called by Bacon
Natural Magic. The art which corresponds to Physics is called
Mechanics.

With the Metaphysics of Forms we have reached the inner
sanctuary of Bacon's philosophy, and we must pause awhile and
make a careful inspection. Let us begin by stating two propositions, one of which would be metaphysical and the other physical. That heat consists of violent irregular molecular movement
is a proposition of Metaphysics. That mixing sulphuric acid
with water generates heat is a proposition of Physics. The particular substances, water and sulphuric acid, are the material
causes; the process of mixing them is the efficient cause. The
notions of material and efficient cause, as used by Bacon, are
thus perfectly clear. But what does he mean by a formal cause?
When we ask: 'What is the formal cause of heat?' we are asking,
not directly how to *produce* heat, but what heat *really is* in Nature

apart from man and his sensations. 'Heat itself,' says Bacon, 'its essence and its quiddity, *is* Motion and nothing else, limited however by certain specific differences.' By the last phrase he means, e.g. that it is irregular and not periodic motion, motion of molecules and not of electrons or of molar masses, and so on. 'Sensible heat', he says, 'is a relative notion and has relation to man not to the Universe. It is correctly defined as merely the *effect* of heat on the animal spirits.'

In order to make Bacon's view quite clear and self-consistent we must draw a threefold distinction which was certainly present in his mind but is never explicitly stated by him. This is the distinction between sensible qualities, physical properties, and metaphysical forms. The sensible quality of hotness is the characteristic quality which is revealed to a human being in sensation when he touches a hot body or is exposed to radiant heat. The metaphysical form of heat is violent and irregular molecular movement. But when a plain man says that a certain body is hot he does not necessarily mean that he or anyone else is receiving a sensibly hot feeling from it, and he certainly is not thinking of molecular movements. He means roughly that the body has the *power* to produce such a feeling in anyone who should touch it, that it has the *power* of expanding the mercury in a thermometer, and so on. This power, or faculty, or disposition is what I mean by the physical property of hotness. Now Bacon asserts that the 'form' of any 'nature', such as hotness, is always present when this nature is present and always absent when this nature is absent. It is evident that this would be a tautology if he identified the nature called *hotness* with the metaphysical form; and it would be glaring falsehood if he identified the nature called *hotness* with the sensible quality. For the kind of movement which is the form of heat might be present in a body and yet the sensible quality of hotness might be absent because no sensitive organism was near enough to this body. I conclude then that, by a 'nature' such as heat, weight, colour, etc., Bacon must mean a physical property, i.e. a power of producing certain kinds of effect under certain assignable circumstances, and among these effects sensations with a certain characteristic sensible quality in presence of a sensitive organism.

We come now to another important assertion which Bacon

makes about forms. The form of a given simple nature is not merely something which is always present when the nature is present and absent when it is absent. The form must in addition be 'a limitation of some more general nature, as of a true and real genus'. The form of heat, e.g. is one species of motion, viz. the violent irregular motion of molecules. The form of colour would be another species of motion, e.g. the periodic variation of electro-magnetic forces. And the form of redness would be a still more specific kind of motion, e.g. a periodic variation of such forces with its frequency confined within a certain narrow range. This is a vitally important point, for it marks the division between medieval and modern Natural Philosophy. A medieval physicist would recognize a large number of different powers in bodies, just as we do. But each of these powers would be for him a distinct and ultimate faculty. In this respect modern psychology, with all its boasting, is in much the same position as medieval physics. For us these various powers of matter reduce to so many specific kinds of minute structure and movement. The whole progress of modern physics depends on the clear recognition of this fundamental fact; and the absence of any similar progress in psychology is due to our inability up to the present to conceive the faculties of the mind in similar terms.

Closely connected with the point which we have been just discussing is the principle which Lord Keynes calls that of *Limited Variety*. Lord Keynes rightly holds that this was recognized by Bacon and that it is essential for the vindication of inductive reasoning. Bacon is not indeed perfectly clear on this point. But there is no doubt that he asserts at least two different forms of this principle. In the first place, he definitely asserts that the same simple nature, e.g. heat, cannot be reduced in some cases (e.g. in fires) to one form, and in other cases (e.g. in the heavenly bodies or in dunghills) to another form. He thus definitely denies that there can be a plurality of forms for a given simple nature. Secondly, Bacon says that 'the forms of simple natures, though few in number, yet in their communications and co-ordinations make all this variety'. It is clear that this is a different sense of the Principle of Limited Variety from that which we have just noticed. It needs, however, some further elucidation. Bacon has said that there is a one-to-one correlation between simple natures and their forms; it follows directly that there must be as many forms as there are simple natures. The explanation is, I think, as follows. By 'simple natures' Bacon evidently means *generic* physical properties, such as colour, temperature, density, etc., in general. He does not include their specific determinations or particular values, such as brick-red, a temperature of 59° C., or a density of 2·73. Now the number of unanalysable generic physical properties with which we are acquainted is quite small, though the number of specific modifications of each is very great, if not infinite. We describe any particular kind of substance, such as gold, and distinguish it from substances of all other kinds, such as silver, by mentioning its generic physical properties and stating the specific modification or value of each which is characteristic of the kind of substance in question.

This being premised, the rather vague statement of Bacon which I have quoted covers four distinct and vitally important cases of Limited Variety within the material world. (1) That the material world is composed of various kinds of substance, such that each kind can be distinguished from all the others by enumerating a comparatively small number of specific properties characteristic of it. This small selection carries with it all the rest of the properties of the kind. E.g. gold can be completely distinguished from all other kinds of substance by mentioning that it is yellow in white light, that its density is 19.26, and that its melting point is 1062° C. Anything that has these few specific properties will have all the other specific properties of gold. (2) That the number of different kinds of material substance is comparatively small, and that the apparent multiplicity of kinds arises from the various proportions in which these few are mixed and compounded. (3) The various specific modifications of a single generic property, such as colour, often differ from each other in such a way that we can immediately recognize the differences but cannot reduce them to any one principle. E.g. we can immediately recognize the differences between red, blue, green, and yellow; but each of these differences is ultimate and incomparable with the others. Now, if the form of colour be a certain kind of periodic change, these ultimate and incomparable differences between the specific colours reduce in the form to the single numerical difference of frequency. (4) The various generic physical properties, such as colour, temperature, etc., are wholly incomparable with each other and cannot be regarded as species of any one genus. But, if the form of colour be periodic motion of particles of a certain order of magnitude, and the form of heat be violent irregular motion of particles of a certain other order of magnitude, it is evident that there is a generic unity among the forms which is lacking among the simple natures themselves.

I do not suggest that Bacon clearly recognized and distinguished these four cases of the second form of the Principle of Limited Variety. But I have little doubt that he meant to assert them all. It is possible to adduce explicit statements for the second and the fourth. In the fragment called *Abecedarium Naturae* he says: 'The nature of things is rich . . . in quantity of matter and variety of individuals; but so limited in . . . species as even to appear scanty and destitute.' And he constantly asserts that the doctrine of forms introduces a hierarchical unity into Nature which is otherwise lacking. He compares Nature to a pyramid, at the apex of which is something which he calls the *Summary Law of Nature*, though he doubts whether this is knowable to man. What is this but an expression of Bacon's personal conviction that the forms of all simple natures are specific modifications of a single generic form?

We now understand what Bacon meant by the Metaphysics of Forms. As he recognizes, it is something very different from what has ordinarily been called Metaphysics. It is an empirical science, and is in fact what we should call the Theoretical Physics of the Microscopic World. The contents of Metaphysics in the traditional sense are distributed by Bacon between First Philosophy and Natural Theology. Let us now consider the art of Natural Magic, which corresponds to the Metaphysics of Forms. Any physical process which induces a certain nature on a body must in fact do so by inducing the form of that nature. But so long as the form is unknown any practical method of inducing this nature can be discovered only by chance. It remains a mere isolated *recipe* which cannot be employed unless certain very special materials and conditions be available. If a man knew merely the rule that heat is produced by mixing sulphuric acid with water he could never produce heat except on the rare occasions when he had these materials to hand. But if he knew that violent molecular motion is the form of heat he would know that *any* way of generating such motion will produce heat, and that nothing else will do so. Thus a knowledge of forms enormously increases our practical control over Nature; it frees us from the contingency and redundancy of rule-of-thumb methods. When we understand exactly what is essential to our purpose we can devise the simplest and most direct means and can avoid all that is irrelevant. In this way, and in this way only, Bacon thought that we might eventually solve the problem of the alchemists, viz. to transmute substances of one kind into substances of another kind. The characteristic properties of mercury depend on a certain complex form; those of gold on a certain other complex form. Now, if these two different forms be different specific modifications of a single generic form or be different mixtures of specific modifications of a few generic forms, we may hope eventually to convert the form of mercury into that of gold and so to transmute the one metal into the other.

The objects of the alchemists, says Bacon, are not absurd; what is absurd is their theories and the means by which they hope to reach their ends. Now transmutation would be the *opus magnum* of Natural Magic; but any case in which we produce profound modifications in the properties of matter by deliberately using our knowledge of the forms of simple natures would be an instance of Natural Magic. Thus Sir J. J. Thomson and Lord Rutherford were profound Metaphysicians in Bacon's sense, whilst the Mendelians who produce new strains of wheat with desired qualities are eminent Natural Magicians. It must be remarked, however, that Bacon sometimes confines the name 'magical' to certain types of physical process in which the material and efficient causes seem very trivial compared with the effect. Examples would be the use of catalysts or enzymes in quickening and improving the yield of chemical reactions, the breaking of great masses by repeated small blows of suitable periodicity, and the propagation of explosive waves in air which is full of inflammable dust.

Now Bacon holds that there is a branch of Physics which is very closely connected with the Metaphysics of Forms and with Natural Magic. This he calls the investigation of the *Latent Processes* and the *Latent Structure* of bodies. No body is ever at rest both as a whole and in its parts; what appears as rest is merely a balance of motions. The efficient and material causes which we recognize in daily life are merely the outstanding and easily perceptible phases in processes which are perfectly continuous and for the most part escape the senses. Every natural result depends on factors which are too small to be perceived by the naked eye, and no one need hope to govern Nature if he confines his attention to macroscopic phenomena. Bacon holds that our present knowledge of Latent Structure is very imperfect, but that our knowledge of Latent Process is far more so. Until we consider Nature in its dynamical as well as its statical aspect we shall neither understand it theoretically nor control it practically. Bacon indeed refuses to call himself an Atomist. But this is partly because he takes the word 'atom' in a very strict philosophical sense, and partly because he takes Atomism to include the doctrine that the spaces between finite bodies are empty of all matter. But it is clear that he accepted a molecular view of matter. Even in the curious tract *Temporis Partus Masculus*, where he deliberately lashes himself into a passion against all other philosophers, calls Plato a crack-brained theologian, and addresses Galen as '*O pestis, o canicula!*' he consents to praise Democritus with faint damns. In many other places he speaks very highly of Democritus, who of course enjoys the double advantage over Aristotle that we know much less about him and that his admirers never succeeded in making him a public nuisance.

The relation of the Metaphysics of Forms and Natural Magic, on the one hand, to the research into Latent Structure and Latent Process, on the other, is as follows. Even if we have an adequate knowledge of the form of a simple nature we shall not be able to devise means of inducing it at will on a given body unless we know the Latent Structure of this body and the Latent Processes involved. On the other hand, a knowledge of Latent Structure and Latent Process will often extend our power of inducing a required simple nature on a body even though we are ignorant of the form of this nature.

I pass now to the third and last division of Philosophy, viz. the Science of Human Nature. This is first divided according as it is concerned with Man as an Individual or with Human Communities. Now the individual man is a composite of soul and body. Hence the Science of Individual Man splits into three parts, one concerned with Man as a composite whole, another with the Human Body, and a third with the Human Soul. Now we can consider either the substance and faculties of the human soul or the right uses and objects of these faculties. The science of the former is Psychology; the latter constitute the subject of Logic, which deals with the right use of our cognitive faculties, and of Ethics, which deals with that of our conative faculties. Logic, in this wide sense, is the subject of Part II of the Great Instauration.

Logic falls into three great divisions. The human mind has both positive faults and negative deficiencies. The first business of Logic is to correct the former, and the second is to supplement the latter. When this is accomplished it can proceed to its main task of supplying the mind with a positive method of discovery. Thus Logic may be divided into a destructive, an auxiliary, and a constructive part. We will now consider these in turn.

There are certain innate sources of error common to the human race. Bacon calls these *Idols of the Tribe*. The most important of them are the following. Men tend to impose certain human ideas of order, fitness, and simplicity on external Nature. They tend to notice facts which support their existing beliefs and to ignore or pervert those which conflict with them. The last thing that they think of doing is deliberately to seek for exceptions so as to try their beliefs as by fire. The human intellect is at once lazy and restless. It still tries to explain and analyse when it has reached what is ultimate and simple, and yet it is content to couch its explanations in terms of what is gross enough for the unaided senses to perceive. It is 'no dry light', but is constantly affected by the will and the emotions. And, finally, it is given to reifying abstractions and to substantializing mere occurrents. Very closely connected in their effects with Idols of the Tribe are those of the *Market-Place*. These are the associations of current words and phrases which have crept insensibly into the mind from infancy through our intercourse with our fellows. Words and phrases represent the analyses of facts which were made by our remote ancestors. Some of them are names for non-existent things or for inappropriate concepts based on bad observations and false theories. They are thus crystallized errors, all the more dangerous because we do not recognize that they embody theories at all. *Idols of the Cave* are innate or acquired sources of error or bias peculiar to individuals. It was, e.g. an Idol of the late Lord Kelvin's Cave to want all physical theories to be capable of representation by mechanical models. Naturally such Idols are too various to be classified. Bacon sums them up by saying that 'whatever one's mind seizes and dwells upon with peculiar satisfaction is to be held in suspicion'.

Bacon admits that the three kinds of Idol just mentioned cannot be altogether eliminated. The best that Logic can do is to point them out to us and thus put us on our guard against them. But there is a fourth kind of Idol which is set up in the mind deliberately and wittingly after we have reached what are ironically termed 'years of discretion'. This kind is called *Idols of the Theatre*. They consist of false systems of Natural Philosophy and arise through applying faulty methods of reasoning to inadequate or badly selected and arranged data. Such Idols can be eliminated, not by refuting the various false systems one by one, but by pointing out the many signs which are unfavourable to the claims of all of them, by giving directions for collecting and arranging an adequate Natural History, and by substituting correct methods of reasoning for those now in use. We have already seen how Bacon deals with the first and second of these tasks. The third leads us from the purely destructive to the auxiliary and constructive parts of Logic. Bacon sums up the destructive part by saying that a man can enter the Kingdom of Nature, like the Kingdom of Heaven, only by becoming as a little child. By a 'little child' he means the ideal infant of Locke and Condillac, not the actual *polymorphe pervers* of the Psychoanalysts. His 'little child', as he well knows, is not born but made by an elaborate process of mental polishing. Even when the first three Idols have been smoothed away from the mind as far as may be, the writings of False Philosophy remain on its surface. And here Bacon says definitely that the analogy to a waxen tablet breaks down. In a tablet we should shave the old writing off the surface before beginning to write anything new. But in the mind the traces of False Philosophy can be erased only by deeply engraving the letters of True Philosophy.

The auxiliary part of Logic consists of three *Ministrations*, one to the Senses, another to the Memory, and a third to the

Reason. The senses have two defects, one positive and the other negative. The positive defect is that there is always a subjective element in sensations; they represent things as they affect a particular organism in a particular place and not simply as they are in Nature. The negative defect is that the senses respond delicately only to a very narrow range of stimuli. They overlook what is very small or distant or swift or slow or weak or intense. Bacon holds that these negative defects can be largely overcome by the use of instruments and by other devices which he discusses very acutely in the *Novum Organum* under the name of *Instances of the Lamp*. The subjective element again can be eliminated by judicious comparisons between one sense and another and one percipient and another. The deliveries of the senses, when thus supplemented and neutralized, are the solid and indispensable foundation of all scientific knowledge. But Bacon adds the extremely important remark that in a well-devised experiment the office of sensation is reduced to a minimum. 'The senses', he says, 'decide touching the experiment only, and the experiment touching the point in Nature and the thing itself.'

The Ministration to the Memory consists of methods of recording observations and tabulating them so that they shall be available when wanted. For this purpose they must be classified from the very first. It is true that our first classifications will be very largely erroneous. But 'truth will emerge more quickly from error than from confusion, and reason will more easily correct a false division than penetrate a confused mass'. We must continually return to our tables and correct and reclassify our results as knowledge grows.

It is difficult to draw a sharp line between the Ministration to Reason and the constructive part of Logic, so I will take them together. Reason may be used either for discovering plausible arguments to persuade others or justify oneself, or in order to understand and master Nature. For the former purpose the existing method of establishing wide generalizations from superficial and unanalysed facts by simple enumeration and then deducing consequences from them by syllogistic reasoning is admirably adapted. We may therefore leave barristers, politicians, preachers, and newspaper editors in happy possession of so useful an instrument. But these methods are perfectly

useless for a serious study of Nature which aims at practical
control. For this purpose three fundamental changes are needed.
(1) The data must be collected, arranged, and analysed according to the rules laid down in the *Parasceve* by men whose minds
have been purged of the Idols and whose senses and memories
have been corrected and supplemented by the Ministrations already mentioned. (2) The order of procedure must be altered.
We must not jump from particular facts to sweeping generalities and then deduce propositions of medium generality from
these. The right process is a very gradual ascent from particulars through middle principles to the highest laws and a very
gradual descent from these to new middle principles and finally
to new particulars. At every stage of the upward process the
generalization is to cover the then known facts and to extend
a very little way beyond them, and this small extension is to be
tested by a fresh appeal to experience. Thus the ascending and
the descending process, like the movements of the angels on
Jacob's ladder, take place side by side; and the latter is the
means of testing the validity of the former. Bacon does, however, allow to the weaker brethren an inferior method, viz. a
direct passage from one experiment to another partly analogous
experiment. This he calls *Instructed Experience*. He enumerates
eight general methods of Instructed Experience, such as applying the old process to new materials or, conversely, applying
the same process a second time to the products of its first application (as in redistillation), inverting one of the agents (e.g. substituting cold for heat), and so on. And he makes extremely
judicious observations on the fallacies to be avoided. He evidently holds that Instructed Experience is a useful preparation
for the true method, which he calls the *Formula of Interpretation*,
but that only the latter will lead to far-reaching discoveries and
inventions.

(3) We must substitute for induction by simple enumeration
a method which makes use of negative instances and arrives
at truth by successive elimination of false alternatives. Our
ultimate aim is to discover the forms of simple natures. But only
God, and perhaps the angels, can have a direct positive knowledge of forms; men must proceed by rejection and exclusion.
Now the form of a simple nature will always be present when
the nature is present, absent when it is absent, and varying

when it varies. We must therefore draw up comparative tables of cases in which the given nature is present, of cases in which it is absent, and of cases in which its degree varies. We shall then know that the form cannot be anything that is absent in the first list or present in the second list or constant in the third list. By this means we may gradually eliminate all other natures and be left with the form which we are seeking.

It is evident that this is equivalent to Mill's Joint Method of Agreement and Difference, supplemented by his Method of Concomitant Variations. Bacon, like Mill, thought that results which are certain and not merely probable could be reached in this way. But he was far more alive to the difficulties than Mill. We cannot be sure that the natures which we take to be simple really are so. And we have not at present any list of the simple natures in the Universe which is known to be exhaustive. Until these defects have been rectified no certain results can be reached, as Bacon clearly sees. Again, unless some means can be found for abridging our Tables the work will be endless; for the Table of Absence will be a mere hotch-potch of heterogeneous items. Bacon therefore enumerates nine 'more powerful aids for the use of the understanding', which he promises to supply. But the promise is very imperfectly fulfilled. Only two of them are treated explicitly, viz. the *Theory of Prerogative Instances* and the *Rules for Preparing a Natural History*. The Theory of Prerogative Instances is designed to abridge our enquiries by teaching us how to choose such instances that a few of them will suffice to eliminate a very large number of suggested forms for the nature under investigation. Bacon has lavished immense care and acuteness on this part of his work, which is full of admirable detail. But we miss the promised *Theory of Prerogative Natures*, which was to abridge enquiry still further by teaching us which subjects to investigate first because they 'hand on a torch to those that come after' on account of their greater generality or certainty or use in practice. And most of all we miss the promised *Synopsis of all the Natures in the Universe*, without which it is evident that no method of successive elimination could ever lead to results that are both positive and certain. It remains only to notice that Bacon held that his method would need modification in detail according to the subject-matter to which it was to be applied, that it would itself develop as more things were discovered by its means, and that we may hope some day to apply it to Psychology and Politics as well as to inanimate nature.

I have now outlined to the best of my ability the Baconian philosophy. To those who know the state of scientific thought in Bacon's time and are capable of estimating philosophical achievement this bare account of his doctrines will be better praise than any studied panegyric. But we are here to bury Bacon as well as to praise him; so I will end with a very brief estimate of what he did and what he did not accomplish.

In the first place, we may set aside as of purely historical interest the attacks on Aristotle and the attempted delimitation of the spheres of reason and faith. We can afford to be fair to Aristotle, for his Natural Philosophy has ceased to be a nuisance and has become a museum specimen embalmed in the rich spices of Oxonian erudition. It was no more possible for Bacon to be meticulously just to him than for an Englishman in 1812 to appreciate the finer shades of character of the Corsican Ogre. And, on the question of reason and faith, those of us who have not personally been favoured with divine revelations have to estimate by ordinary human reason the revelations which are alleged to have been vouchsafed to others. The one test that Bacon suggests, viz. that the contents of a divine revelation may be expected to be shocking to reason, is obviously insufficient in a world so replete as ours with every form of fantastic lunacy.

Setting these points aside, let us ask and try to answer the following questions. (1) Was Bacon a great scientist who discovered new facts and established physical theories which form the basis of modern science? Most certainly not. As regards experiment and observation he 'never said a foolish thing and never did a wise one'. He seems to have been an incompetent but pertinacious experimenter; and in his Natural Histories he breaks all his own rules, copying quite uncritically a jumble of facts and fables from other writers. His incapacity in mathematics prevented him from understanding the best work of his contemporaries, and *a fortiori* made it impossible for him to state or work out far-reaching physical theories himself.

(2) Granted that modern science does not owe any important facts or special theories to Bacon, does it derive its general

methods and its general outlook on the world from him? This is a question of historical causation which must be answered with a decided negative. So far as I can see, the actual course which science has taken, even if it has been in accord with Bacon's principles and has led to the results which he desired and antici- pated, has been influenced little if at all by his writings. I sus- pect that the popularity of the opposite view is due to the mag- nificent advertisement which Bacon received from D'Alembert and the French Encyclopaedists, who found it convenient to march into battle under his ensign. If then Bacon be the father of the method and outlook of modern science he is so by spiritual affinity rather than by natural generation.

(3) Granted that Bacon's actual influence has been over- rated, did he in fact discover and state explicitly those methods and principles of scientific research and inductive proof which scientists implicitly use with so much success? It seems to me that the honours of stating these methods and principles are pretty evenly divided between Bacon and Descartes. Up to a point they cover much the same ground. There is considerable analogy between the destructive part of Bacon's method and Descartes' systematic doubt. Here Bacon can be praised with- out reserve; he discusses in far greater detail than Descartes the causes of human error and the remedies for it, and his treat- ment is exhaustive, profound, and illuminating. Again, Des- cartes, in the *Regulae*, agrees with Bacon in recognizing the importance of the Principle of Limited Variety. After this point the two methodologies diverge, and the truth is divided between them. Each is strong where the other is weak. Bacon is paralysed whenever he touches mathematics, pure or applied. He has no theory of mathematical reasoning and was ignorant of the swift advances that pure mathematics was making. He verbally recognizes the importance of applied mathematics; but he failed to see how predominant a part mathematical state- ment and deduction must play in physics if anything like his theory of forms is to work. Here Descartes is strong with the strength of a man who has himself invented a method which in his own hands has revolutionized geometry and mechanics. On the other hand, Descartes is as helpless over induction as Bacon is over mathematical deduction. In his analysis of inductive arguments Bacon was, so far as I know, breaking new ground,

and all later discussion has followed on his lines. That the constructive side of his method is incomplete is admitted by himself. We can see that its main defects are the following. Under the most favourable circumstances possible Bacon's method of exclusions would not suffice to discover the form of a simple nature, but at most empirical laws connecting one simple nature with another. A form is not one among the physical properties which can be perceived to be present or absent in a thing; it is the hypothetical structural and motional basis of a perceptible property. It follows that forms can be established only by hypothesis, mathematical deduction of observable consequences, and subsequent verification of these by actual observation. Closely connected with this fact is Bacon's other great defect. He never clearly distinguished between approaching facts with a prejudice and approaching them with a working hypothesis. He is so anxious to avoid the former that he fails to see that no progress can be made without the latter. Whewell's great contribution to the theory of induction was to point out the importance of the appropriate colligating concept and the fruitful working hypothesis. And these are just the points at which rules and methods fail us and the insight of individual genius comes into its own, though the genius must be trained in the methods and soaked with the facts of science.

(4) Lastly, did Bacon provide any logical justification for the principles and methods which he elicited and which scientists assume and use? He did not, and he never saw that it was necessary to do so. There is a skeleton in the cupboard of Inductive Logic, which Bacon never suspected and Hume first exposed to view. Kant conducted the most elaborate funeral in history, and called Heaven and Earth and the Noumena under the Earth to witness that the skeleton was finally disposed of. But when the dust of the funeral procession had subsided and the last strains of the Transcendental Organ had died away, the coffin was found to be empty and the skeleton in its old place. Mill discreetly closed the door of the cupboard, and with infinite tact turned the conversation into more cheerful channels. Mr. Johnson and Lord Keynes may fairly be said to have reduced the skeleton to the dimensions of a mere skull. But that obstinate *caput mortuum* still awaits the undertaker who will give it Christian burial. May we venture to hope that when Bacon's

next centenary is celebrated the great work which he set going will be completed; and that Inductive Reasoning, which has long been the glory of Science, will have ceased to be the scandal of Philosophy?

THE NEW PHILOSOPHY:
BRUNO TO DESCARTES

I HAVE been asked to speak to-day on the 'new philosophy' which arose and gradually triumphed in the period between the birth of Bruno in 1548 and the death of Descartes in 1650. I propose to put a fairly wide interpretation on the word 'philosophy', as did all the great thinkers of our period. And I propose to begin by giving a fairly full, though necessarily very imperfect, synopsis of the old philosophy against which the new doctrines reacted and which they superseded. What I shall describe with the name of the 'old philosophy' is the theory of the universe which St. Thomas had elaborated on the basis of such knowledge of the works of Aristotle as was available to him. This, for example, is what Descartes would have learnt from his highly intelligent teachers at La Flèche; and it was the intellectual background of all educated men in our period.

It is necessary to devote what may seem to be a disproportionate part of to-day's lecture to the old philosophy, simply because the victory of the new was in the end so complete and has for so long been unchallenged. The conception of the world, of man, and of man's place in nature, which was common to all educated persons at the beginning of our period, is now for most of us a curiosity in a museum which we have never visited. That which was then new and revolutionary has for generations been as familiar and unnoticed as the air which we breathe. As a result we are liable to be unfair to both. The old, taken out of its context, seems to be a mere childish fairy-tale too ridiculous to have ever been sincerely believed; and the new, when ex-

plicitly stated, seems so trite and trivial that we cannot understand why the innovators made such a fuss about it. Yet the
Thomistic synthesis is one of the greatest achievements of the
human mind; and the transition from the old to the new was,
in many respects, the most radical change in theory and the
most fruitful (for good and for ill) in practice of which we have
any record.

Let us begin with the old account of the structure and composition of the Macrocosm. If the position and motion of the
sun, the moon, and the planets are observed from the earth
night after night over a long period, they are found to form a
spatio-temporal pattern whose rhythmic complexity cannot be
better summarized than in Milton's words:

> Mazes intricate, eccentric, intervolved, yet regular—
> Then most when most irregular they seem.

Now the Greek astronomers set to themselves the problem of
describing on a single uniform plan all the observed motions of
all the heavenly bodies and of enabling their position at any
assigned past or future date to be inferred. The problem was
set under the following three conditions: (1) that the earth was
to be taken as fixed and other bodies as moving round it, (2)
that the only fundamental motion which was to be admitted
was to be *circular*, and (3) that every circular motion was to take
place with *uniform* speed.

The problem was solved by Hipparchus and Ptolemy by two
devices, viz. the theory of *Eccentrics* and that of *Epicycles*. According to the former theory it is not the earth itself, but a point at
some distance from it and fixed with respect to it, which is the
centre of all the ultimate uniform circulations. According to the
latter, each member of the solar system circulates uniformly
about a centre peculiar to it; this centre is not at rest, but itself
circulates uniformly about another centre, which may in turn
be circulating uniformly about another, and so on. Such a
series ends with a centre which circulates uniformly about the
fixed centre of the cosmos. The ultimate circles with this common fixed centre are called *Deferents*, the others are called
Epicycles.

By providing each heavenly body with enough epicycles, and
by suitably choosing the rates of circulation in its deferent and

in each of its epicycles, all the long-term geometrical and kinematic appearances of the heavens can be accounted for to any degree of approximation. Finally, the short-term appearances, which are due to the daily rotation of the earth on its own axis, are explained by supposing that the system of planets, luminaries, and fixed stars rotates as a rigid whole about an axis through the poles of the earth once in every twenty-four hours.

In itself this scheme is simply a mathematical solution of a mathematical problem. As such, it is a marvellous achievement, and it can be criticized only on the ground that equally effective and much simpler schemes can be devised. This had been done in one way, just before our period, by Copernicus; and it was done in another way during our period by Tycho Brahe; though neither of them could dispense with epicycles. But unfortunately it was treated as a physical theory. The fixed stars were regarded as attached to the inside of a rotating spherical shell which encloses the universe, and the deferent of each planet was associated with a concentric spherical shell rotating on an axis whose axle-boxes are attached to the inside of the starry sphere. For reasons which need not be considered here two additional spheres—the Crystalline Sphere and the Primum Mobile—were assumed to be located outside that of the fixed stars. And for most purposes the theory of eccentrics was often ignored, and the centre of the earth was identified with that of the universe.

According to this theory there is an absolute sense of 'up' and 'down'. Motion *up* is radial motion from the centre of the universe to its circumference; motion *down* is radial motion in the opposite direction. The first rotating shell above the earth is that associated with the moon's deferent. This divides the universe into a sublunary and a celestial region. It was held that there is a profound difference between sublunary substances and their changes, on the one hand, and celestial substances and their changes, on the other. The stars and planets and their spheres are composed of a superior kind of substance called the *Fifth Element* or *Quintessence*. This is not subject to generation or corruption. The only kind of change of which it is susceptible is perpetual circular motion with constant speed.

So much for the structure of the Macrocosm; now for the composition of the sublunar world. Everything in this is ultimately composed of four elements, to which the names *Earth*, *Air*, *Fire* and *Water* were given. In each of the four elements we can distinguish in thought two correlative factors, viz. substratum and quality. The substratum of all four is the same and is called *Materia Prima*. The quality of each element is conceived in the following way. There are two fundamental pairs of opposite qualities, viz. *hot and cold*, *moist and dry*. Of these *hot* is considered positive as compared with *cold*, and *moist* is considered positive as compared with *dry*. This opinion was, no doubt, based on the fact that germination and growth are fostered by warmth and moisture and checked by cold and drought. Now there are four possible combinations of these qualities, viz. *CD*, *CM*, *HM*, and *HD*. Each such combination characterizes one of the four elements. *Earth* is *materia prima* qualified by coldness and dryness. The corresponding qualities for the other elements are: *Fire*, hot and dry; *Air*, hot and moist; *Water*, cold and moist. There is thus a maximum opposition between *Earth* (*CD*) and *Air* (*HM*), and also between *Fire* (*HD*) and *Water* (*CM*).

It is impossible for any portion of *materia prima* to exist without being qualified by one or other of these four pairs of qualities; and it is equally impossible for these qualities to exist except as qualifying some portion of *materia prima*. *Materia prima* is ingenerable and indestructible, and it occupies continuously the whole sphere of the material universe. It might therefore be compared with the ether of the nineteenth-century physicists or the substantival absolute space of Newton. The elements can be and are transformed into each other and back again, but there is no loss or gain of stuff in this process.

Each of the four elements has a certain natural position in the universe. When it is in that position it rests there quietly. When it is out of that position it has a natural tendency to move radially towards its proper place. The proper place of *Fire* is at the circumference of the universe, and so it tends to move upwards. The proper place of *Earth* is at the centre, and so it tends to move downwards. The proper places of *Air* and *Water* are intermediate; *Air* below *Fire* and above *Water*, and *Water* below *Air* and above *Earth*.

This is as much as I need say about the scholastic physics. I pass now to the metaphysics. This is formulated in terms of three pairs of correlates, viz. *Essence and Existence*, *Stuff and Form*, and *Potentiality and Actuality*. I will now try to give a rough account of them.

(1) The essence of any substance is that set of interconnected qualities, powers, modes of behaviour, etc., which together constitute its nature and mark it out from other substances. Thus an essence defines a possible substance or species of substances. But there are possible substances, e.g. dragons, which do not exist. So in any actually existing substance we can distinguish in thought the two factors of essence and existence. Now there are two cases of the union of essence and existence to be considered. Generally the connexion between the two factors is contingent. There are lions and there are no dragons; but there is nothing in the essence of the lion to necessitate that there should be lions, and nothing in the essence of the dragon to make it impossible for there to be dragons. This contingent connexion between essence and existence is characteristic of all created substances. On the other hand, we can conceive that there might be an essence or essences which could not fail to be endowed with existence. Any substance whose essence was of this kind would be eternal. It would not just exist throughout unending time; its existence would be altogether non-temporal, and the two factors of essence and existence in it would be distinguishable but logically inseparable, like the equilateralness and the equiangularity of an equilateral triangle. There is one and only one substance of this kind, viz. God; and the existence of every other substance depends on the creative act by which God has instantiated its essence.

(2) I pass now to the notions of *Stuff and Form*. We have already had an instance of them in the theory of the elements. I think that this notion arose from two kinds of empirical fact, and was then generalized into a metaphysical concept. The first fact is that a workman or artist can deliberately impose various forms, of which he already has ideas, on different portions of the same previously undifferentiated stuff. Thus he may make a coin, a kettle, and a ring out of a lump of copper. In all such cases we have first, in the external world, stuff which has not yet received a certain form; and, in the artificer's mind, the idea of a certain form which has not yet been imposed on the stuff. Then, in consequence of his idea and his desire for its external embodiment, a series of changes is set up which ends by the

form being imposed on the stuff and a new kind of substance being produced.

The second empirical fact is the reproduction, growth, and self-repair of living plants and animals. Corresponding to each species there is a characteristic shape, size, internal organization and so on. This constitutes the form of any member of the species. Now each such individual, beginning as an embryo, gradually acquires the adult form of its species by a certain characteristic process of development. Then it maintains this form for a longer or shorter time by continually converting foreign stuff, viz. food, drink, and air, into various tissues, and imposing its own characteristic organization on them. Eventually it performs these operations less and less efficiently, and finally it fails to do so at all. The body then loses the form of a living plant or animal, and becomes a corpse. This is a mere aggregate of various kinds of informed stuff of a lower order, and it soon breaks down into its components. Generally while an individual is mature it reproduces others which go through the same cycle of growth, maturity, reproduction, decay, and dissolution.

In these biological examples it cannot be said that the concept of the form is present in the mind of an external artificer. Yet everything proceeds as if each individual were striving, and for a time succeeding, and eventually failing to impose the form of its species on the alien materials which it ingests and to propagate it in new individuals which will take its place. In the elements this unconscious striving takes the specially simple form of a tendency in each to move towards its appropriate sphere, if displaced from it, and to rest there.

Now in every substance known to us, including ourselves, there are the two factors of stuff and form. But there can be, and, according to the Scholastics, there are in fact, substances which are pure forms without stuff. The stuff-factor is absent, not only in God, but also in a whole series of created intelligent beings, viz. angels, which rise in a hierarchy above men. In each angel there are the two factors of existence and essence, and these are not merely two inseparable though distinguishable aspects, as they are in God. For angels, like men, are finite created beings; and it is logically possible that God should never have endowed with existence that essence which is the nature of a certain angel, e.g. Gabriel, whom he has in fact created. But an angel, though composite in respect of essence and existence, has nothing in it corresponding to that factor of stuff which is the vehicle of form in all lower creatures. The fact that most of us think of angels only as epicene winged figures on Christmas cards, whilst they play an indispensable part in the Scholastic philosophy, is a typical example of the breach between the medieval and the modern *Weltanschauung*.

(3) The third pair of correlative concepts to be considered is *Potentiality and Actuality*. Every substance has certain powers and dispositions, active or passive, original or acquired, which are characteristic of it. Each of these may remain latent or may manifest itself in a certain number of alternative and mutually exclusive possible ways. The circumstances which prevail at any moment within the substance itself and in its neighbours determine whether a disposition shall manifest itself or remain latent. If they determine that a certain disposition shall be manifested at a certain moment, they determine also which one of its alternative possible manifestations shall then be actualized. The actual history of any substance consists in two kinds of process. (1) The passage of this, that, or another of its dispositions from latency to actuality or *vice versa*; and (2) the passage from potentiality to actuality and *vice versa* of this, that, and the other alternative possible manifestation of a disposition which is already in action. The explosion of a mass of nitro-glycerine when struck would be an example of the first. The change from the solid to the liquid and then to the gaseous state of a mass of wax when the temperature varies beyond certain characteristic limits would be an example of the second. So at every moment in the history of a substance there are the two correlated factors of potentiality and actuality. On the side of actuality we count the manifestations of any of its dispositions which are active at the moment. On the side of potentiality we count any of its dispositions which may be latent at the moment (e.g. the inflammability of petrol that is shut up in a tin), and also all the alternative possible manifestations of each disposition which is active at the moment (e.g. the potential solidity and the potential gaseousness of this petrol, which is now in fact liquid because the temperature is above its freezing-point and below its boiling-point).

Now in respect of actuality and potentiality there are two extremes. At the one end is God and at the other *materia prima*. God has no history. There is therefore no sense in ascribing latent dispositions to him, or in suggesting that he has dispositions which manifest themselves now in one way and now in another according to circumstances. He is therefore described as *Actus Purus*. On the other hand, unformed *materia prima*, which is an ideal limit and not an actual existent, would have no positive powers of its own. It would simply have the passive capacity to receive any and every form. Every substance between these two extremes has at any moment both unmanifested potentialities and powers in action. The general rule is that the higher the position of any substance in the scale of being, the more extensive is the range of its powers and the more intensely and continuously are they manifested. In men and the substances below them there are always many dispositions latent at any moment; and the dispositions manifest themselves in a succession of variegated total states which make up the history of the substance. For example, at any moment most of one's knowledge exists only in a latent potential form; and what is explicitly before one's mind varies from moment to moment, as now one and now another cognitive disposition is brought into action.

Here again there is a characteristic difference between angels and God, on the one hand, and lower created substances, on the other. Angels are neither timeless, like God, nor do they have a variegated life-history, like men and the substances below men. In angelic cognition there is nothing comparable to the distinction between waking and drowsing and sleeping, or to that between remembering, perceiving, and anticipating. It is all of the nature of perceiving, though it is not sense-perception but intellectual intuition. Again, there is nothing like our experience of turning attention now to one thing and now to another, or gradually acquiring rational cognition about a subject by a series of deductive steps. Thus the notion of potentiality has a rather special and limited application in reference to angels.

In discussing the notions of Form and Stuff and of Potentiality and Actuality we have met with particular instances of a certain general conception which is of great importance in the old philosophy. This is the doctrine of the *Hierarchy of Being*. It goes back at least to the Neo-Platonists, and one form of it is very clearly stated by Proclus. This doctrine continually crops up in human thought in one form or another. It appears in the Jewish Cabbalists, in Spinoza, in Leibniz, and in modern times in Bradley. I think that it is derived, *inter alia*, from analogy with the radiation of light from a point-source with decrease of intensity and purity as the distance from the source increases. In the philosophy of St. Thomas, God is conceived as in some ways like a point-source of white light. In him there is infinite energy and absolute simplicity. The process of creation is analogous in some respects, though not in all, to the perpetual streaming out of an influence from a centre with diminution of intensity and a consequent loss of purity, growth in complexity, and gradual hardening and coarsening. Thus there emerges a descending hierarchy of being, which is ordered in accordance with the following two rules. (1) That which is higher in the scale can do and experience all and more than all that can be done or experienced by what is lower. (2) The higher in the scale the greater is the activity and intensity of life and yet the greater is the internal simplicity. It is a mark of imperfection to use complicated means to an end. Compare, for example, the fussiness of an unskilled rider or tennis-player or fencer with the effortless ease of a skilled agent who accomplishes his purpose efficiently without a single superfluous movement. An angel sees at a glance the truth of complex propositions of geometry and their connexion with the axioms and with other propositions. A man has to argue step by step and to use all kinds of extraneous devices, such as co-ordinates, diagrams, and constructions. In general, items which are dispersed and disorganized in the lower levels of the scale of being are fused and integrated into simple and more efficient units at the higher levels.

Next we must consider the view which the old philosophy took of man, the Microcosm. It recognized more fully than its successors the fact that men are highly paradoxical creatures. We are both sensuous and rational, and the two sides of our nature are indispensable to each other in this life, and yet they constantly conflict. We thus lack the elegant simplicity either of the mere animal or of the angel. The Thomistic explanation is that we come at an important dividing point in the hierarchy of being. We are the lowest kind of intellectual creature and the highest kind of sensitive being. Above us are angels, which are pure intelligences without sensation and without bodies. Below us are mere animals, which are living and sensitive but have no intellectual powers. Our anomalous nature is the sign of our peculiar position in the hierarchy.

According to this philosophy a soul is a form whose stuff is a living body. Neither a soul nor its body is a substance. A body without its soul is a mere aggregate of material substances, a carcass and not an organism. On the other hand, to talk of a soul as a substance which might exist by itself without a body is like talking of the life of a living organism as something which might exist by itself. This is the whole truth about the relation of soul to body in the case of animals; but there are further complications in the case of men.

There is one profound difference between a man and a mere animal. Both have powers of sensation and sense-perception; but the man has in addition a power which no animal has, viz. that of intellectual cognition. This includes the capacity to think of universals, to know or believe general propositions, to contemplate unrealized possibilities, to see logical connexions, and to draw inferences. Even these powers, and the corresponding acts, belong to the human individual as a single unit composed of soul and body, and not to a certain purely mental part of him called his soul. But the cognitive powers and acts, such as seeing and feeling, which we share with animals, take place by means of specialized bodily organs, e.g. the eye and the skin. Intellectual cognition, though it is equally the act of an individual composed of soul and body, does not take place by means of any special bodily organ.

It was held that the fact that a human being has certain cognitive powers which do not depend on a special bodily organ for their exercise leaves open the possibility that each human soul may in some sense survive the death of its body. That this possibility is in fact realized is guaranteed by revelation to Christians. But honest and acute thinkers, like St. Thomas, recognized that the theory that the soul is the form of the living body does not fit at all easily into the doctrine of human survival which they accepted as Christians. They admitted and asserted that the condition of a human soul when it is not animating a human body is anomalous and unnatural. The fact that even the higher cognitive processes belong, not to the soul alone, but to the human individual as a unit of soul and body, makes the condition of the soul after the death of its body to be one of suspended activity. St. Thomas based on this difficulty an argument in favour of the specifically Christian doctrine of the resurrection of the body and its reunion with the soul at the Last Judgment. It is only after this reunion that the soul is once more in its natural and proper state.

I have now devoted as much of the time at my disposal as I can spare to describing the old philosophy, in which all the men of our period, conservatives and radicals alike, were brought up. We have next to consider why it ceased to give satisfaction. The reaction began in Italy and travelled northward, and there were many causes of it which were not good reasons. At the earlier stages the attack came mainly from scholars and literary men, and it consisted in an appeal from one authority to another rather than an independent attempt to interrogate nature and construct an alternative philosophy. St. Thomas's predecessors had had to be content with Latin versions of Arabian translations of Aristotle's works. St. Thomas himself had worked with direct translations from the Greek which he had made for him, but he could not read Aristotle in the original for himself. After the revival of learning direct access to the Greek sources of Aristotle's writings and to the early commentators upon them became easy for scholars. Again, the works of Plato and the Neo-Platonists, and the fragments of earlier Greek philosophers such as Democritus, became available in properly edited texts; so these thinkers could be appealed to as alternative authorities of no less reputable antiquity than Aristotle himself. There was a general stir in men's minds owing to a variety of causes, such as the development of printing and the discovery of the New World. The Thomistic philosophy, which had rightly been regarded as a revolutionary innovation, and had been resisted as such when it was first formulated, was now associated with everything that was stuffy and old-fashioned. Lastly, many humanists, with a new-found enthusiasm for correct Latinity, seem to have thought that the fact that the Latin in which the scholastic philosophy was written contained words and constructions unknown to Cicero was enough to condemn it without reprieve.

As a professional philosopher, and not a historian, I shall confine myself to the grounds of dissatisfaction which were also good reasons. We cannot do better than begin with Galileo, who, though not a philosopher in the modern sense of that word, was a man of genius with the most profound physical insight and great experimental and mathematical ability.

The following quotation from Galileo is typical. 'Philosophy is written in that very great book—the Universe—which is always open before our eyes. But we cannot understand it unless we first learn to understand the language and the characters in which it is written. It is written in *mathematical* language, and the characters are triangles, circles, and other geometrical figures, without which means it is impossible, humanly speaking, to understand a word of it.' Accordingly, Galileo rejects all such sensible qualities as colour, taste, smell, sound, etc., from the physical world and ascribes to it only extension, figure, position, motion, and mass, which can be measured and treated mathematically.

His investigation of the law of falling bodies is the first instance of the kind of combination of reasoning and experiment which is characteristic of modern science. He sees that when a body falls from rest it travels with increasing velocity, and he puts forward the two simplest mathematical hypotheses that he can think of as to the law of this increase. One is that the velocity is proportional to the distance fallen through; the other is that it is proportional to the time which has elapsed since the body began to fall. Before attempting any experiments he tries to deduce by mathematical reasoning the consequences which should be observable on each of these hypotheses. He persuades himself, by reasoning which is in fact fallacious but which could easily be replaced by a valid argument, that the hypothesis that the velocity is proportional to the distance fallen leads to impossible consequences. So he rejects that hypothesis and proceeds to deduce mathematically certain consequences of the alternative supposition that the velocity is proportional to the time which has elapsed. In doing this he performs quite correctly what is in fact an integration, and reaches the result that the distance fallen should be proportional to the square of the time which has elapsed since the body began to fall.

He now proceeds to test this result by observation, and here both his practical ability and his physical insight are displayed.

He has first to devise a method of measuring short lapses of time, and he does this by using a wide vessel with a small hole in the bottom which he can open and shut at will with his finger. He fills the vessel with water; and assumes that, since in a short period the level of the liquid in the vessel does not alter appreciably, the weight of water discharged will be proportional to the time which has elapsed between opening and shutting the hole.

Next he finds that bodies falling freely take too little time for him to be able to test his conclusions accurately by direct experiments on them. So he turns his attention to the case of bodies rolling down inclined planes, where, by making the slope of the plane gentle enough he can make the time of descent long enough to be measured accurately. He finds that his deductions are fully confirmed by observation in such cases.

Then comes another layer of reasoning which displays his physical insight. He argues that the velocity which a body acquires in rolling down an inclined plane must depend only on the vertical distance through which it has descended and not on the slope of the plane. For, as he shows, if this were not so, it would be possible by a suitable system of inclined planes to make a body raise itself above its starting point by the momentum which it has acquired in rolling down from that point. This he sees to be physically impossible. So he can now transfer his results from the case of the body rolling down an inclined plane to that of a body falling freely, which is the limiting case of an inclined plane whose angle is 90° to the horizontal.

Next he makes another application of the principle of continuity. Imagine a body which has rolled down an inclined plane and attained a certain velocity in doing so. Let it then start to roll up another inclined plane. Apart from air-resistance to friction, it will travel upwards, gradually losing velocity, until it stops at the same height as that from which it originally started on the first plane. Now imagine the slope of this second inclined plane made gradually less and less, until in the limiting case it becomes zero. The body will travel farther and farther, and lose velocity more and more slowly, as the slope is diminished. Therefore in the limiting case it will lose no velocity, but with travel on for ever with its original speed. Thus Galileo arrives at a particular case of the Law of Inertia or First Law of Motion.

Galileo now applies his results on falling bodies to the then unsolved problem of the path of a projectile. This seems to me to be one of his greatest triumphs of physical insight and sound reasoning. The body is projected upwards at an angle to the horizontal. Galileo by a stroke of genius sees that this motion can be regarded as compounded of two motions, one horizontal and one vertical, each of which follows its own laws and goes on independently of the other. The horizontal component continues throughout with unchanged velocity in accordance with the law of inertia. The vertical component follows exactly the same law as if the body had been thrown straight upwards, and, after losing its initial velocity, had then fallen straight downwards. This law has already been established in the way which I have explained. Finally, Galileo shows by geometrical reasoning that a body endowed simultaneously with such a horizontal and such a vertical motion will describe a parabola.

Galileo also did much to undermine the medieval astronomy, considered as a physical theory of the structure and motion of the heavens. His invention of the telescope enabled him to observe irregularities and imperfections on the surface of the moon, and to discover that Jupiter has satellites which are plainly related to it as the moon is related to the earth. He himself accepted the Copernican system, according to which the earth and all the planets move in circles round the sun. He argued against the Ptolemaic system, which I have already described; and against that of Tycho Brahe, according to which the sun circulates round the earth and the other planets round the sun. Remembering the fate of Bruno, who had been burnt alive by the Inquisition in 1600, he very sensibly went through the form of recanting these opinions when threatened with prosecution at the same hands; and so he died at the ripe age of seventy-eight in 1642.

I pass now from Galileo to Descartes. Descartes was an eminent mathematician, and he was the only thinker in our period who was of first-rate importance as a philosopher, not only in the wider sense, but also in the narrower meaning in which we now use that word. In his *Discourse on Method* he has given us a kind of philosophical autobiography which is of extreme interest.

Descartes was brought up at La Flèche in the old philosophy

and the old physics. New discoveries were not ignored or despised by his teachers, and he was a brilliant pupil; but he nevertheless felt profoundly dissatisfied. His complaint is that nothing, outside pure mathematics, was proved; everything in natural science and metaphysics was a matter of opinion and controversy. He therefore set himself to seek for a general method by which problems could be attacked and absolutely certain solutions obtained.

Now the search for a general method, and the belief that, if only it could be found, unlimited progress in knowledge and practice would automatically follow, is highly characteristic of the new philosophy. Bacon (1561–1626) and Descartes (1596–1650) speak in the same terms of it and use almost the same metaphors. Both of them hold that there are no great innate differences of intellectual capacity among men; and they compare the right method to a pair of compasses by using which a quite unskilled person can be sure of drawing a more perfect circle than the best artist can draw without one. Descartes was also convinced that one and the same method is necessary and sufficient for solving problems in every subject.

Starting with these convictions, he naturally began by inspecting and analysing the one subject in which it was admitted that men had reached genuine non-controversial knowledge which was continually growing. This was mathematics, and in particular geometry and arithmetic. If we can discover and formulate explicitly the method by which mathematicians attack and solve their problems, we shall have discovered the general method by which anyone can attack and solve any problem.

But Descartes was at once struck by the fact that even within mathematics there seem to be different methods used in geometry, on the one hand, and arithmetic and algebra on the other. And, although the results are equally certain in both, the solution of geometrical problems seems to depend on the luck or individual insight which enables a geometer to hit on the right construction. Descartes was persuaded that this difference could not be ultimate. He saw clearly that inferences must depend on formal relationships and not on the question whether the terms are geometrical figures or numbers or what not. He was thus led to make one of the most important discoveries in technique that has ever been made, viz. that of analytical geometry. He realized that points can be represented by triads of numbers, that the distance between two points can be represented by a certain algebraical relation between the numbers which represent the points, and that every geometrical proposition must therefore have an algebraical analogue. Conversely, any algebraical relation between numbers can be represented by a geometrical diagram. In geometry, then, he really had found a method which would enable anyone who would follow the rules and had patience to manipulate the symbols to solve any problem however complicated.

We come now to Descartes' treatment of physics. Here, again, his general position was characteristic of the new philosophy in contrast to the old. He rejects the secondary qualities, such as colour, sound, smell, taste, etc., from external nature, and holds that everything must be explained mechanically and mathematically in terms of shape, extension, position, and motion. We have already seen that Galileo had formulated this principle. It is quite explicit in Hobbes, who tried to construct a complete system of mechanistic materialism. And Bacon, who is less radical, nevertheless explains sensible heat, for example, as due to concealed motion of particles, and makes the search for minute structure and process to be an essential part of the true method of science.

But Descartes, being a philosopher in the technical sense, is not content to reject the scholastic physics because it is unfruitful and to adopt the mechanical and mathematical view of nature because it is found to work. He wants to see precisely what was the mistake that the old philosophy made; to explain why we are so liable to make it; to eradicate the last lurking traces of it; and to find an irrefragable positive basis for the new mechanical physics. This involves him in a very elaborate series of reflexions which I shall now try to trace in rough outline.

Plainly the defect of the old philosophy of nature is, not that it does not rest on experience, but that it accepts the rather superficial data of every-day experience too naïvely and interprets nature too anthropomorphically. The geocentric astronomy, the doctrine of the elements and their oppositions and transformations, and the theory that different elements have their own natural place which they seek to regain, are all transcriptions of readily observable superficial facts and explanations of them in terms of something like willing and striving in the inorganic world. In order to account for colour, weight, heat, and so on it postulates different powers and dispositions in matter, very much as psychologists still postulate various instincts in men and animals. Each of these dispositions is conceived only as the concealed cause of a certain observable effect, and nothing is asserted of them by which they can be connected with each other or from which other observable results can be deduced. All these points had been made also by Bacon before Descartes.

Now it appeared to Descartes after long reflexion that this erroneous view about the external world is bound up with a fundamental muddle about the nature of the human soul and the human body, which the old philosophy had fallen into. Descartes found on reflexion that it was perfectly possible for him to doubt the existence of matter, including his own body, whilst it was utterly impossible for him to doubt the existence of himself and his own doubts and his other experiences. He concluded from this that his self or soul must be something entirely different from his body and must be something which could have existed even if he never had had a body. Hence the scholastic doctrine that the soul is the form of the living organism must be rejected. The soul is a substance of one kind, and the body is a substance of a radically different kind, though in this life a substance of the former kind is most intimately and mysteriously connected with one of the latter kind.

He then proceeds to reflect on the notions of soul and body, or mind and matter, in order to see what is essential and what is only adventitious to each. His conclusion is as follows. The only essential attribute of a mind is the power of cognition. A mind could be conceived which had no feelings or sensations or images or volitions; but it cannot be conceived as being without cognition. Moreover, feeling, sensation, volition, etc., if present, all presuppose cognition. Similarly, the only essential attribute of a bit of matter is extension, which of course carries with it the notion of having some shape, size, and position, and of being capable of motion or rest either as a whole or in its smaller parts. Our concepts of these two fundamental attributes, cognition and extension, are perfectly clear and distinct; and we can see quite clearly that they are mutually exclusive. What is extended cannot think, and what thinks cannot be extended.

Now the notion of extension is not only clear and distinct but is also fruitful. We know with complete certainty very simple axioms about extension, and from these we can pass gradually by perfectly clear reasoning to an unlimited number of more and more complex propositions. Since we have this complete insight into the nature of extension and its logical independence of consciousness, we can see that there can be no contradiction in the notion of a world of extended objects, obeying the laws of geometry and kinematics. Such a world is known to be at least possible. But our ideas of colour, temperature, sound, etc., though impressive and obtrusive, are not intellectually clear. Here, then, we have no such insight. We cannot be sure that the very notion of an independent world of coloured and hot objects, of noises, of smells, and so on, may not involve a latent contradiction. Such a world may then, for all that we know, be a logical impossibility.

Granted, then, that an independent world of extended movable matter, obeying the laws of geometry and kinematics, is a possible existent, can we be certain that it actually does exist? Descartes has two different lines of argument on this question.

(1) He points out that, although we are thinking beings, we are not (as it is logically possible that we might have been) pure intellects. We have sensations, bodily feelings, emotions, and imagery, and not just pure imageless dispassionate cognition. This is a contingent fact, and it has to be explained somehow. Now each of us believes that his mind is very intimately connected with a certain extended material substance, viz. his own body. If this belief were true, we should have an explanation of those contingent peculiarities of human experience which I have indicated; and it is difficult to think of any other explanation. So it is at least a very highly probable hypothesis that there really are those extended material substances which we call human bodies. And if there are these, then there is no reason to doubt that there are others.

(2) Descartes' second line of argument is more fundamental, and it is liable to strike modern readers as peculiar. The fact is that the notion of God, and the proof of God's existence, play an essential part in Descartes' physics and metaphysics. It is a foundation-stone of the whole system, not an ornament which could be dispensed with. Descartes claims to prove the existence

of an infinitely wise and powerful creative being by several arguments. Most of them were current in the Scholastic philosophy; but he resuscitates one, viz. the Ontological Argument, which was invented by St. Anselm and had been rejected by St. Thomas. He also provides a new proof of his own. The essence of this is as follows. Each of us has the idea of an infinitely wise and powerful creative being, and this fact has to be accounted for. He argues that the idea is not a composite one, like that of a mermaid, constructed by combining ideas derived from various objects which we have perceived and by dropping out the limitations which we found in them. The infinity ascribed to God is positive, not negative; and the unity of the various factors in this idea is intrinsic and is not imposed by us as when we construct the idea of a mermaid from that of a woman's body and a fish's tail. Descartes concludes that our capacity to think of so exalted an object can have been derived from no less a source than a being answering to that idea. Hence God exists, and our innate capacity to form an idea of God may be compared to the mark which an artist puts on a picture or statue to show that it is his handiwork.

Now, since our minds are the work of an infinitely wise and good and powerful maker, we can be sure that all their *original* equipment will be perfect. We shall have no *innate* ideas which are fictitious, and no *genuinely instinctive* beliefs which are false. Error is to be found only in ideas and beliefs which we have acquired in the course of our lives. But we have all acquired many ideas and beliefs so early or so imperceptibly that we are liable to think that we never acquired them at all and that they are innate and instinctive. These are what Bacon picturesquely called *Idols of the Tribe*.

Now the belief that our sensations arise from the action of foreign extended movable objects upon our own bodies is genuinely instinctive and innate. Therefore it must have been implanted in us by God when he created us, and so it must be true. So the existence of a world of extended and movable objects, which surround our bodies and interact with them and with each other, may now be accepted as not merely possible but certain.

But, it may be said, we all ascribe to these objects colour, temperature, etc., as well as extension, figure and motion. Are not these beliefs equally instinctive, and must not they also be therefore accepted as implanted in us by God and thus guaranteed to be true? Here Descartes draws an important distinction. The function of sensations of colour, temperature, taste, smell, etc., is not to supply scientific theoretical knowledge of the nature and laws of the external world as it is in itself. Their only function is to give us biologically useful practical hints about the properties of external things which may make them useful or harmful to us. That is why God gave us the capacity to have sensations of various kinds, including pleasantly and painfully toned organic sensations, and why he implanted in us the belief that every sensible quality is a sign of some correlated quality in the material world. That belief is genuinely instinctive and is true. But the belief that this correlation is identity, that material things are literally coloured and hot and squeaky, is not genuinely instinctive and is nonsensical. It is a confused superstition; which we acquired in childhood, when we accepted uncritically everything that our elders told us and had not clearly recognized the radical distinction and opposition between mind and matter. The Scholastic physics has never grown up. It still ascribes literally to extended, and therefore essentially non-mental, objects qualities which belong only to sensations and therefore can occur only in connexion with minds. That which corresponds in external bodies to the colours, temperatures, etc., which we become aware of when they act on our sense-organs can be nothing but peculiarities of minute structure or motion in substances which are themselves without colour or temperature.

Descartes' extremely sharp distinction between mind and matter makes the connexion between the soul and the body of an individual into an embarrassing problem for him. On the one hand, a living body is simply an extended substance among others, and no properties may be ascribed to it and its parts except extension, figure, and motion. It is just a highly complicated machine, and all vital phenomena must be explained in purely mechanical terms. On the other hand, a soul is an independent substance which has no spatial characteristics, and therefore it is meaningless to ascribe to it shape, size, position, or motion. Yet we know that in the case of a human being these two utterly disparate substances are somehow intimately yoked together for a time. The fact of rational speech and writing shows that a human mind affects by its thoughts and its volitions some of the movements of its body; and the fact that we have sensations, emotions, and images, shows that certain movements within the body affect the mind. How can we conceive of the bond between two such disparate yoke-fellows? And how can we reconcile the principle of the Conservation of Momentum in the material world with the fact that certain movements, e.g. those of the tongue and the fingers in speech and writing, are determined in part by non-material causes?

Descartes restricts the range of this embarrassment by roundly denying that animals have souls. They are mere machines, and their cries when injured are just the squeaks and clatter of ill-oiled or damaged machinery. But he cannot take this view of men, and all that he can do is to argue that the mind's sole action on the body is to guide and control transformations of momentum within the latter, but neither to increase nor diminish the total quantity of momentum in the material world.

This brings me to the general principles of Descartes' mechanical physics. He is not content to establish the fundamental laws of motion, as Galileo might have done, by putting forward alternative hypotheses in mathematical terms, deducing from each a train of consequences which would be observable under assignable conditions if it were true, and then fulfilling these conditions experimentally and seeing whether the inferred consequences do or do not follow. For this would lead at best to highly probable opinion; and, on such fundamental matters Descartes can be content with nothing less than knock-down proof and *a priori* knowledge. So God is again called in aid.

Since God is immutable and eternal we must ascribe to his creation only the bare minimum of change that is compatible with observation. Now we know that there is change of the first-order, viz. motion, and therefore that God has deliberately introduced this into the extended world when he created it. But we are entitled to conclude that at the next level, God will have restored stability. The changes will be subject to unchanging *laws*, and the fundamental law of change will be one of *conservation*. So Descartes derives his first law that the total amount of motion in the world remains at all times the same as it was when God first created it. All changes are simply redistributions of this unalterable original stock of motion. By another bit of *a priori* reasoning Descartes deduces the complete Law of Inertia, i.e. the following proposition: At any moment at which a body is not acted upon from without it will, if at rest, remain at rest; and, if in motion, continue to move with unaltered velocity along the instantaneous tangent to the curve in which it has been moving. I believe that Descartes is the first person to have stated this law fully and correctly. Galileo certainly did neither.

Next, Descartes professes to prove seven laws about the motion of bodies after impact with each other under various initial conditions. Here he is less fortunate. I have worked through all the cases, and I find that some of his laws hold only when the bodies are perfectly elastic, others only when they are perfectly inelastic, and others under no conditions whatever.

It remains to consider Descartes' view of the place of experiments in science. His position is this. We know *a priori* that every natural phenomenon, inorganic or organic, must be capable of a mechanical explanation, and that no other kind of explanation is admissible or intelligible. We can prove *a priori* the fundamental laws of motion; so, although experience is in accord with them, it would be fatuous to base them on experiment. But in the case of a complicated natural phenomenon, e.g. the circulation of the blood, we may be able to think of a number of alternative mechanical explanations, any one of which will explain the observed facts as well as any other. In such cases and in such only experiment becomes important. Although all the mechanical hypotheses under consideration agree in accounting for the natural phenomenon to explain which they were put forward, it will generally be possible to deduce further consequences from each of them; and these will not all be the same under similar conditions. Thus we may be able to devise what Bacon calls 'crucial experiments', which between them will reduce the number of admissible alternatives and perhaps leave only one of them standing.

I will end by attempting very briefly to sum up the strong and the weak points of Descartes' philosophy. He was a man of genius with an extreme dislike for anything misty and confused. So difficulties which were latent in the new philosophy, and which its practical success tended to conceal, stand out clearly in the light of his penetrating and synoptic intellect.

Descartes' absolutely sharp separation of mind and matter, and his denial of all qualities and powers to matter except extension, position, shape and motion was extremely important at the time for the progress of physiology and still more of physics. The sharp separation of mind and body encouraged people to pursue the study of anatomy and physiology as purely physical sciences and to attempt to explain what goes on in living organisms in terms of the mechanical processes which go on in inorganic matter. The extrusion of colour, temperature, and other sensible qualities, and of quasi-psychological strivings and tendencies, from matter enabled scientists to elaborate a system of mathematical physics, and to explain all that happens in the inorganic world on geometrical and mechanical principles. We have only to compare the sciences in which this has been done with others, like psychology and sociology in which nothing of the kind has proved feasible, to appreciate the enormous importance of this step.

The defects were not at the time so obvious, but by now they are fairly clear.

(1) Even within physics itself Descartes was too much of a purist. In his reaction from the scholastic luxuriance of powers and strivings and faculties he did not allow enough activities and potentialities to matter even for dynamical purposes. Dynamics cannot proceed without the notion of inertial mass in addition to that of extension and motion. And Descartes' system has no room for this. Still less could it have admitted Newton's conception of gravitation, as an ultimate active power in matter. To Descartes this would have seemed a deplorable return of the sow that had been washed to her wallowing in the Scholastic mire of occult qualities and substantial forms.

(2) In biology it is simply not helpful to regard living organisms as automatic machines, and biologists have in fact always used other categories beside those of mathematical physics. Moreover, the sharp division which Descartes necessarily makes between men and animals, and between psychology and biology was probably in some respects detrimental to the progress of both these sciences.

(3) Lastly, it is quite impossible to believe that Descartes' theory can be ultimately true in philosophy. It is clear and distinct; but distinctly odd and clearly incredible. It leaves on our

hands the appearances of colour, sound, temperature, etc., and the various organic sensible qualities. Physics may ignore these for its own purposes; but they are part of the contents of the world, and philosophy cannot ignore them. On such a theory as Descartes', they occupy an ambiguous position between the unextended thinking substances and the extended material substance. Somehow, if he is right, we misperceive external bodies as coloured, hot, etc., and we misperceive our own bodies as qualified by aches, ticklings, and so on. That is, we perceive things as having qualities which, if he is right, belong neither to mind nor to matter; and yet there is no third kind of thing for these qualities to belong to.

Descartes' only explanation is that these misperceptions occur in our minds because the latter are so intimately linked with certain portions of matter, viz. our bodies. But this helps not at all. In the first place, the connexion between the human soul and the human body is completely mysterious on this theory. The human soul becomes a kind of Thomistic angel, doomed for a time to haunt a penny-in-the-slot machine, and permitted very occasionally and within very strict limits to interfere with the works. And, secondly, whatever the nature of this curious and discreditable liaison between minds and certain natural machines may be, it does not explain why the former should perceive the latter as having qualities, such as colour and achiness, which in fact belong to nothing in the universe.

The main lesson to be learned is this. At certain periods in the development of human knowledge it may be profitable and even essential for generations of scientists to act on a theory which is philosophically quite ridiculous. And the success of this procedure may blind people for centuries to the fact that its assumptions are quite incredible if taken to be the whole truth and nothing but the truth.

LIEBNIZ'S LAST CONTROVERSY
WITH THE NEWTONIANS

IN this paper I shall give a critical account of the famous series of controversial letters which Leibniz exchanged at the end of his life with Dr. Samuel Clarke. In this correspondence Clarke is the very able representative of Newton and the Newtonians, and Leibniz is engaged in controverting certain fundamental points in the Newtonian philosophy of nature. Questions of pure mathematics, such as Fluxions and Differentials, play no important part in these letters.

I shall begin with a few elucidatory remarks about the persons concerned and the historical background of the controversy. Newton does not appear in person upon the scene, but Clarke is his deputy and advocate.

It will suffice to say a very few words by way of reminder about Newton and Leibniz, but it will be desirable to give a little more detail about Clarke. Newton was born on Old Christmas Day 1642; he entered Trinity College, Cambridge, as a subsizar in June 1661 and became a Fellow of the College in 1667 and Lucasian Professor of Mathematics in Cambridge University in 1669; he published his *Philosophiae Naturalis Principia Mathematica* in the summer of 1687; he became Master of the Mint in 1699 and lived thereafter in London until his death on 20th March 1727. He was seventy-three years old when Leibniz wrote the letter which opened this controversy.

Leibniz was born on 21st January 1646, at Leipzig. He was appointed Librarian to the Duke of Brunswick at Hanover in 1676, and he held that post until his death on 14th November

1716. He was, to the best of my belief, the greatest pure intellect of whom we have any record. He was sixty-nine years old when he started this controversy and he died in the midst of it.

Samuel Clarke was born at Norwich on 11th October 1675. Though not a man of genius, like Newton and Leibniz, he was a person of first-rate mathematical and philosophical ability. He entered Caius College, Cambridge, in 1691, and became a very distinguished undergraduate known to his contempories as 'the lad of Caius'. He soon became an enthusiastic adherent of the Newtonian system in opposition to that of Descartes. At that time one of the best textbooks of mathematical physics was Rohault's *Physique*, written from the Cartesian standpoint. On the advice of his tutor, Clarke translated it into Latin and provided it with copious critical notes in which its Cartesian errors were indicated and corrected on Newtonian principles. Clarke's translation of Rohault became the standard textbook in Cambridge. It was later translated into English by Clarke's brother John, and remained in use until at least 1730.

Clarke became a clergyman of the Church of England, like his father before him, and in 1709 was appointed Chaplain in Ordinary to Queen Anne. In that year he took his D.D. degree at Cambridge. In order to do this he defended before the University the thesis that no article of the Christian faith is contrary to reason. His academic opponent was Dr. James, the Regius Professor of Divinity. It was usual for the Professor on such occasions to conclude the exercise by saying to the candidate *Probe te exercui*; on this occasion Dr. James substituted the phrase *Probe me exercuisti*. A Dr. Yarborough, who had been present, said many years afterwards when he was an old clergyman living at a great distance: 'Though I am seventy-seven years old, I would gladly ride to Cambridge to hear such another act.'

Clarke was probably the ablest philosophical theologian in England in the early eighteenth century. He is famous for his attempt to found a purely rationalistic and axiomatic system of ethics. His theological and ethical theories are stated with great force and clearness in the course of Boyle Lectures which he delivered in London in 1704–5. He was offered the Mastership of the Mint on Newton's death in 1727, but decided it was an unsuitable office for a clergyman. He himself died on 17th May 1729.

There is another person to be mentioned, though she, like Newton, remains behind the scenes. This is Caroline of Anspach, at that time Princess of Wales and afterwards Queen of England as Consort to George II. She was the very intelligent and highly astute wife of a rather stupid and tiresome husband. She managed George admirably in his own interests; making no needless fuss over the regular mistresses whom he thought it due to his position to keep at home, or the occasional infidelities abroad which he was wont to describe in great detail in the eloquent and affectionate letters which he would write to her from Hanover; and getting her own way by proposing the opposite course and relying on his habit of automatically contradicting what he believed to be her wishes. Though Caroline was accustomed to call a spade a spade, and, to judge from Lord Hervey's *Memoirs*, had a fondness for highly spiced conversation, she also took a genuine delight in the company of philosophers and theologians, and seems to have been capable of following and appreciating their arguments. She had been friendly with Leibniz in Hanover; when she came to England after the death of Queen Anne she saw much of Clarke; and in her later years she conversed with Berkeley and befriended Butler, the two great philosophic bishops whose works are still read by philosophers throughout the western world.

The controversy between Leibniz and Clarke began with a letter written by the former to the Princess of Wales in November 1715. In this letter Leibniz made some provocative remarks about the decay of religion and the growth of materialism in England, and attributed this to certain doctrines of Newton and of Locke which he specifies. Caroline handed the letter to Clarke who answered it in some detail. Leibniz replied, and a general engagement along the whole philosophical line followed. Each party wrote five letters, of gradually increasing length and acerbity. Clarke may be said to have remained in possession of the field, since Leibniz died in November 1716 before he could answer Clarke's fifth letter.

The central subject under discussion in these letters is the nature of Space and Time. Newton, as is well known, held a form of the Absolute Theory of Space and Time. This was because he thought that certain dynamical phenomena both enable and compel us to distinguish between absolute and relative rotation in particular and between absolute and relative acceleration in general. He held that absolute rotation and acceleration entail absolute space and time. Leibniz rejected the Absolute Theory and was one of the first persons to state the alternative Relational Theory clearly. His main grounds for rejecting the Absolute Theory were that it conflicts, in his opinion, with two general philosophical principles which he set great store by, viz. the Principle of Sufficient Reason and the Identity of Indiscernibles.

Closely connected with this central topic are certain subsidiary questions. Is the material universe limited or unlimited in extension? Is the created world limited or unlimited in duration? Are there empty regions within the material world, or is it a plenum? On all these questions the Newtonians held certain views and Leibniz was opposed to them.

Much of the controversy is conducted in theological terms. This is partly adventitious; many of the questions which are stated and discussed in theological terminology are independent of it and could easily be translated into non-theological language. But this is not true of all of them. Both Leibniz and the Newtonians were convinced theists, who took the notion of God as creator and sustainer of the world seriously, and there are many assertions about God and his operations in Newton's *Principia*. Newton had thrown out the suggestion that Absolute Space might be the *sensorium* of God, i.e. roughly speaking the medium in and through which God perceives created things. Leibniz attacks this bitterly and somewhat tediously as leading to consequences which are theologically unacceptable. But it develops into the more general and interesting question: 'How does God perceive material things; how do men perceive them; and how are the two modes of perception interrelated?' On these questions Leibniz held highly original and rather paradoxical views which Clarke could not accept. Again, to any theist the question: 'How are Space and Time related to God?' is of fundamental importance; and it is plain that, whatever the answer may be, it will be very different according as the Absolute or the Relational theory is presupposed.

Two other central questions in the correspondence are the Newtonian Theory of Attraction and what I shall describe by an intentionally vague expression as the 'Conservation or Non-

Conservation of Active Force'. Newton's theory of gravitation as a not further explicable property of matter seemed to Leibniz radically unscientific; it was for him a betrayal of the hardly and recently won principle that all genuine explanation of natural phenomena must be in mechanical terms, and a reversion to the purely verbal explanations of the medieval scholastic philosophers. On the second question the Newtonians held that the created universe is automatically running down; whilst Leibniz, on metaphysical grounds, had formulated and asserted what we should now call the 'Conservation of Vis Viva', and thought that this disproved the Newtonian contention. The discussion of both these subjects led straightway to the theological topic of the nature of miracles, i.e. the distinction between the natural and super-natural action of God on the created world. Leibniz said that the only way to make sense of the Newtonian theory of attraction would be to suppose that, when one material particle is moving in the neighbourhood of another, God diverts the former from the straight line which it would otherwise traverse with uniform velocity in accordance with the Law of Inertia. This, he says, is to introduce a continual miracle into the ordinary course of nature. He also said that it is discreditable to the skill of God as maker of the world-machine to suppose that he needs every now and then to clean it and wind it up miraculously.

I think that this should suffice to give a general idea of the contents of the correspondence. I shall now state the Newtonian view of Space and Time, as it gradually emerges in Clarke's letters under the stimulus of Leibniz's criticisms. I suspect that it was much vaguer in many respects when it left Newton's hands than it became when Clarke had to defend it against a critic of Leibniz's ability.

(1) The first and most fundamental point is that Space is logically prior to matter, and Time is logically prior to events or processes. There could not have been matter unless there had been Space for it to occupy and to rest or move in and Time for it to endure through. There could not have been events or processes unless there had been Time in which they have their dates and their durations. But there would have been Space, in precisely the same literal categorical sense, even if there had never been any matter; and there would have been Time, in

precisely the same literal and categorical sense, even if there had never been any events or processes.

(2) We must distinguish between the space occupied by a body at any moment or for any period and the volume of that body; for the body could occupy different spaces at different times without changing its volume. The volume of a body is a property of it, but the space which it occupies at any time is not. Limited spaces are not properties of limited bodies, even if they happen to be occupied by such; they are just parts of the one unlimited Space in which these limited substances exist. Even if it were the case that the whole of infinite Space were continuously occupied by matter, still Space would not be a property of that infinite body. The infinite mass of matter would still merely be *in* Space as finite bodies are in it.

It is plain that Clarke takes a similar view, *mutatis mutandis*, about Time and events or processes in Time; though I think that he ought to have paid more attention to the fact that it is meaningless to suppose that an event or process should shift its position in Time as a body can shift its position in Space without change of volume or shape.

(3) Strictly speaking Space is indivisible. One can indeed talk of parts of Space, i.e. different regions actually or in imagination marked out by containing certain material objects or by being traced in pencil or ink. But the parts of Space are in principle inseparable. Two adjoined regions of Space are inseparable, not merely in the sense that there is no force in nature which could overcome their mutual adhesion. This would be the case with two adjoined parts of an old-fashioned extended solid atom. But two adjoined regions of Space are inseparable in the logical sense that it is *meaningless* to talk of any region coming to occupy a different position, and it is therefore *meaningless* to suggest that two regions which are adjoined might be separated. In the same way Space is in principle continuous. It is a contingent question whether there are or are not holes in matter; it is nonsensical to suggest that there might be holes in Space. Similar remarks apply, *mutatis mutandis*, to Time.

(4) Space is actually, and not just potentially, infinite. Of course neither Clarke nor Leibniz ever entertained the notion that the geometry of nature might be non-Euclidean and that straight lines might return into themselves like the great-circles

on a sphere. The same is true of Time; it had no beginning and will have no end.

(5) The points of Space and the moments of Time are not perceptible; only the things and events which occupy Space and Time can be perceived. But, since Time is quite independent of the events and processes which happen to occupy it, it is intelligible to suggest that the universe might have been created at an earlier or a later moment than that at which it was in fact created. Again, since Space is quite independent of the things and events which happen to occupy it, both the following suggestions are intelligible on the supposition that the material universe is of finite extent. (i) That without any difference in its internal structure it might *have been* created in a different region of Space. (ii) That it might *be* moved as a whole by God from one part of Space to another, or be given an absolute rotation about any direction of Space. If this rectilinear motion of the universe were accelerated or decelerated, or if the universe were subjected to an absolute rotation, these absolute motions would betray themselves by observable forces within the world. Otherwise they would remain unobservable.

(6) Absolute motion involves absolute Space and absolute Time; and the existence of absolute motion and its distinction from relative motion is evidenced by the existence of centrifugal forces, by the flattening of the earth at the poles, and so on. Clarke points out two consequences of the theory that all motion is relative which are certainly most paradoxical and which seem to him enough to refute the theory. One is that, if a body happened to be the only one that existed, it would be meaningless to suggest that it could either be at rest or in motion whether translatory or rotational. The other is that, if all the matter outside a rotating body, such as the earth, were annihilated, it would at once become meaningless to say that it was rotating; and therefore presumably all the observable effects which are attributed to the rotation of the earth would cease to happen.

(7) A region of Space or a stretch of time has an absolute magnitude, viz. volume in the one case and duration in the other. Different regions can be compared in respect of their volumes, and different stretches in respect of their duration.

(8) The last topic which must be discussed here is Clarke's

account of what might be called the 'ontological status' of Absolute Space and Time. The following are the main points. (i) They are not substances, but attributes. (ii) They are attributes, not of any created substance, but of God himself. Absolute Space is that attribute of God which theologians call 'Immensity'; Absolute Time is that attribute of God which they call 'Eternity'. Clarke says, somewhat rashly in my opinion, that no meaning can be attached to 'immensity' except space without bounds, and no meaning can be attached to 'eternity' except time without beginning or end. (iii) Absolute Space and Time are said to be, not only attributes of God, but also immediate and necessary consequences of his existence. Since they are attributes which follow necessarily from the existence of a Being whose existence is necessary, their ontological status is much more assured than that of any material thing or event. For the existence of the latter is contingent, depending as it does on the will of God to create it. (iv) God does not 'exist in' Space and Time in the sense in which created things and events do so. For Space and Time are logically prior to created things and events, and, if a certain region of Space happens to be occupied for a certain stretch of time by a certain thing or process, that is simply because God chose to create such a thing or process at a certain place and date. Obviously God is not 'in' Space and Time, which are his own attributes, in this special way. Nevertheless God is immediately present throughout the whole of unending time to every part of unbounded space. By this omnipresence he is continually aware of all created things and he acts upon them, but they do not react upon him.

I pass now to Leibniz's criticisms on the Newtonian theory of Space and Time and to the alternative Relational Theory of them which he upheld in its stead. I shall begin with an account of his two principles of Sufficient Reason and the Identity of Indiscernibles.

Leibniz distinguished sharply between necessary and contingent truths. A truth is necessary if and only if all the apparent alternatives to it are impossible because self-contradictory. Thus e.g. the proposition that the square-root of 2 is irrational is a necessary truth. For the supposition that there is a fraction m/n, in its lowest terms, such that $m^2 = 2n^2$ can be shown to be self-contradictory. A truth is contingent if and only if there are real alternatives to it which, though in fact false, are logically possible because internally consistent. Thus, e.g. it is a contingent singular truth that Julius Caesar decided to cross the Rubicon on a certain occasion, and it is a contingent general truth that the sine of the angle of incidence bears a constant ratio to the sine of the angle of refraction for light of a given wave-length travelling from a certain medium to a certain other.

It is clear that the Principle of Non-Contradiction is the guarantee of necessary truths, and it is equally clear that it is not the guarantee of contingent truths. Now Leibniz held that in the case of any contingent truth, there is always a sufficient reason why that preposition is true and why the logically possible alternatives to it are false. He also held that the ultimate reason for the truth of any true contingent proposition is always of the same kind. If we trace this doctrine backwards in the letters to Clarke, we find that it rests on the following two inter-connected principles. (i) Every choice is determined by mo-tives. (ii) Any being who is capable of choosing always chooses that alternative which seems to him at the time to be the most good or the least bad of those open to him. In comparing alter-natives from this point of view he will consider, not only the intrinsic qualities of each, but also its relations to contemporary and past events and its future consequences. He will choose that one which seems to him to be most good or least bad on the whole when all these factors are taken into account.

Now these general principles of choice apply to God as well as to created intelligent beings such as men or angels. But there are certain important differences between God and any created being in this matter. God is fully aware of all the possible alter-natives, and can see all the relationships and foresee all the consequences of each. But a created being is always limited in the extent of his knowledge and is always liable to have mistaken beliefs about matters of fact. Moreover what seems best on the whole to God is always what is really best on the whole. But a creature is always liable to be biased by passion or impulse, so that what seems best to him may not really be so even if he makes no mistakes or omissions about matters of fact.

Now the ultimate reason for the truth of any true contingent proposition is this. God foresaw that a world in which this proposition would be true would on the whole contain more good or less evil than any possible alternative world in which it would be false. He therefore chose to create a world in which this proposition would be true, and to leave uncreated all the equally possible worlds in which this proposition would be false and one or other of the possible alternatives to it would have been true. What I have just been explaining is, I think, what Leibniz meant by the *Principle of Sufficient Reason*.

We come now to the other Principle, viz. the *Identity of Indiscernibles*. McTaggart used to say, rightly in my opinion, that a better name for the principle would be the *Dissimilarity of the Diverse*. Leibniz held that we can know for certain that there are not, never have been, and never will be two things in nature which are exactly alike. If there is numerical diversity, there is certainly some kind and degree of qualitative dissimilarity. He undoubtedly meant this much by the Identity of Indiscernibles. What is uncertain is whether he held that the very supposition that there might be two things exactly alike is self-contradictory and meaningless; or whether he held that, although it is not logically impossible that there should be two such things, we can be quite sure that God would not create them. As Clarke pointed out, Leibniz seems now to say the one thing and now the other. In his Fourth Letter, e.g. he says that 'to suppose two indiscernible things is to suppose the *same* thing under two names'. This certainly suggests that he held that the supposition, if taken literally, is self-contradictory and meaningless. But elsewhere in this Letter, and still more explicitly in the Fifth, he seems to take the other view. For instance, in the Fifth Letter he says that he does *not* maintain that it is absolutely impossible to suppose that there are two bodies which are indiscernible from each other, but only that it would be *contrary to God's wisdom* to create two such bodies and therefore we can be certain that there are not two such.

I think that there are two things to be said about this apparent inconsistency. (i) Plainly there is a sense in which it is possible to make and to argue correctly and intelligibly from a supposition which is, in another sense, impossible. That is precisely what happens, e.g. when one proves by a *reductio ad absurdum* that there cannot be a rational fraction in its lowest terms whose square is equal to 2. (ii) Leibniz might merely be making a concession, for the sake of argument, to his opponent. His position might, perhaps, be expressed as follows: 'I can see that the supposition that there are two things exactly alike is self-contradictory; but, even if you will not grant me this, I can show from the Principle of Sufficient Reason that God never would create two such things and therefore that the supposition will always be false.'

We can now pass from the statement of Leibniz's two philosophical principles to the use which he makes of them in attacking the Newtonian doctrine of Absolute Space and Absolute Time. We will consider first his attempt to prove from the Principle of Sufficient Reason that there are not, never have been, and never will be two precisely similar material particles. The argument may be put as follows.

Suppose, if possible, that there are two co-existing material particles A and B, exactly alike in all their qualities and dispositional properties. They would have to be at different places. Suppose that A is at P and B at Q. For the present purpose it does not matter whether we assume the absolute or the relational theory of Space. If P and Q are points of Absolute Space there could be no possible reason for preferring to put A at P and B at Q rather than B at P and A at Q. But a similar consequence follows on the relational theory. In that case the point P is defined by certain spatial relations to a certain set of material particles chosen as a system of reference, and the point Q is defined by certain other spatial relations to the same set of material particles. Now, if the two particles A and B are precisely alike in all their qualities and dispositional properties, there can be no possible reason for preferring to put A into the former set of relations and B into the latter rather than doing the opposite with them. If, then, God were to create two such particles, he would (i) be bound to put them in different places, and yet (ii) would have no reason for choosing between the two alternatives which would arise by imagining the two particles transposed. Since God never acts without a sufficient reason, we can conclude that he never will create two precisely similar co-existing particles and therefore that there never will be two such particles.

The importance of this conclusion for the present purpose is the following. Leibniz used the Principle of Sufficient Reason as the basis of one of his main arguments against the theory of Absolute Space and Time. Suppose that the Absolute Theory of Space were true and that the material universe is of finite extent. Then it is intelligible to suggest that, without any difference in the mutual relations of various parts, the material universe as a whole might have been created by God in this, that, or another region of Absolute Space. But there could be no reason for preferring to create it in one region rather than in another. Therefore God would be faced with either (i) the alternative of not creating a material universe at all, or (ii) creating it in one or another of a number of alternative places between which he would have no possible ground for deciding. Since the material universe does in fact exist, we know that God has in fact created it. Since it is contrary to the nature of an intelligent being to make an unmotivated choice, we can be sure that God was not really faced with the alternatives which would have confronted him if the Absolute Theory of Space had been true. Now, if the Relational Theory were true, these so-called alternative ways of placing the world would not be genuine possibilities; for there could be no space prior to the existence of matter. On that theory God creates space in creating and arranging matter. So, Leibniz concludes, we can reject the Absolute Theory and accept the Relational Theory of Space.

A very similar argument can be used against Absolute Time. On the Absolute Theory it is intelligible to suggest that God might have created the world, with exactly the same contents and exactly the same subsequent history, at an earlier or a later moment of absolute time than that at which he in fact created it. Yet he could have no possible reason for preferring one moment to another at which to start the created world. The argument then proceeds as before. On the Relational Theory of time these so-called alternatives do not exist; for time begins with the first event.

Now Clarke had answered by pointing out that God would be in precisely the same kind of difficulty on the Relational Theory if he created two exactly similar particles. And he assumed that Leibniz would admit that there might be, and in fact are, precisely similar particles, e.g. various atoms of the same substance. As we have seen, Leibniz's reaction was to accept Clarke's argument and to conclude that God would not create two precisely

similar particles and therefore that the supposition that there
are such particles may be rejected.

The logical position at this point is the following. Leibniz
has tried to refute the Absolute Theory and support the Relational Theory by showing that a certain situation, which would
conflict with the Principle of Sufficient Reason, *would* arise if
the former theory were true and *could not* arise if the latter were
true. Clarke counters this by saying that, if there are material
particles which are precisely alike, a similar conflict with the
Principle of Sufficient Reason will arise even on the Relational
Theory; and concludes that Leibniz's argument cannot be
decisive in favour of the latter. Leibniz counters this by accepting all Clarke's premises except that there are precisely similar
material particles, and concludes that God will never create
such particles and that therefore there never will be such.

Clarke is not satisfied with this answer. He points out that
a person might know that it would be much better to actualize
one or other of two alternatives A and A' than to actualize *neither*
of them, whilst at the same time he may see that it is a matter
of complete indifference whether it should be A or A' that is
realized. On Leibniz's principle a person in this position will
realize *neither*, simply because he has no reason to prefer one
to the other, although he has a very good reason for preferring
to realize *one or other* of them to realizing neither. Clarke
says that in such a case of indifference a free agent chooses a
certain one of the indifferent alternatives by a 'mere act of will'.
Leibniz answers that, if this were possible, which it is not, such
motiveless choice would be indistinguishable from pure objec-
tive chance. I might remark that a man in this kind of situation
would probably decide to associate the head of a coin with one
of the alternatives and the tail with the other and to spin the
coin and choose that alternative which was associated with the
side that should fall uppermost. But this expedient would not
be open to God; for he would know beforehand how the coin
would fall, and so he would already be deciding on a certain
alternative when he associated it with the face which he foresaw would fall uppermost.

I think that this part of Leibniz's argument might fairly be
summarized as follows. Let us grant, for the sake of argument,
that the Absolute Theory of Space and Time is in some sense

an intelligible hypothesis and not just meaningless verbiage. If that theory were true the created universe could have occupied, without being in any way different internally, a different stretch of time or a different region of space. Now there would have been no possible reason for preferring to put it in one stretch of time or one region of space rather than another. Therefore God, who never makes a choice without a sufficient reason, would not have created a universe at all. But, since there is a universe, we know that he has created one. Therefore we can be certain that the Absolute Theory is false if it is not meaningless.

Like Clarke I find it hard to decide whether Leibniz would have gone further and said that the Absolute Theory is just meaningless verbiage. The following remarks in his Fifth Letter are typical. The supposition of the universe as a whole being moved is (i) meaningless, since there is no space outside it; and (ii) even if it were intelligible it would be pointless for 'there would happen no change which could be observed by any person whatever'. He adds the following remark: 'Mere mathematicians, who are only taken up with the conceits of imagination are apt to forge such notions, but they are destroyed by superior reasons.' In the same letter he says that real change must be *in principle* observable. Motion need not be actually observed; but there is no motion where there is no change that *could be* observed, and there is no change where none *could be* observed.

All this has a very modern ring, and might have been said by any contemporary Logical Positivist. Nevertheless I do not feel quite sure how to interpret it. It seems to me that it is fairly susceptible of either of the following two interpretations. (i) The Absolute Theory, and various questions which arise in connexion with it, are *intrinsically* meaningless; and so we must accept the Relational Theory. (ii) Even though the Absolute Theory be *not intrinsically* meaningless, and though these questions be intelligible in terms of it, yet we can reject it and accept the Relational Theory because of the argument founded on the Principle of Sufficient Reason. And *in terms of the Relational Theory* these questions *are* meaningless. I am inclined to suspect that Leibniz himself held the first view, but contented himself with the second for controversial purposes.

It is now convenient to give Leibniz's positive account of what is meant by 'Space' and 'Time'. He introduces this topic in the Fourth Letter and goes into considerable detail about Space in the Fifth. He does not discuss Time in similar detail; no doubt he thought, as so many writers on these topics have done, that what holds for Space can be applied automatically to Time. This is, in my opinion, a dangerous assumption, for the unlikenesses are at least as important as the likenesses.

According to Leibniz, Space is an order of coexistences and Time is an order of sequences. This seems to me plainly inadequate; for events may be contemporary as well as successive, and we can give no account of either rest or motion unless we conceive of identity of place at different times as well as difference of place at the same time. However, Leibniz is fully aware of the latter point and deals explicitly with it in the full account of Space which he gives in the Fifth Letter. This may be summarized as follows.

Suppose that certain bodies, X, Y, Z . . ., etc., do not change their mutual spatial relations during a certain interval. Suppose further that, if there is a change during this interval in their spatial relations to certain other bodies, then the cause of it has not been in themselves. Then we can say that the bodies X, Y, Z . . ., etc., have constituted a 'rigid fixed system' during the interval in question. Suppose that, at some moment within this period, a certain body A stood in certain spatial relations to the bodies of this system; that at a later moment within the period it ceased to stand in those relations to them; and that at some later moment within the period a certain other body B began to stand to those bodies in precisely similar relations to those in which A had formerly stood. Then we can say that 'B had come to *occupy the same place as A* formerly occupied'. If and only if the cause of these changes of relative position have been in A and in B, we can say that A and B have 'been in motion'.

Leibniz then defines 'a place' in terms of the relation of 'occupying the same place', and he defines 'space' as the collection of all places. He makes several interesting comments on this procedure.

(1) He remarks that, in making the notion of sameness of place primary and defining 'place' in terms of it, he follows the procedure of Euclid who starts by defining the statement that A

has *the same ratio* to *B* as *C* has to *D* and does not begin by defining 'ratio'.

(2) He remarks that, if *B* occupies the same place as *A* did, we must not say that the present relation of *B* to the system of reference is *the same* as the previous relation of *A* to that system. Two different things cannot literally stand in the same relationship. We must say that the relationships are precisely alike. He then adds the following remark. 'The mind, not contented with an agreement, looks for an identity—for something that should be truly the same; and conceives it as being extrinsic to the subject; and this is what we here call "place" and "space". But this can only be an ideal thing; containing a certain *order* wherein the mind conceives the application of relations.'

The upshot of the matter is this. Speaking in the terminology of contemporary Cambridge logicians we may say that Leibniz regards Space as a logical construction out of places, and regards a place as a logical construction out of facts about relative spatial position. And he holds that the notion of Absolute Space and absolute places is a fallacy of misplaced concreteness. The *word* 'Space' is a substantive and occurs as the grammatical subject of such sentences as 'Space is three-dimensional'. This suggests that it is, like the word 'Cambridge', the proper name of a particular existent, though one of a peculiar kind. But, according to Leibniz, this suggestion is misleading.

It will be noticed that, in defining 'sameness of place at different times', Leibniz has had to introduce the condition that the system of reference shall not have moved during the interval. It will also be noticed that he gives a causal criterion for judging whether a body or system of bodies which has changed its relative position shall be said to have moved or not. The criterion is whether the cause of the change of relative position is or is not in the body itself. He uses this criterion in order to answer Newton's empirical arguments for absolute rotation based on the existence of centrifugal forces. In reference to this argument he says that there is nothing in it that proves the reality of Absolute Space. There is a difference, even on the Relational Theory, between what he calls 'an absolute true motion of a body' and what he calls 'mere relative change of its situation with respect to another body'. But this difference, he says, consists in whether 'the immediate cause' of the change of relative position 'is in the body itself' or not. I take it that his view is that centrifugal forces are connected with 'absolute true motions' thus defined.

It seems to me that a *prima facie* objection to this criterion is that, according to the First Law of Motion, the cause of an accelerated or a curvilinear motion of a body never is in that body itself. Leibniz would not have accepted this objection because he had a general metaphysical principle that all the changes in any substance are caused by its own previous states, and that the appearance of interaction between different substances is delusive. He attempts to construct a system of dynamics in accordance with that principle, but it would take us outside our present limits to discuss it.

We can now pass to another point in the controversy. Clarke in his Third Letter said that space and time are magnitudes, whilst order and situation are not, and he made this an objection to the relational theory. He reiterates this objection in his Fourth Letter and complains that Leibniz has made no attempt to answer it. Leibniz deals with the objection in his Fifth Letter. He says there that relations can have magnitude. The examples which he gives are ratios between numbers. E.g. the ratio of 28 to 7 is equal to the ratio of 16 to 4 and is greater than that of 15 to 5. Now ratios are relations, and any pair of terms of which it is intelligible to say that one is equal to, greater than, or less than another is a magnitude. He adds that the magnitudes of ratios are measured by their logarithms. I suppose that this is because, if the ratio of x to y is l and that of y to z is m and that of x to z is n, then $\log l + \log m = \log n$. Clarke answers that ratios are not magnitudes because they are not additive. I think that the point is that $x/y + y/z$ is not in general equal to x/z. He considers the reference to the additive property of logarithms irrelevant. And, in any case, he says, time and space are not of the nature of ratios. They are absolute magnitudes which have ratios among themselves.

It seems to me that the questions at issue are confused by Leibniz's reference to the example of ratios in arithmetic. Presumably the fundamental relations on the Relational Theory are (i) the relation of *distance* between two material particles, and (ii) that of *angular divergence* between the lines joining one pair of material particles and another pair. I see no objection to saying that these are magnitudes. In certain special cases, viz. if three particles x, y, and z are collinear and y is between x and z, the distance between x and z is the sum of the distances between x and y and between y and z. But in general the relationship is more complex. Similar remarks, *mutatis mutandis*, apply to angular divergence between lines. So far Leibniz seems to be in the right. On the other hand, we have also to consider area and volume; and Clarke seems to be right in calling these absolute magnitudes which have ratios among themselves. But I do not think that this would be any reason for accepting the Absolute Theory of Space and rejecting the Relational Theory, though it might show that the Relational Theory needs certain supplements.

The next point that I shall consider is the question of the finitude or infinitude of the material world in space and of whether it is a plenum or contains empty regions within it. The Newtonians held that the material world is of finite extent and that outside it there is a boundless expanse of Absolute Space. They also held that within the universe there are regions of Absolute Space which contain no matter. Leibniz denied both these propositions. According to him the material universe continuously occupies an unlimited expanse.

The details of the controversy are rather tedious, so I shall try to state briefly in my own way what I believe to be the facts of the case. (1) The only alternatives among those just mentioned which would have a meaning on the Absolute Theory (assuming that the theory is itself intelligible) and would be meaningless on the Relational Theory are the following. (i) That the universe as a whole should rotate or not rotate about an axis. (ii) That, if the universe be finite in extent, it should as a whole either have a motion of translation or be translationally at rest.

(2) On the Relational Theory it is *prima facie* intelligible that the universe should be either finite or infinite in extent. The former alternative would mean that, if you take the distance between any two particles P and Q as your unit, then there is a finite integer N such that the distance between any two particles in the universe is less than N times the distance between P and Q. The latter alternative would mean that, if you take the distance between any two particles P and Q as your unit

and measure in any direction from any assigned particle O, then, whatever finite integer N may be, there is always a particle in that direction at a greater distance from O than N times the distance between P and Q. (I call this *prima facie* intelligible, because it involves no internal contradiction. Whether this kind of actual infinity be not unintelligible in some *other* important sense is a question which I cannot discuss here.)

(3) If the universe is of finite extent, it is intelligible on the Relational Theory to say (i) that it *might have been* bigger or smaller at a given moment than it in fact was then, and (ii) that it might *become* bigger or smaller in future than it now is. For this means simply that the finite integer N, mentioned above in the definition of the finitude of the universe, might have been bigger or smaller than it in fact was or might become bigger or smaller than it now is.

(4) On the Relational Theory it is equally intelligible to suggest that matter is continuous or that there are holes in it. We could define an 'empty linear segment' as a pair of particles P and Q such that there was no particle between them. Having done this we should have no difficulty in principle, though there would be considerable difficulties in detail, in defining an 'empty area' and an 'empty volume'.

It seems to me then that there is no close logical connexion between the controversy about Absolute and Relative Space, on the one hand, and these controversies about the finite or infinite extent of the universe and the existence or non-existence of empty spaces within it, on the other. In the end Leibniz says explicitly that he does not maintain either that God *could not* have limited the quantity of matter or that he *certainly has not* done so. He asserts only that it is *very unlikely* that a perfectly wise and benevolent creator would have done so. This is his position in the latter part of the Fifth Letter. But earlier in the same letter he uses phrases which suggest that the Relational Theory suffices to settle the question in favour of the infinity and continuity of matter. He says: 'Since space in itself is an ideal thing . . . space outside the world must needs be imaginary. . . . The case is the same with empty space within the world, which I take also to be imaginary. . . .' Immediately after this passage he goes on to discuss the allegation that Guerike of Magdeburg had produced a vacuum in the receiver of his air-pump.

If Leibniz meant merely that, on the Relational Theory, space does not exist, in the sense in which the Newtonians thought it did, either outside the material universe, if that be finite, or inside the receiver of an air-pump, he was no doubt right. But, if he thought that this has any tendency to prove that the material universe cannot be finite in extent and cannot have empty holes in it, he was, as I hope I have shown, quite mistaken.

I have now stated the arguments which Leibniz used and the conclusions which he drew in his *Letters to Clarke* about the absolute and relational theories of Space and Time. But it is important to remember that this controversy is conducted at what Leibniz would regard as an intermediate level of philosophical rigour and thoroughness. It is indeed a philosophical, and not merely a physical, discussion. But in it Leibniz is granting for the sake of argument certain assumptions which he would claim to have refuted in his more elaborate and professional philosophical writings. He is granting here the reality of extended substances and of spatial relations between them, but in fact he believes himself to have shown that the notion of an extended substance involves a contradiction, and that there can be no relations between substances. According to his considered opinion, what we misperceive as an endlessly divisible extended material thing is really a collection of an infinite number of unextended mental substances, and what we misperceive as a relation between two things is really certain qualities in the things which we misperceive as interrelated. I shall end this paper by showing that, at this deeper level, Leibniz's view is in an important sense a form of the absolute theory.

In order to do this I must first explain a distinction which was originally pointed out by the Cambridge philosopher, W. E. Johnson, in his *Logic*. I shall put it in my own way. In controversies about the absolute *versus* the relational theory of space and time there are two questions to be distinguished: (1) Is position a pure quality or a relational property? (2) Does position belong to material particles *directly*; or does it belong primarily to particulars of another kind, viz. points of space, and only in a derivative sense to material particles in virtue of their occupation of points of space? The first question may properly be put in the form: 'Is spatial position qualitative or relational?'

The second may properly be put in the form: 'Is space adjectival or substantival in character?' Johnson pointed out, quite rightly, in my opinion, that these two questions were never clearly distinguished by protagonists in the controversy about 'absolute' *versus* 'relative' space.

We can begin by dividing possible theories into (1) Substantival, and (2) Adjectival. The essential features of all forms of the Substantival Theory are the following. There are particulars which together constitute a single complex particular, viz. Space. These and only these have spatial characteristics in the primary and underived sense. And each of them has timelessly or sempiternally all the spatial qualities and relational properties that it has. It is meaningless to talk of a point of Space, in this sense, changing its position; or of a volume of Space, in this sense, changing its size or shape. Now, besides Space and its regions or points, there are material things or particles. Each material particle at any moment occupies a certain point of Space, and each body at any moment occupies a certain region of Space. At different moments the same material particle or body may occupy the same or different points or regions of Space. The statement that a certain body has at a certain moment a certain position, shape, size, etc., is always derivative and analysable. It means that at this moment that body occupies a region of space which timelessly or sempiternally has a certain position, shape, size, etc. A body can change in respect of its spatial characteristics because (i) it can occupy different regions of Space at different times, and (ii) these regions must differ timelessly or sempiternally in position and may differ timelessly or sempiternally in shape and size.

The essential features of all forms of the Adjectival Theory are the following. The only subjects of spatial characteristics are material particles or bodies. There is not another kind of particular existent called 'Space' beside matter. The spatial characteristics which a material particle or a body has at any moment belong to it in a primary and underived sense. So there are no timeless or sempiternal spatial characteristics. A body may happen to keep the same position, shape, and size for a long time, or it may happen to change quickly and continuously in respect of some or all of these characteristics. But there can be no question of analysing such a change into a relation of occupance to a series of terms of an entirely different kind, each of which has all its spatial characteristics timelessly or sempiternally.

I think there is no doubt that the Newtonians held, and that Leibniz rejected at all levels of his thinking, the *substantival* theory of Space and Time.

We can now consider the other pair of opposites, viz. (1) Qualitative and (2) Relational, theories. We will confine ourselves here to the characteristic of spatial position, and not consider shape or size. I think that the Qualitative Theory may be put most clearly as follows. There is a certain determinable quality, which we will call 'Spatial Position'. We might compare this to the determinable Sound-quality. The determinates under it form a continuous three-dimensional manifold of qualities. These may be compared (though the analogy must not be pressed in detail) with the manifold of determinate sound-qualities which can be arranged in respect of pitch, loudness, and timbre. Any two particulars which have simultaneously two different determinate forms of the determinable quality of Spatial Position will *ipso facto* stand to each other in certain determinate relations of distance, direction, etc. This may be compared with the fact that any two sounds which have simultaneously two different determinate forms of the determinable Sound-quality will *ipso facto* stand to each other in certain relations of harmony or disharmony, of relative loudness, and so on. Thus spatial relations are *founded upon* the determinate positional qualities of the related terms; just as musical relationships are founded upon the determinate sound-qualities of the notes struck.

The essential features of the Relational Theory are the following. There is no *quality* of spatial position. The fundamental positional characteristics of any term are its *relations* of distance and direction to other terms. These relations are not founded upon qualities in the related terms, as the musical relations between notes are founded upon their determinate sound-qualities. To say that a certain particular has a certain position is simply to state its relations of distance and direction to certain other particulars of the same kind chosen arbitrarily as terms of reference.

Now it would be possible theoretically to combine either the

Substantival or the Adjectival theory with either the Qualitative or the Relational theory. But in fact the usual combinations have been Substantival Qualitative and Adjectival Relational. I think there is little doubt that the Newtonians held a form of the Substantival Qualitative theory, and it is certain that Leibniz in the letters to Clarke is asserting a form of the Adjectival Relational theory.

But this is not the theory that Leibniz really held. What he really held, when he was not arguing *ad hominem* against Clarke and the Newtonians, was a form of Adjectival Qualitative theory. That this must be so is obvious in view of his general principle that what we take to be relations between terms are really qualities in the terms which we partially misperceive. But we need not confine ourselves to such general considerations; for Leibniz has told us explicitly what is the determinable quality, present in some determinate form in every monad at every moment, which is the basis of the appearance of spatial relations. It is what he calls 'Point of View'. It is true that he would not allow us to identify point of view with the quality of spatial position; but point of view is a quality, and every difference in the apparent spatial position of apparently extended objects is correlated with a real difference in the point of view of the monads which we misperceive as those extended objects.

Suppose that we were to drop the distinction between the quality of Point of View and the quality of Spatial Position, and to speak wholly in terms of the latter. Then the Adjectival Qualitative theory of spatial position could be formulated as follows. There is a determinable quality of Spatial Position, and under it there is a three-dimensional manifold of determinate positional qualities. At each moment each material particle has one and only one of these. At two different moments the same material particle may have the same or different determinate positional qualities. At any moment any two material particles will stand in a determinate relation of relative position, which is founded upon the determinate positional qualities possessed at the moment by each of them. Absolute motion of a particle consists in its having, at each of a continuous series of moments, a different one of a continuous series of positional qualities. Relative motion of one material particle with respect to another entails that at least one of them is in absolute motion;

but the same relative motion could arise in connexion with very different absolute motions of the two particles concerned. It seems to me that this is the kind of view of space and motion which we ought to ascribe to Leibniz when we dig beneath the position which he occupies in his controversy with Clarke.

SECTION III

ETHICS

DETERMINISM, INDETERMINISM, AND LIBERTARIANISM

The Implications of Obligability

W E often make retrospective judgments about the past actions of ourselves or other people which take the form: 'You ought not to have done the action X, which you in fact did; you ought instead to have done the action Y, which in fact you did not.' If I make such a judgment about a person, and he wants to refute it, he can take two different lines of argument. (1) He may say: 'I could have done Y instead of X, but you are mistaken in thinking that Y was the action that I ought to have done. In point of fact, X, the action that I did, was the one that I ought to have done. If I had done Y, I should have done what I ought not to have done.' (2) He may say: 'I could not help doing X,' or he may say: 'Though I need not have done X, I could not possibly have done Y.'

If the accused person makes an answer of the first kind, he is admitting that the alternatives 'ought' and 'ought not' apply to the actions X and Y, but he is objecting to my applying 'ought' to Y and 'ought not' to X. He is saying that 'ought' applies to X, and 'ought not' to Y. It is as if two people, who agree that X and Y are each either black or white, should differ because one holds that X is black and Y white whilst the other holds that X is white and Y black. If the accused person makes an answer of the second kind, he is denying the applicability of the alternatives 'ought' and 'ought not'. If he says: 'I could not help doing X,' he assumes that his critic will admit that neither 'ought' nor 'ought not' has any application to an action which the agent

o   195

could not help doing. If he says: 'Though I need not have done *X*, yet I could not possibly have done *Y*,' he assumes that his critic will admit that neither 'ought' nor 'ought not' has any application to an action which the agent could not have done. It is as if one person should say that *X* is black and *Y* is white, and the other should answer that at least one of them is un-extended and therefore incapable of being either black or white.

Obligability Entails Substitutability

Now we are concerned here only with the second kind of answer. The essential point to notice is that it is universally admitted to be a *relevant* answer. We all admit that there is some sense or other of 'could' in which 'ought' and 'ought not' entail 'could'. We will now try to get clear about the connexion between these two notions.

Judgments of obligation about past actions may be divided into two classes, viz. (1) judgments about actions which were actually done, and (2) judgments about conceivable actions which were not done. Each divides into two sub-classes, and so we get the following fourfold division. (1·1) 'You did *X*, and *X* was the action that you ought to have done.' (1·2) 'You did *X*, and *X* was an action that you ought not to have done.' (2·1) 'You did not do *X*, and *X* was the action that you ought to have done.' And (2·2) 'You did not do *X*, and *X* was an action that you ought not to have done.' Now both judgments of the first class entail that you could have helped doing the action which you in fact did. If the action that you did can be said to be one that you ought to have done, or if it can be said to be one that you ought not to have done, it must be one that you *need not* have done. And, since you actually did it, it is obviously one that you *could have* done. Both judgments of the second class entail that you could have done an action which you did not in fact do. If a conceivable action which you did not do can be said to be one which you ought to have done, or if it can be said to be one that you ought not to have done, it must be one that you *could have* done. And, since you actually failed to do it, it is obviously one that you *need not* have done.

It is worth while to notice that the common phrases: 'You ought to have done so and so' and 'You ought not to have done so and so' are generally equivalent to our judgments (2·1) and (1·2) respectively. The former is generally used to mean: 'You did not do so and so, and that was an action which you ought to have done.' The latter is generally used to mean: 'You did so and so, and that was an action which you ought not to have done.' But we often need to express what is expressed by our judgments (1·1) and (2·2). We often want to say that a person did what he ought on a certain occasion, and we often want to say that a person avoided doing something which he ought not to have done on a certain occasion. For this is exactly the state of affairs which exists when a person has in fact done an unpleasant duty in face of a strong temptation to shirk it by lying.

Now the importance of this connexion between 'ought' and 'ought not', on the one hand, and 'could', on the other, is very great. People constantly make judgments of obligation of the four kinds which we have distinguished, and such judgments have constantly been made throughout the whole course of human history. Every single one of these judgments has been false unless there have been cases in which actions which *were* done could have been left undone and actions which *were not* done could have been done. And these judgments would all have been false in principle, and not merely in detail. They would have been false, not in the sense that they asserted 'ought' where they should have asserted 'ought not', or *vice versa*. They would be false in the sense that nothing in the world has ever had that determinable characteristic of which 'ought to be done' and 'ought not to be done' are the determinate specifications. They would be false in the sense in which all judgments which predicated redness, blueness, etc., of any object would be false in a world which contained no objects except minds and noises.

It will be convenient to call an action 'obligable' if and only if it is an action of which 'ought to be done' or 'ought not to be done' can be predicated. It will be convenient to call an action 'substitutable' if, either it was done but could have been left undone, or it was left undone but could have been done. We may then sum up the situation by saying that an action is obligable if and only if it is, in a certain sense, substitutable; that, unless all judgments of obligations are false in principle, there are obligable actions; and therefore, unless all judgments of obligation are false in principle, there are actions which are, in this sense, substitutable.

Various Senses of 'Substitutable'

This is one aspect of the case. The other aspect is the following. There are several senses of 'could' in which nearly everyone would admit that some actions which were done could have been left undone, and some actions which were left undone could have been done. There are thus several senses of 'substitutable' in which it would commonly be admitted that some actions are substitutable. But, although an action which was *not* substitutable in these senses would *not* be obligable, it seems doubtful whether an action which was substitutable *only* in these senses *would be* obligable. It seems doubtful whether an action would be obligable unless it were substitutable in some further sense.

At this stage two difficulties arise. (i) It is extremely difficult to grasp and to express clearly this further sense of 'substitutable', i.e. this further sense of 'could' in which an action that was done could have been left undone or an action which was not done could have been done. Many people would say that they can attach no meaning to 'substitutable' except those meanings in which it is insufficient to make an action obligable. (ii) Even if this other meaning of 'substitutable' can be grasped and clearly expressed, many people would say that no action is substitutable in this sense. They would claim to see that no act on which has been done could have been left undone, and that no action which was not done could have been done, in that sense of 'could' which is required if an action is to be obligable.

Now anyone who holds these views is in a very awkward position. On the one hand, it is not easy to believe that every judgment of obligation is false, in the sense in which every judgment ascribing colour to an object would be false in a world containing only minds and noises. On the other hand, it is highly depressing to have to admit that there is a sense of 'could' which you can neither grasp nor clearly express. And it is equally unsatisfactory to have to believe that some actions *are* substitutable in a sense in which it seems to you self-evident that no action *could be* substitutable.

There are two problems to be tackled at this point. (i) To try to discover and state the sense of 'substitutable' in which being substitutable is the necessary and sufficient condition of being obligable. And (ii), if we can do this, to consider whether any action could be substitutable in this sense.

Voluntary Substitutability

Let us begin by considering an action which has actually been performed. In some cases we should say that the agent 'could not have helped' performing it. We should certainly say this if we had reason to believe that the very same act would have been performed by the agent in these circumstances even though he had willed that it should not take place. It is obvious that there are actions which are 'inevitable', in this sense, since there are actions which take place although the agent is trying his hardest to prevent them. Compare, e.g. the case of a conspirator taken with an uncontrollable fit of sneezing.

Next consider a conceivable action which was not in fact performed. In some cases we should say that the agent 'could not possibly' have performed it. We should certainly say this if the act would not have taken place in these circumstances no matter how strongly the agent had willed it. It is obvious that there are conceivable acts which are 'impossible' in this sense, since there are cases where such an act fails to take place although the agent is trying his hardest to bring it about. Compare, e.g. the case of a man who is bound and gagged, and tries vainly to give warning to a friend.

We will call acts of these two kinds 'not voluntarily substitutable'. It is plain that an act which is not voluntarily substitutable is not obligable. No one would say that the conspirator ought not to have sneezed, or that the bound and gagged man ought to have warned his friend. At most we may be able to say that they ought or ought not to have done certain things in the past which are relevant to their present situation. Perhaps the conspirator ought to have sprayed his nose with cocaine before hiding behind the presumably dusty arras, and perhaps the victim ought not to have let himself be lured into the house in which he was gagged and bound. But these are previous questions.

We see then that to be voluntarily substitutable is a *necessary* condition for an action to be obligable. But is it a *sufficient* condition? Suppose I performed the action A on a certain occasion. Suppose that I should not have done A then if I had willed with a certain degree of force and persistence not to do it. Since I did A, it is certain that I *did not* will with this degree of force and persistence to avoid doing it. Now suppose that at the time I *could not* have willed with this degree of force and persistence to avoid doing A. Should we be prepared to say that I ought not to have done A?

Now take another case. Suppose that on a certain occasion I failed to do a certain conceivable action B. Suppose that I should have done B if I had willed with a certain degree of force and persistence to do it. Since I did not do B, it is certain that I *did not* will with this degree of force and persistence to do it. Now suppose that at the time I *could not* have willed with this degree of force and persistence to do B. Should we be prepared to say that I ought to have done B? It seems to me almost certain that, under the supposed conditions, we should not be prepared to say either that I ought not to have done A or that I ought to have done B.

Consider, e.g. the case of a man who gradually becomes addicted to some drug like morphine, and eventually becomes a slave to it. At the early stages we should probably hold that he could have willed with enough force and persistence to ensure that the temptation would be resisted. At the latest stages we should probably hold that he could not have done so. Now at every stage, from the earliest to the latest, the hypothetical proposition would be true: 'If he had willed with a certain degree of force and persistence to avoid taking morphine, he would have avoided taking it.' Yet we should say at the earlier stages that he ought to have resisted, whilst, at the final stages, we should be inclined to say that 'ought' and 'ought not' have ceased to apply.

Primary and Secondary Substitutability

An action which was in fact done, but would not have been done if there had been a strong and persistent enough desire in the agent not to do it, will be called 'primarily avoidable'. Suppose, in addition, that there could have been in the agent at the time a desire of sufficient strength and persistence to prevent the action being done. Then the action might be called 'secondarily avoidable'. If this latter condition is not fulfilled, we shall say that the action was 'primarily avoidable, but secondarily inevitable'. Similarly, an action which was not in fact done, but would have been done if there had been in the agent a strong and persistent enough desire to do it, will be called 'primarily possible'. Suppose, in addition, that there could have been in the agent at the time a desire of sufficient strength and persistence to ensure the action being done. Then the action may be called 'secondarily possible'. If this latter condition is not fulfilled, we shall say that the action is 'primarily possible, but secondarily impossible'. An action will be called 'primarily substitutable' if it is either primarily avoidable or primarily possible. It will be secondarily substitutable if it is either secondarily avoidable or secondarily possible. In order that an action may be obligable it is not enough that it should be primarily substitutable, it must be at least secondarily substitutable.

We are thus led on from the notion of voluntarily substitutable *actions* to that of substitutable *volitions*. Suppose that, on a certain occasion and in a certain situation, a certain agent willed a certain alternative with a certain degree of force and persistence. We may say that the volition was substitutable if the same agent, on the same occasion and in the same circumstances, could instead have willed a different alternative or could have willed the same alternative with a different degree of force and persistence. Now there is one sense of 'could' in which it might plausibly be suggested that many volitions are substitutable. It seems very likely that there are many occasions on which I *should* have willed otherwise than I did, *if* on previous occasions I had willed otherwise than I did. So it seems likely that many volitions have been voluntarily substitutable.

It is necessary to be careful at this point, or we may be inadvertently granting more than we are really prepared to admit. Obviously it is often true that, if I had willed otherwise than I did on certain earlier occasions, I should never have got into the position in which I afterwards made a certain decision. If, e.g. Julius Caesar had decided earlier in his career not to accept the command in Gaul, he would never have been in the situation in which he decided to cross the Rubicon. This, however, does not make his decision to cross the Rubicon substitutable. For a volition is substitutable only if a different volition could have occurred in the agent in the *same* situation. Again, it is often true that, if I had willed otherwise than I did on certain earlier occasions, my state of knowledge and belief would have been different on certain later occasions from what it in fact was. In that case I should have thought, on these later occasions, of certain alternatives which I did not and could not think of in my actual state of knowledge and belief. Suppose, e.g. that a lawyer has to decide what to do when a friend has met with an accident. If this man had decided years before to study medicine instead of law, it is quite likely that he would now think of, and perhaps choose, an alternative which his lack of medical knowledge prevents him from contemplating. This, however, does not make the lawyer's volition in the actual situation substitutable. For, although the external part of the total situation might have been the same whether he had previously decided to study medicine or to study law, the internal part of the total situation would have been different if he had decided to study medicine, instead of deciding, as he did, to study law. He would have become an agent with different cognitive powers and dispositions from those which he in fact has. No one would think of saying that the lawyer ought to have done a certain action, which he did not and could not contemplate, merely because he would have contemplated it and would have decided to do it if he had decided years before to become a doctor instead of becoming a lawyer.

Having cleared these irrelevances away, we can now come to the real point. A man's present conative-emotional dispositions, and what we may call his 'power of intense and persistent willing', are in part dependent on his earlier volitions. If a person has repeatedly chosen the easier of the alternatives open to him, it becomes increasingly difficult for him to choose and to persist in pursuing the harder of two alternatives. If he has formed a habit of turning his attention away from certain kinds of fact, it will become increasingly difficult for him to attend fairly to alternatives which involve facts of these kinds. This is one aspect of the case. Another, and equally important, aspect is the following. If a man reflects on his own past decisions, he may see that he has a tendency to ignore or to dwell upon certain kinds of fact, and that this had led him to make unfair or unwise decisions on many occasions. He may decide that, in future, he will make a special effort to give due, and not more than due, weight to those considerations which he has a tendency to ignore or to dwell upon. And this decision may make a difference to his future decisions. On the other hand, he may see that certain alternatives have a specially strong attraction for him, and he may find that, if he pays more than a fleeting attention to them, he will be rushed into choosing them, and will afterwards regret it. He may decide that, in future, he will think as little as possible about such alternatives. And this decision may make a profound difference to his future decisions.

We can now state the position in general terms. Suppose that, if the agent had willed differently on earlier occasions, his conative-emotional dispositions and his knowledge of his own nature would have been so modified that he would now have willed differently in the actual external situation and in his actual state of knowledge and belief about the alternatives open to him. Then we can say that his actual volition in the present situation was 'voluntarily avoidable', and that a volition of a different kind or of a different degree of force and persistence was 'voluntarily possible'. An action which took place was secondarily avoidable if the following two conditions are fulfilled. (i) That this action would not have been done if the agent had willed with a certain degree of force and persistence to avoid it. (ii) That, if he had willed differently in the past, his conative-emotional dispositions and his knowledge of his own nature would have been such, at the time when he did the action, that he would have willed to avoid it with enough force and persistence to prevent him doing it. In a precisely similar way we could define the statement that a certain conceivable action, which was not done, was secondarily possible. And we can thus define the statement that an action is secondarily substitutable.

Can we say that an action is obligable if it is secondarily substitutable, in the sense just defined, though it is not obligable if it is only primarily substitutable? It seems to me that the same difficulty which we noticed before reappears here. Suppose that the agent could not have willed otherwise than he did in the remoter past. It is surely irrelevant to say that, *if* he had done so, his conative dispositions *would* have been different at a later stage from what they in fact were then, and that he *would* have willed otherwise than he then did. One might, of course, try to deal with this situation by referring back to still earlier volitions. One might talk of actions which are not only primarily, or only secondarily, but are tertiarily substitutable. But it is quite clear that this is useless. If neither primary nor secondary substitutability, in the sense defined, suffice to make an action obligable, no higher order of substitutability, in this sense, will suffice. The further moves are of exactly the same nature as the second move. And so, if the second move does not get us out of the difficulty, none of the further moves will do so.

Categorical Substitutability

The kind of substitutability which we have so far considered may be called 'conditional substitutability'. For at every stage we have defined 'could' to mean 'would have been, if certain conditions had been fulfilled which were not'. Now I have concluded that merely conditional substitutability, of however high an order, is not a sufficient condition for obligability. If an action is to be obligable, it must be *categorically* substitutable. We must be able to say of an action, which was done, that it could have been avoided, in some sense of 'could' which is not definable in terms of 'would have, if'. And we must be able to say of a conceivable action, which was not done, that it could have been done, in some sense of 'could' which is not definable in terms of 'would have, if'. Unless there are some actions of which such things can truly be said, there are no actions which are obligable. We must therefore consider whether any clear meaning can be attached to the phrase 'categorically substitutable', i.e. whether 'could' has any clear meaning except 'would have, if'. And, if we can find such a meaning, we must enquire whether any actions are categorically substitutable.

Various Senses of 'Obligable'

Before tackling these questions I must point out that the words 'ought' and 'ought not' are used in several different senses. In some of these senses obligability does not entail categorical substitutability.

(i) There is a sense of 'ought' in which we apply it even to inanimate objects. It would be quite proper to say: 'A car ought to be able to get from London to Cambridge in less than three hours,' or: 'A fountain-pen ought not to be constantly making blots.' We mean by this simply that a car which did take more than three hours would be a poor specimen of car, or would be in a bad state of repair. And similar remarks apply to the statement about the fountain-pen. We are comparing the behaviour of a certain car or fountain-pen with the average standard of achievement of cars or fountain-pens. We are not suggesting that *this* car or *this* pen, in its present state of repair, unconditionally could go faster or avoid making blots. Sometimes when we make such judgments we are comparing an individual's achievements, not with those of the *average* member, but with those of an *ideally perfect* member, of a certain class to which it belongs. We will call 'ought', in this sense, 'the comparative ought'. And we can then distinguish 'the average-comparative ought' and 'the ideal-comparative ought'.

(ii) Plainly 'ought' and 'ought not' can be, and often are, used in this sense of human actions. But, in the case of human actions, there is a further development. Since a human being has the power of cognition, in general, and of reflexive cognition, in particular, he can have an idea of an average or an ideal man. He can compare his own achievements with those of the average, or the ideal, man, as conceived by him. And he will have a more or less strong and persistent desire to approximate to the ideal and not to fall below the average. Now it is part of the notion of an ideal man that he is a being who would have a high ideal of human nature and would desire strongly and persistently to approximate to his ideal. Obviously it is no part of the notion of an ideal horse or an ideal car that it is a being which would have a high ideal of horses or cars and a strong and persistent desire to live up to this. When we say that a man ought not to cheat at cards we often mean to assert two things. (a) That the average decent man does not do this, and that anyone who does falls in this respect below the average. And (b) that a man who does this either has a very low ideal of human nature or a very weak and unstable desire to approximate to the ideal which he has. So that, in this further respect, he falls below the average.

Now neither of these judgments implies that a particular person, who cheated on a particular occasion, categorically could have avoided cheating then; or that he categorically could have had a higher ideal of human nature; or that he categorically could have willed more strongly and persistently to live up to the ideal which he had. For an action to be obligable, in this sense, it is plain enough that it should be secondarily substitutable, in the sense already defined.

The Categorical Ought

Some philosophers of great eminence, e.g. Spinoza, have held that the sense of 'ought' which I have just discussed is the only sense of it. Plainly it is a very important sense, and it is one in which 'ought' and 'ought not' can be applied only to the actions of intelligent beings with power of reflexive cognition, emotion, and conation. I think that a clear-headed Determinist should hold either that this is the only sense; or that, if there is another sense, in which obligability entails *categorical* substitutability, it has no application.

Most people, however, would say that, although we often do use 'ought' and 'ought not' in this sense, we quite often use them in another sense, and that in this other sense they entail categorical substitutability. I am inclined to think that this is true. When I judge that I ought not to have done something which I in fact did, I do not as a rule seem to be judging merely that a person with higher ideals, or with a stronger and more persistent desire to live up to his ideals, would not have done what I did. Even when this is part of what I mean, there seems to be something more implied in my judgment, viz. that I *could* have had higher ideals or *could* have willed more strongly and persistently to live up to my ideals, where 'could' does not mean just 'would have, if'. Let us call this sense of 'ought' the 'categorical ought'. It seems to me then that we must distinguish between an action being obligable in the comparative sense and being obligable in the categorical sense; and that, if any action were categorically obligable, it would have to be categorically substitutable.

Analysis of Categorical Substitutability

We can now proceed to discuss the notion of categorical substitutability. It seems to me to involve a negative and a positive condition. I think that the negative condition can be clearly formulated, and that there is no insuperable difficulty in admitting that it may sometimes be fulfilled. The ultimate difficulty is to give any intelligible account of the positive condition. I will now explain and illustrate these statements.

Suppose that, on a certain occasion, I willed a certain alternative with a certain degree of force and persistence, and that, in consequence of this volition, I did a certain voluntary action which I should not have done unless I had willed this alternative with this degree of intensity and persistence. To say that I categorically could have avoided doing this action implies at least that the following negative condition is fulfilled. It implies that the process of my willing this alternative with this degree of force and persistence was not completely determined by the nomic, the occurrent, the dispositional, and the background conditions which existed immediately before and during this process of willing. In order to see exactly what this means it will be best to contrast it with a case in which we believe that a process is completely determined by such conditions.

Suppose that two billiard-balls are moving on a table, that they collide at a certain moment, and that they go on moving in modified directions with modified velocities in consequence of the impact. Let us take as universal premises the general laws of motion and of elastic impact. We will call these 'nomic premises'. Let us take as singular premises the following propositions. (i) That each ball was moving in such and such a direction and with such and such a velocity at the moment of impact. We will call this an 'occurrent premiss'. (ii) That the masses and co-efficients of elasticity of the balls were such and such. We will call this a 'dispositional premiss'. (iii) That the table was smooth and level before, at, and after the moment of impact. We will call this a 'background premiss'. Lastly, let us take the proposition that the balls are moving, directly after the impact, in such and such directions with such and such velocities. Then this last proposition is a *logical consequence* of the conjunction of the nomic, the occurrent, the dispositional, and the background premisses. That is to say, the combination of these premisses with the denial of the last proposition would be *logically inconsistent*. It is so in exactly the sense in which the combination of the premisses of a valid syllogism with the denial of its conclusion would be so.

The Negative Condition

We can now work towards a definition of the statement that a certain event *e* was completely determined in respect of a certain characteristic. When we have defined this statement it will be easy to define the statement that a certain event was not completely determined in respect of a certain characteristic. I will begin with a concrete example, and will then generalize the result into a definition.

Suppose that a certain flash happened at a certain place and date. This will be a manifestation of a certain determinable characteristic, viz. colour, in a certain perfectly determinate form. It may, e.g. be a red flash of a certain perfectly determinate shade, intensity, and saturation. We may call shade, intensity, and saturation the three 'dimensions' of colour, and we shall therefore symbolize the determinable characteristic colour by a three-suffix symbol C_{123}. When we want to symbolize a certain perfectly determinate value of this we shall use the symbol C_{123}^{abc}. This means that the shade has the determinate value a, that the intensity has the determinate value b, and that the saturation has the determinate value c. Each *index* indicates the determinate value which the dimension indicated by the corresponding *suffix* has in the given instance.

Now the statement that this flash was completely determined in respect of colour has the following meaning. It means that there is a set of true nomic, occurrent, dispositional, and background propositions which together entail the proposition that a manifestation of colour, of the precise shade, intensity, and saturation which this flash manifested, would happen at the place and time at which this flash happened. To say that this flash was *not* completely determined in respect of colour means that there is *no* set of true nomic, occurrent, dispositional, and background propositions which together entail the proposition that a manifestation of colour, of the precise shade, intensity, and saturation which this flash manifested, would happen at the place and time at which this flash happened.

There are two remarks to be made at this point. (i) It seems to me that the second statement is perfectly *intelligible*, even if no such statement be ever true. (ii) It is a purely *ontological* statement, and not in any way a statement about the limitations of our knowledge. Either there is such a set of true propositions, or there is not. There may be such a set, even if no one knows that there is; and there may be no such set, even if everyone believes that there is.

We can now give a general definition. The statement that a certain event e was completely determined in respect of a certain determinable characteristic C_{123} is equivalent to the conjunction of the following two propositions. (i) The event e was a manifestation of C_{123} in a certain perfectly determinate form C_{123}^{abc} at a certain place and date. (ii) There is a set of true nomic, occurrent, dispositional, and background propositions which together entail that a manifestation of C_{123} in the form C_{123}^{abc} would happen at the place and date at which e happened. The statement that e was *not* completely determined in respect of C_{123} is equivalent to the conjoint assertion of (i) and denial of (ii).

The next point to notice is that an event might be partly determined and partly undetermined in respect of a certain characteristic. As before, I will begin with a concrete example. Our flash might be completely determined in respect of shade and saturation, but not in respect of intensity. This would be equivalent to the conjunction of the following two statements. (i) That there is a set of true propositions, of the kind already mentioned, which together entail that a flash, of precisely the shade and saturation which this flash had, would happen at the place and date at which this flash happened. (ii) There is no such set of true propositions which together entail that a flash, of precisely the intensity which this flash had, would happen at the time and place at which this flash happened. We thus get the notion of 'orders of indetermination' in respect of a given characteristic. If an event is undetermined in respect of one and only one dimension of a certain determinable characteristic, we say that it has 'indetermination of the first order' in respect of this characteristic. If it is undetermined in respect of two and only two dimensions of a certain determinable characteristic, we say that it has 'indetermination of the second order' in respect of this characteristic. And so on.

It is obvious that there is another possibility to be considered, which I will call 'range of indetermination in respect of a given dimension of a given characteristic'. Suppose that our flash is undetermined in respect of the intensity of its colour. There may be a set of true propositions, of the kind mentioned, which together entail that a flash, whose intensity falls within certain limits, would happen at the time and place at which this flash happened. This range of indetermination may be wide or narrow. Complete determination in respect of a given dimension of a given characteristic is the limiting case where the range of indetermination shuts up to zero about the actual value of this dimension for this event. Thus the 'extent of indetermination' of an event with respect to a given characteristic depends in general upon two factors, viz. (i) its order of indetermination with respect to the dimensions of this characteristic, and (ii) its range of indetermination with respect to those dimensions for which it is not completely determined.

We can now define the statement that a certain event e was completely determined. It means that e has zero range of indetermination for every dimension of every determinable characteristic of which it is a manifestation. The statement that a certain event e was *not* completely determined can now be defined. It means that e had a finite range of indetermination for at least one dimension of at least one of the characteristics of which it was a manifestation.

And now at last we can define 'Determinism' and 'Indeterminism'. Determinism is the doctrine that *every* event is completely determined, in the sense just defined. Indeterminism, is the doctrine that some, and it may be all, events are not completely determined, in the sense defined. Both doctrines are, *prima facie*, intelligible, when defined as I have defined them.

There is one other point to be noticed. An event might be completely determined, and yet it might have a 'causal ancestor' which was not completely determined. If Y is the total cause of Z, and X is the total cause of Y, I call both Y and X 'causal ancestors' of Z. Similarly, if W were the total cause of X, I should call Y, X, and W 'causal ancestors' of Z. And so on. If at any stage in such a series there is a term, e.g. W, which contains a cause-factor that is not completely determined, the series will stop there, just as the series of human ancestors stops with Adam. Such a term may be called the 'causal progenitor' of such a series. If Determinism be true, every event has causal ancestors, and therefore there are no causal progenitors. If Indeterminism be true, there are causal progenitors in the history of the world.

We can now state the negative condition which must be fulfilled if an action is to be categorically substitutable. Suppose that, at a certain time, an agent deliberated between two alternatives, A and B, and that he actually did A and not B. Suppose that the following conditions are fulfilled. (i) The doing of A by this agent at this moment was completely determined. (ii) The total cause of A being done contained as cause-factors a desire of a certain strength and persistence for A and a desire of a certain strength and persistence for B. (iii) These two desires were not completely determined in respect of strength and persistence. (iv) The range of indetermination was wide enough to include in it, as possible values, so strong and persistent a desire for B or so weak and fleeting a desire for A as would have determined the doing of B instead of the doing of A. Conditions (iii) and (iv) are the negative conditions which must be fulfilled if B is to be categorically substitutable for A. They amount to the following statement. It is consistent with (a) the laws of nature, including those of psychology, (b) the facts about the agent's dispositions and the dispositions of any other agent in the world at the moment of acting, (c) the facts about what was happening within and without the agent at that moment, and (d) the facts about the general background conditions at that moment, that the strength and persistence of the desires mentioned in (ii) should have any value that falls within the range mentioned in (iv).

Before we go further there is one point to be mentioned.

Strictly speaking, what I have just stated are the negative conditions for *primary* categorical substitutability. For I have supposed the incomplete determination to occur at the *first* stage backwards, viz. in one of the cause-factors in the total cause of the action A. It would be quite easy to define, in a similar way, the negative conditions for secondary, or tertiary, or any other order of categorical substitutability. All that is needed is that, at *some* stage in the causal ancestry of A, there shall be a total cause which contains as factors desires of the agent answering to the conditions which I have stated. That is to say, all that is necessary is that A shall have a causal ancestor which is a causal progenitor, containing as a factor an incompletely determined desire of the agent's.

We come now to the final question. Supposing that this negative condition were fulfilled, would this *suffice* to make an action categorically obligable? It seems to me plain that it would not. Unless some further and positive condition were fulfilled, all that one could say would be the following: 'The desire to do A happened to be present in me with such strength and persistence, as compared with the desire to do B, that I did A and avoided B. The desire to do B might have happened to be present in me with such strength and persistence, as compared with the desire to do A, that I should have done B and avoided A.' Now, if this is all, the fact that I did A and not B is, in the strictest sense, an *accident*, lucky or unlucky as the case may be. It may be welcomed or it may be deplored, but neither I nor anything else in the universe can properly be praised or blamed for it. It begins to look as if the categorical ought may be inapplicable, though for different reasons, both on the hypothesis that voluntary actions have causal progenitors and on the hypothesis that none of their causal ancestors are causal progenitors.

The Positive Condition

Let us now try to discover the positive conditions of categorical obligability. I think that we should naturally tend to answer the sort of objection which I have just raised in the following way. We should say: 'I deliberately identified myself with my desire to do A, or I deliberately threw my weight on the side of that desire. I might instead have made no particular effort in one direction or the other; or I might have identified myself with, and thrown my weight on the side of, my desire to do *B*. So my desire to do *A* did not just happen to be present with the requisite strength and persistence, as compared with my desire to do *B*. It had this degree of strength and persistence because, and only because, I *reinforced* it by a deliberate effort, which I need not have made at all and which I could have made in favour of my desire to do *B*.' Another way of expressing the same thing would be this: 'I forced myself to do *A*; but I need not have done so, and, if I had not done so, I should have done *B*.' Or again: 'I might have forced myself to do *B*; but I did not, and so I did *A*.'

It is quite plain that these phrases express a genuine positive experience with which we are all perfectly familiar. They are all, of course, metaphorical. It will be noticed that they all attempt to describe the generic fact by metaphors drawn from specific instances of it, e.g. deliberately pressing down one scale of a balance, deliberately joining one side in a tug-of-war, deliberately thrusting a body in a certain direction against obstacles, and so on. In this respect they may be compared with attempts to describe the generic facts about time and change by metaphors drawn from specific instances, such as flowing streams, moving spots of light, and so on. The only use of such metaphors is to direct attention to the sort of fact which one wants one's hearers to contemplate. They give no help towards analysing or comprehending this fact. A metaphor helps us to understand a fact only when it brings out an analogy with a fact of a *different* kind, which we already understand. When a generic fact can be described only by metaphors drawn from specific instances of itself it is a sign that the fact is unique and peculiar, like the fact of temporal succession and the change of events from futurity, through presentness, to pastness.

Granted that there is this unique and peculiar factor of deliberate effort or reinforcement, how far does the recognition of it help us in our present problem? So far as I can see, it merely takes the problem one step further back. My doing of *A* is completely determined by a total cause which contains as factors my desire to do *A* and my desire to do *B*, each of which has a certain determinate strength and persistence. The preponderance of my desire to do *A* over my desire to do *B*, in respect of strength and persistence, is completely determined by a total cause which contains as a factor my putting forth a certain amount of effort to reinforce my desire for A. This effort-factor is not completely determined. It is logically consistent with all the nomic, occurrent, dispositional, and background facts that no effort should have been made, or that it should have been directed towards reinforcing the desire for B instead of the desire for A, or that it should have been put forth more or less strongly than it actually was in favour of the desire for A. Surely then we can say no more than that it just happened to occur with a certain degree of intensity in favour of the desire for A.

I think that the safest course at this stage for those who maintain that some actions are categorically obligable would be the following. They should admit quite frankly what I have just stated, and should then say: 'However paradoxical it may seem, we do regard ourselves and other people as morally responsible for accidents of this unique kind, and we do not regard them as morally responsible, in the categorical sense, for anything but such accidents and those consequences of them which would have been different if the accidents had happened differently. Only such accidents, and their causal descendants in the way of volition and action, are categorically obligable.' If anyone should take up this position, I should not know how to refute him, though I should be strongly inclined to think him mistaken.

This is not, however, the position which persons who hold that some actions are categorically obligable generally do take at this point. I do not find that they ever state quite clearly what they think they believe, and I suspect that is because, if it were clearly stated, it would be seen to be impossible. I shall therefore try to state clearly what I think such people want to believe, and shall try to show that it is impossible. I suspect that they would quarrel with my statement that, on their view, the fact that one puts forth such and such an effort in support of a certain desire is, in the strictest sense, an accident. They would like to say that the putting forth of a certain amount of effort in a certain direction at a certain time *is* completely determined, but is determined in a unique and peculiar way. It is literally determined *by the agent or self*, considered as a substance or continuant, and not by a total cause which contains as factors *events in* and *dispositions of* the agent. If this could be maintained, our puttings-forth of effort would be completely determined, but their causes would neither be events nor contain events as cause-factors. Certain series of events would then originate from causal progenitors which are continuants and not events. Since the first event in such a series would be completely determined, it would not be an accident. And, since the total cause of such an event would not be an event and would not contain an event as a cause-factor, the two alternatives 'completely determined' and 'partially undetermined' would both be inapplicable to it. For these alternatives apply only to events.

I am fairly sure that this is the kind of proposition which people who profess to believe in Free Will want to believe. I have, of course, stated it with a regrettable crudity, of which they would be incapable. Now it seems to me clear that such a view is impossible. The putting-forth of an effort of a certain intensity, in a certain direction, at a certain moment, for a certain duration, is quite clearly an event or process, however unique and peculiar it may be in other respects. It is therefore subject to any conditions which self-evidently apply to every event, as such. Now it is surely quite evident that, if the beginning of a certain process at a certain time is determined at all, its total cause *must* contain as an essential factor another event or process which *enters into* the moment from which the determined event or process *issues*. I see no *prima facie* objection to there being events that are not completely determined. But, in so far as an event *is* determined, an essential factor in its total cause must be other *events*. How could an event possibly be determined to happen at a certain date if its total cause contained no factor to which the notion of date has any application? And how can the notion of date have any application to anything that is not an event?

Of course I am well aware that we constantly use phrases, describing causal transactions, in which a continuant is named as the cause and no event in that continuant is mentioned. Thus we say: 'The stone broke the window,' 'The cat killed the mouse,' and so on. But it is quite evident that all such phrases are elliptical. The first, e.g. expresses what would be more fully expressed by the sentence: 'The coming in contact of the moving stone with the window at a certain moment caused a process of disintegration to begin in the window at that moment.' Thus the fact that we use and understand such phrases casts no doubt on the general principle which I have just enunciated.

Let us call the kind of causation which I have just described and rejected 'non-occurrent causation of events'. We will call the ordinary kind of causation, which I had in mind when I defined 'Determinism' and 'Indeterminism', 'occurrent causation'.

Now I think we can plausibly suggest what may have made some people think they believe that puttings-forth of effort are events which are determined by non-occurrent causation. It is quite usual to say that a man's putting-forth of effort in a certain direction on a certain occasion was determined by 'Reason' or 'Principle' or 'Conscience' or 'The Moral Law'. Now these impressive names and phrases certainly do not denote events or even substances. If they denote anything, they stand for propositions or systems of propositions, or for those peculiar universals or systems of universals which Plato called 'Ideas'. If it were literally true that puttings-forth of effort are determined by such entities, we should have causation of events in time by timeless causes. But, of course, statements like 'Smith's putting-forth of effort in a certain direction on a certain occasion was determined by the Moral Law' cannot be taken literally. The Moral Law, as such, has no causal efficacy. What is meant is that Smith's *belief* that a certain alternative would be in accordance with the Moral Law, and his *desire* to do what is right, were cause-factors in the total cause which determined his putting-forth of effort on the side of that alternative. Now this belief was an event, which happened when he began to reflect on the alternatives and to consider them in the light of the moral principles which he accepts and regards as relevant. And this desire was an event, which happened when his conative-emotional moral dispositions were stirred by the process of reflecting on the alternatives. Thus the use of phrases about action being 'determined by the Moral Law' may have made some people think they believe that some events are determined by non-occurrent causation. But our analysis of the meaning of such phrases shows that the facts which they express give no logical support to this belief.

DETERMINISM, ETC.

Libertarianism

We are now in a position to define what I will call 'Libertarianism'. This doctrine may be summed up in two propositions. (i) Some (and it may be all) voluntary actions have a causal ancestor which contains as a cause-factor the putting-forth of an effort which is not completely determined in direction and intensity by occurrent causation. (ii) In such cases the direction and the intensity of the effort are completely determined by non-occurrent causation, in which the self or agent, taken as a substance or continuant, is the non-occurrent total cause. Thus, Libertarianism, as defined by me, entails Indeterminism, as defined by me; but the converse does not hold.

If I am right, Libertarianism is self-evidently impossible, whilst Indeterminism is *prima facie* possible. Hence, if categorical obligability entails Libertarianism, it is certain that no action can be categorically obligable. But if categorical obligability entails only Indeterminism, it is *prima facie* possible that some actions are categorically obligable. Unfortunately, it seems almost certain that categorical obligability entails more than Indeterminism, and it seems very likely that it entails Libertarianism. It is therefore highly probable that the notion of categorical obligability is a delusive notion, which neither has nor can have any application.

EGOISM AS A THEORY OF
HUMAN MOTIVES

THERE seem *prima facie* to be a number of different kinds of ultimate desire which all or most men have. Plausible examples would be the desire to get pleasant experiences and to avoid unpleasant ones, the desire to get and exercise power over others, and the desire to do what is right and to avoid doing what is wrong. Very naturally philosophers have tried to reduce this plurality. They have tried to show that there is one and only one kind of ultimate desire, and that all other desires which seem at first sight to be ultimate are really subordinate to this. I shall call the view that there really are several different kinds of ultimate desire *Pluralism of Ultimate Desires*, and I shall call the view that there is really only one kind of ultimate desire *Monism of Ultimate Desires*. Even if a person were a pluralist about ultimate desires, he might hold that there are certain important features common to all the different kinds of ultimate desire.

Now much the most important theory on this subject is that all kinds of ultimate desire are *egoistic*. This is not in itself necessarily a monistic theory. For there might be several irreducibly different kinds of ultimate desire, even if they were all egoistic. Moreover, there might be several irreducibly different, though not necessarily unrelated, senses of the word 'egoistic'; and some desires might be egoistic in one sense and some in another, even if all were egoistic in some sense. But the theory often takes the special form that the only kind of ultimate desire is the desire to get or to prolong pleasant experiences, and to avoid or to cut

EGOISM AS A THEORY OF HUMAN MOTIVES

short unpleasant experiences, for oneself. That *is* a monistic theory. I shall call the wider theory *Psychological Egoism*, and this special form of it *Psychological Hedonism*. Psychological Egoism might be true, even though psychological hedonism were false; but, if psychological egoism be false, psychological hedonism cannot be true.

I shall now discuss Psychological Egoism. I think it is best to begin by enumerating all the kinds of desire that I can think of which might reasonably be called 'egoistic' in one sense or another.

(1) Everyone has a special desire for the continued existence of himself in his present bodily life, and a special dread of his own death. This may be called *Desire for Self-preservation*. (2) Everyone desires to get and to prolong experiences of certain kinds, and to avoid and to cut short experiences of certain other kinds, because the former are pleasant to him and the latter unpleasant. This may be called *Desire for one's own Happiness*. (3) Everyone desires to acquire, keep, and develop certain mental and bodily powers and dispositions, and to avoid, get rid of, or check certain others. In general he wants to be or to become a person of a certain kind, and wants not to be or to become a person of certain other kinds. This may be called *Desire to be a Self of a certain kind*. (4) Everyone desires to feel certain kinds of emotion towards himself and his own powers and dispositions, and not to feel certain other kinds of reflexive emotion. This may be called *Desire for Self-respect*. (5) Everyone desires to get and to keep for himself the exclusive possession of certain material objects or the means of buying and keeping such objects. This may be called *Desire to get and to keep Property*. (6) Everyone desires to get and to exercise power over certain other persons, so as to make them do what he wishes, regardless of whether they wish it or not. This may be called *Desire for Self-assertion*. (7) Everyone desires that other persons shall believe certain things about him and feel certain kinds of emotion towards him. He wants to be noticed, to be respected by some, to be loved by some, to be feared by some, and so on. Under this head come the *Desire for Self-display*, for *Affection*, and so on.

Lastly, it must be noted that some desires, which are concerned primarily with other things or persons, either would not exist at all or would be very much weaker or would take a different form if it were not for the fact that those things or persons already stand in certain relations to oneself. I shall call such relations *egoistic motive-stimulants*. The following are among the most important of these. (i) The relation of ownership. If a person owns a house or a wife, e.g. he feels a much stronger desire to improve the house or to make the woman happy than if the house belongs to another or the woman is married to someone else. (ii) Blood-relationship. A person desires, e.g. the well-being of his own children much more strongly than that of other children. (iii) Relations of love and friendship. A person desires strongly, e.g. to be loved and respected by those whom he loves. He may desire only to be feared by those whom he hates. And he may desire only very mildly, if at all, to be loved and respected by those to whom he feels indifferent. (iv) The relationship of being fellow-members of an institution to which one feels loyalty and affection. Thus, e.g. an Englishman will be inclined to do services to another Englishman which he would not do for a foreigner, and an Old Etonian will be inclined to do services to another Old Etonian which he would not do for an Old Harrovian.

I think that I have now given a reasonably adequate list of motives and motive-stimulants which could fairly be called 'egoistic' in some sense or other. Our next business is to try to classify them and to consider their inter-relations.

(1) Let us begin by asking ourselves the following question. Which of these motives could act on a person if he had been the only person or thing that had ever existed? The answer is that he could still have had desires for *self-preservation*, for *his own happiness*, to be a *self of a certain kind*, and for *self-respect*. But he could not, unless he were under the delusion that there were other persons or things, have desires for *property*, for *self-assertion*, or for *self-display*. Nor could he have any of those desires which are stimulated by family or other alio-relative relationships. I shall call those desires, and only those, which could be felt by a person who knew or believed himself to be the only existent in the universe, *Self-confined*.

(2) Any desire which is not self-confined may be described as *extra-verted*; for the person who has such a desire is necessarily considering, not only himself and his own qualities, dispositions, and states, but also some other thing or person. If the desire is

egoistic, it will also be *intro-verted*; for the person who has such a desire will also be considering himself and his relations to that other person or thing, and this will be an essential factor conditioning his experience. Thus a self-confined desire is purely intro-verted, whilst a desire which is egoistic but not self-confined is both intro-verted and extra-verted. Now we may subdivide desires of the latter kind into two classes, according as the primary emphasis is on the former or the latter aspect. Suppose that the person is concerned primarily with himself and his own acts and experiences, and that he is concerned with the other thing or person only or mainly as an object of these acts or experiences or as the other term in a relationship to himself. Then I shall call the desire *Self-centred*. I shall use the term *Self-regarding* to include both desires which are self-centred and those which are self-confined. Under the head of self-centred desires come the desire for *property*, for *self-assertion*, for *self-display*, and for *affection*.

(3) Lastly, we come to desires which are both intro-verted and extra-verted, but where the primary emphasis is on the other person or thing and its states. Here the relationship of the other person or thing to oneself acts as a strong egoistic motive-stimulant, but one's primary desire is that the other person or thing shall be in a certain state. I will call such desires *Other-regarding*. A desire which is other-regarding, but involves an egoistic motive-stimulant, may be described as *Self-referential*. The desire of a mother to render services to her own children which she would not be willing to render to other children is an instance of a desire which is other-regarding but self-referential. So, too, is the desire of a man to inflict suffering on one who has injured him or one whom he envies.

Having thus classified the various kinds of egoistic desire, I will now say something about their inter-relations.

(1) It is obvious that self-preservation may be desired as a necessary condition of one's own happiness; since one cannot acquire or prolong pleasant experiences unless one continues to exist. So the desire for self-preservation *may* be subordinate to the desire for one's own happiness. But it seems pretty clear that a person often desires to go on living even when there is no prospect that the remainder of his life will contain a balance of pleasant over unpleasant experiences. This attitude is expressed

very strongly in the loathsome lines of Maecenas which Seneca has handed down to posterity:

> Debilem facito manu, debilem pede coxo
> tuber adstrue gibberum, lubricos quate dentes;
> vita dum superest, bene est; hanc mihi, vel acuta
> si sedeam cruce, sustine.

(2) It is also obvious that property and power over others may be desired as a means to self-preservation or to happiness. So the desire to get and keep property, and the desire to get and exert power over others, *may* be subordinate to the desire for self-preservation or for one's own happiness. But it seems fairly certain that the former desires are sometimes independent of the latter. Even if a person begins by desiring property or power only as a means—and it is very doubtful whether we always do begin in that way—it seems plain that he often comes to desire them for themselves, and to sacrifice happiness, security, and even life for them. Any miser, and almost any keen politician, provides an instance of this.

It is no answer to this to say that a person who desires power or property enjoys the experiences of getting and exercising power or of amassing and owning property, and then to argue that therefore his ultimate desire is to give himself those pleasant experiences. The premiss here is true, but the argument is self-stultifying. The experiences in question are pleasant to a person only in so far as he desires power or property. This kind of pleasant experience presupposes desires for something other than pleasant experiences, and therefore the latter desires cannot be derived from desire for that kind of pleasant experience.

Similar remarks apply to the desire for self-respect and the desire for self-display. If one already desires to feel certain emotions towards oneself, or to be the object of certain emotions in others, the experience of feeling those emotions or of knowing that others feel them towards one will be pleasant, because it will be the fulfilment of a pre-existing desire. But this kind of pleasure presupposes the existence of these desires, and therefore they cannot be derived from the desire for that kind of pleasure.

(3) Although the various kinds of egoistic desire cannot be reduced to a single ultimate egoistic desire, e.g. the desire for

one's own happiness, they are often very much mixed up with each other. Take, e.g. the special desire which a mother feels for the health, happiness, and prosperity of her children. This is predominantly other-regarding, though it is self-referential. The mother is directly attracted by the thought of her child as surviving, as having good dispositions and pleasant experiences, and as being the object of love and respect to other persons. She is directly repelled by the thought of his dying, or having bad dispositions or unpleasant experiences, or being the object of hatred or contempt to other persons. The desire is therefore other-regarding. It is self-referential, because the fact that it is *her* child and not another's acts as a powerful motive-stimulant. She would not be prepared to make the same sacrifices for the survival or the welfare of a child which was not her own. But this self-referential other-regarding motive is almost always mingled with other motives which are self-regarding. One motive which a woman has for wanting her child to be happy, healthy and popular is the desire that other women shall envy her as the mother of a happy, healthy and popular child. This motive is subordinate to the self-centred desire for self-display. Another motive, which may be present, is the desire not to be burdened with an ailing, unhappy, and unpopular child. This motive is subordinate to the self-contained desire for one's own happiness. But, although the self-referential other-regarding motive is nearly always mixed with motives which are self-centred or self-confined, we cannot plausibly explain the behaviour of many mothers on many occasions towards their children without postulating the other-regarding motive.

We can now consider the various forms which Psychological Egoism might take. The most rigid form is that all human motives are ultimately egoistic, and that all egoistic motives are ultimately of one kind. That one kind has generally been supposed to be the desire for one's own happiness, and so this form of Psychological Egoism may in practice be identified with Psychological Hedonism. This theory amounts to saying that the only ultimate motives are *self-confined*, and that the only ultimate self-confined motive is *desire for one's own happiness*.

I have already tried to show by examples that this is false. Among self-confined motives, e.g. is the desire for self-preservation, and this cannot be reduced to desire for one's own happiness. Then, again, there are self-regarding motives which are self-centred but not self-confined, such as the desire for affection, for gratitude, for power over others, and so on. And, finally, there are motives which are self-referential but predominantly other-regarding, such as a mother's desire for her children's welfare or a man's desire to injure one whom he hates.

It follows that the only form of Psychological Egoism that is worth discussing is the following. It might be alleged that all ultimate motives are *either* self-confined *or* self-centred *or* other-regarding but self-referential, some being of one kind and some of another. This is a much more modest theory than, e.g. Psychological Hedonism. I think that it covers satisfactorily an immensely wide field of human motivation, but I am not sure that it is true without exception. I shall now discuss it in the light of some examples.

Case A. Take first the case of a man who does not expect to survive the death of his present body, and who makes a will, the contents of which will be known to no one during his lifetime.

(1) The motive of such a testator cannot possibly be the expectation of any experiences which he will enjoy after death through the provisions of his will being carried out; for he believes that he will have no more experiences after the death of his body. The only way in which this motive could be ascribed to such a man is by supposing that, although he is intellectually convinced of his future extinction, yet in practice he cannot help imagining himself as surviving and witnessing events which will happen after his death. I think that this kind of mental confusion is possible, and perhaps not uncommon; but I should doubt whether it is a plausible account of such a man's motives to say that they all involve this mistake.

(2) Can we say that his motive is the desire to enjoy during his life the pleasant experience of imagining the gratitude which the beneficiaries will feel towards him after his death? The answer is that this may well be *one* of his motives, but it cannot be primary, and therefore cannot be the only one. Unless he desired to be thought about in one way rather than another after his death, the present experience of imagining himself as becoming the object of certain retrospective thoughts and emotions on the part of the beneficiaries would be neither attractive nor repulsive to him.

(3) I think it is plain, then, that the ultimate motive of such a man cannot be desire for his own happiness. But it might be desire for power over others. For he may be said to be exercising this power when he makes his will, even though the effects will not begin until after his death.

(4) Can we say that his motive in making the will is simply to ensure that certain persons will think about him and feel towards him in certain ways after his death? In that case his motive would come under the head of self-display. (This must, of course, be distinguished from the question, already discussed, whether his motive might be to give himself the pleasant experience of imagining their future feelings of gratitude towards him.) The answer is that self-display, in a wide sense, may be a motive, and a very strong one, in making a will; but it could hardly be the sole motive. A testator generally considers the relative needs of various possible beneficiaries, the question whether a certain person would appreciate and take care of a certain picture or house or book, the question whether a certain institution is doing work which he thinks important, and so on. In so far as he is influenced by these considerations, his motives are other-regarding. But they may all be self-referential. In making his will he may desire to benefit persons only in so far as they are *his* relatives or friends. He may desire to benefit institutions only in so far as *he* is or has been a member of them. And so on. I think that it would be quite plausible to hold that the motives of such a testator are all either self-regarding or self-referential, but that it would not be in the least plausible to say that they are all self-confined or that none of them are other-regarding.

Case B. Let us next consider the case of a man who subscribes anonymously to a certain charity. His motive cannot possibly be that of self-display. Can we say that his motive is to enjoy the pleasant experience of self-approval and of seeing an institution in which he is interested flourishing? The answer is, again, that these motives may exist and may be strong, but they cannot be primary and therefore cannot be his only motives. Unless he wants the institution to flourish, there will be nothing to attract him in the experience of seeing it flourish. And, unless he subscribes from some other motive than the desire to enjoy a feeling of self-approval, he will not obtain a feeling of self-approval. So here, again, it seems to me that some of his motives must be other-regarding. But it is quite possible that his other-regarding motives may all be self-referential. An essential factor in making him want to benefit this institution may be that it is *his* old college or that a great friend of *his* is at the head of it.

The question, then, that remains is this. Are there any cases in which it is reasonable to think that a person's motive is not egoistic in any of the senses mentioned? In practice, as we now see, this comes down to the question whether there are any cases in which an other-regarding motive is not stimulated by an egoistic motive-stimulus, i.e. whether there is any other-regarding motive which is not also and essentially self-referential.

Case C. Let us consider the case of a person who deliberately chooses to devote his life to working among lepers, in the full knowledge that he will almost certainly contract leprosy and die in a particularly loathsome way. This is not an imaginary case. To give the Psychological Egoist the longest possible run for his money I will suppose that the person is a Roman Catholic priest, who believes that his action may secure for him a place in heaven in the next world and a reputation for sanctity and heroism in this, that it may be rewarded posthumously with canonization, and that it will redound to the credit of the church of which he is an ordained member.

It is difficult to see what self-regarding or self-referential motives there could be *for* the action beside desire for happiness in heaven, desire to gain a reputation for sanctity and heroism and perhaps to be canonized after death, and desire to glorify the church of which one is a priest. Obviously there are extremely strong self-confined and self-centred motives *against* choosing this kind of life. And in many cases there must have been very strong self-referential other-regarding motives *against* it. For the person who made such a choice must sometimes have been a young man of good family and brilliant prospects, whose parents were heart-broken at his decision, and whose friends thought him an obstinate fool for making it.

Now there is no doubt at all that there was an other-regarding motive, viz. a direct desire to alleviate the sufferings of the lepers. No one who was not dying in the last ditch for an over-simple theory of human nature would deny this. The only questions that are worth raising about it are these. (1) Is this other-regarding motive stimulated by an egoistic motive-

226

stimulus and thus rendered self-referential? (2) Suppose that this motive had not been supported by the various self-regarding and self-referential motives *for* deciding to go and work among the lepers, would it have sufficed, in presence of the motives *against* doing so, to ensure the choice that was actually made?

As regards the first question, I cannot see that there was any special pre-existing relationship between a young priest in Europe and a number of unknown lepers in Asia which might plausibly be held to act as an egoistic motive-stimulus. The lepers are neither his relatives nor his friends nor his benefactors nor members of any community or institution to which he belongs.

As regards the sufficiency of the other-regarding motive, whether stimulated egoistically or not, in the absence of all self-regarding motives tending in the same direction, no conclusive answer can be given. I cannot prove that a single person in the whole course of history *would* have decided to work among lepers, if all the motives against doing so had been present, whilst the hope of heaven, the desire to gain a reputation for sanctity and heroism, and the desire to glorify and extend one's church had been wholly absent. Nor can the Psychological Egoist prove that *no* single person would have so decided under these hypothetical conditions. Factors which cannot be eliminated cannot be shown to be necessary and cannot be shown to be superfluous; and there we must leave the matter.

I suspect that a Psychological Egoist might be tempted to say that the intending medical missionary found the experience of imagining the sufferings of the lepers intensely unpleasant, and that his primary motive for deciding to spend his life working among them was to get rid of this unpleasant experience. This, I think, is what Locke, e.g. would have had to say in accordance with his theory of motivation. About this suggestion there are two remarks to be made.

(1) This motive cannot have been primary, and therefore cannot have been the only motive. Unless this person desired that the lepers should have their sufferings alleviated, there is no reason why the thought of their sufferings should be an unpleasant experience to him. A malicious man, e.g. finds the thought of the sufferings of an enemy a very pleasant experi-

ence. This kind of pleasure presupposes a desire for the well-being or the ill-being of others.

(2) If his primary motive were to rid himself of the unpleasant experience of imagining the sufferings of the lepers, he could hardly choose a less effective means than to go and work among them. For the imagination would then be replaced by actual sense-perception; whilst, if he stayed at home and devoted himself to other activities, he would have a reasonably good chance of diverting his attention from the sufferings of the lepers. In point of fact one knows that such a person would reproach himself in so far as he managed to forget about the lepers. He would *wish* to keep them and their sufferings constantly in mind, as an additional stimulus to doing what he believes he ought to do, viz. to take active steps to help and relieve them.

In this connexion it is important to notice the following facts. For most people the best way to realize the sufferings of strangers is to imagine oneself or one's parents or children or some intimate and beloved friend in the situation in which the stranger is placed. This, as we say, 'brings home to one' his sufferings. A large proportion of the cruelty which decent people applaud or tolerate is applauded or tolerated by them only because they are either too stupid to put themselves imaginatively into the position of the victims or because they deliberately refrain from doing so. One important cause of their deliberately refraining is the notion of retributive justice, i.e. the belief that these persons, or a group taken as a collective whole to which they belong, have *deserved* suffering by wrongdoing, and the desire that they shall get their deserts. Another important cause of this deliberate refrainment is the knowledge that one is utterly powerless to help the victims. However this may be, the fact that imagining oneself in their position is often a necessary condition of desiring to relieve the sufferings of strangers does not make that desire self-referential. Imagining oneself in their place is merely a condition for becoming vividly *aware of* their sufferings. Whether one will then desire to relieve them or to prolong them or will remain indifferent to them, depends on motives which are not primarily self-regarding or self-referential.

I will now summarize the results of this discussion.

(1) If Psychological Egoism asserts that all ultimate motives

are self-confined; or that they are all either self-confined or self-centred, some being of one kind and some of the other; or that all self-confined motives can be reduced to the desire for one's own happiness; it is certainly false. It is not even a close approximation to the truth.

(2) If it asserts that all ultimate motives are either self-regarding or self-referential, some being of one kind and some of the other; and that all other-regarding motives require a self-referential stimulus, it is a close approximation to the truth. It is true, I think, that in most people and at most times other-regarding motives are very weak unless stimulated by a self-referential stimulus. As England's wisest and wittiest statesman put it in his inimitable way: 'Temporal things will have their weight in the world, and, though zeal may prevail for a time and get the better in a skirmish, yet the war endeth generally on the side of flesh and blood, and will do so until mankind is another thing than it is at present.'[1]

(3) Nevertheless, Psychological Egoism, even in its most diluted form, is very doubtful if taken as a universal proposition. Some persons at some times are strongly influenced by other-regarding motives which cannot plausibly be held to be stimulated by a self-referential stimulus. It seems reasonable to hold that the presence of these other-regarding motives is *necessary* to account for their choice of alternatives which they do choose, and for their persistence in the course which they have adopted, though this can never be conclusively established in any particular case. Whether it is also *sufficient* cannot be decided with certainty, for self-regarding and self-referential components are always present in one's total motive for choosing such an action.

I think that the summary which I have just given fairly represents the results of introspection and reflection on one's own and other men's voluntary action. Yet Psychological Egoism in general and Psychological Hedonism in particular have seemed almost self-evident to many highly intelligent thinkers, and they do still seem highly plausible to nearly everyone when he first begins to speculate on human motivation. I believe that this depends, not on empirical facts, but on certain verbal ambiguities and misunderstandings. As so often happens in philosophy, clever people accept a false general principle on *a priori*

[1] Halifax: *The Character of a Trimmer*

grounds and then devote endless labour and ingenuity to explaining away plain facts which obviously conflict with it. A full discussion of the subject would require an analysis of the confusions which have made these theories seem so plausible; but this must be omitted here.

I must content myself with the following remarks in conclusion. I have tried to show that Psychological Egoism, in the only form in which it could possibly fit the facts of human life, is not a monistic theory of motives. On this extended interpretation of the theory the only feature common to all motives is that every motive which can *act on* a person has one or another of a large number of different kinds of special *reference to* that person. I have tried to show that this certainly covers a very wide field, but that it is by no means certain that there is even this amount of unity among *all* human motives. I think that Psychological Egoism is much the most plausible attempt to reduce the *prima facie* plurality of ultimate kinds of desire to a unity. If it fails, I think it is most unlikely that any alternative attempt on a different basis will succeed.

For my part I am inclined to accept an irreducibly pluralistic view of human motives. This does not, of course, entail that the present irreducible plurality of ultimate motives may not have evolved, in some sense of that highly ambiguous word, out of fewer, either in the history of each individual or in that of the human race. About that I express no opinion here and now.

Now, if Psychological Hedonism had been true, all conflict of motives would have been between motives of the *same kind*. It would always be of the form 'Shall I go to the dentist and certainly be hurt now but probably avoid thereby frequent and prolonged toothache in future? Or shall I take the risk in order to avoid the certainty of being hurt by the dentist now?' On any pluralistic view there is also conflict between motives of irreducibly *different kinds*, e.g. between aversion to painful experience and desire to be thought manly, or between a desire to shine in conversation and aversion to hurting a sensitive person's feelings by a witty but wounding remark.

It seems to me plain that, in our ordinary moral judgments about ourselves and about others, we always unhesitatingly assume that there can be and often is conflict between motives of radically different kinds. Now I do not myself share that superstitious reverence for the beliefs of common sense which many contemporary philosophers profess. But I think that we must start from them, and that we ought to depart from them only when we find good reason to do so. If Psychological Hedonism, or any other monistic theory of motives had been true, we should have had to begin the study of Ethics by recognizing that most moral judgments which we pass on ourselves or on others are made under a profound misapprehension of the psychological facts and are largely vitiated thereby. If Psychological Hedonism, e.g. had been true, the only ethical theory worth discussing would have been an egoistic form of Ethical Hedonism. For one cannot be under an obligation to attempt to do what is psychologically impossible. And, on the hypothesis of Psychological Hedonism, it is psychologically impossible for anyone ultimately to desire anything except to prolong or acquire experiences which he knows or expects to be pleasant and to cut short or avoid experiences which he knows or expects to be unpleasant. If it were still possible to talk of having duties at all, each person's duties would be confined within the limits which that psychological impossibility marks out. And it would clearly be impossible to suppose that any part of anyone's ultimate motive for doing any act is his belief that it would be right in the circumstances together with his desire to do what is right as such. For, if Psychological Hedonism were true, a desire to do what is right could not be ultimate, it must be subordinate to the desire to get or prolong pleasant experiences and to avoid or cut short unpleasant ones.

Now it is plain that such consequences as these conflict sharply with common-sense notions of morality. If we had been obliged to accept Psychological Egoism, in any of its narrower forms, on its merits, we should have had to say: 'So much the worse for the common-sense notions of morality!' But, if I am right, the morality of common sense, with all its difficulties and incoherences, is immune at least to attacks from the basis of Psychological Egoism.

OUGHT WE TO FIGHT FOR
OUR COUNTRY IN THE NEXT WAR?

T HE question before us is of the general form: 'What
ought such and such people (e.g. males of military age)
to do under such and such circumstances (e.g. when
their country is involved in a war)?' I shall first point out the
general conditions which govern all attempts to answer such
questions.

Any argument on the subject will have to use premises of two
utterly different kinds, viz. *Purely Factual* and *Ethical*. An ethical
proposition is one which involves the notion of good or bad,
right or wrong, ought or ought not. A purely factual proposition
is one which involves no such notions. That deliberate homicide
is wrong is an ethical proposition, true or false. It is a purely
factual proposition that, if a man is shot through the heart, he
will almost certainly be dead very soon afterwards.

Now the purely factual premises are of two kinds, viz.
(1) Statements of alleged particular facts about the past or the
present. These may be called *Instantial Premisses.* And (2) statements of alleged general laws or tendencies. These may be
called *Nomic Premisses.* An example of the first kind is the proposition that Japan has spent such and such a proportion of her
revenue on her navy for the past ten years. An example of the
second is the proposition, true or false, that an increase of
armaments tends to produce war. Now everyone admits that
what a person ought or ought not to do at a given moment
depends *either* on his present state and circumstances and his

past history *or* on the probable consequences of the various alternative actions open to him at the time; and most people believe that it depends to some extent on *both*. In order to conjecture the probable consequences of various alternative actions which might be done in a given situation it is always necessary to use both kinds of factual premiss. Therefore everyone would admit that factual premisses of the instantial kind are needed, and the vast majority of people would admit that factual premisses of the nomic kind are also needed, if we are to have any rational argument about such questions as we are asking.

But it is equally certain that ethical premisses are also needed in any argument about an ethical question. Now ethical propositions are of two kinds, which I will call *Pure* and *Mixed*. It is always difficult to be sure that a given ethical proposition is pure, but it is easy to give examples of ethical propositions which are certainly mixed. Suppose I assert that a classical education is a good thing. I mean (*a*) that it is likely to produce in those subjected to it certain experiences and dispositions, which could be described on purely psychological and non-ethical terms; and (*b*) that such experiences and dispositions are good. The first of these two constituents of the original proposition is a purely factual statement of the nomic kind. The second is an ethical proposition. Whether it is *purely* ethical is another question. But, at any rate, the original proposition is certainly a mixed ethical one, and its ethical component is certainly a nearer approximation to a purely ethical one. When mixed ethical propositions are used as premisses in ethical arguments they are always liable to lead to mistakes and misunderstandings. If we are to avoid these, it is essential that we should split up such propositions, so far as we can, into their purely ethical and their purely factual components. For two disputants who agree about one of the components may differ about the other; and, if they fail to recognize and distinguish the two, they are bound to be at cross-purposes and to produce crooked answers.

There is another important division of ethical propositions which cuts across the division into pure and mixed. Ethical propositions are of three kinds, which may be expressed respectively by sentences of the three forms:

ETHICS

'You *ought* (or ought not) to do so-and-so in such and such circumstances'; 'Such and such an action would be *right* (or wrong) in such and such circumstances'; and 'Such and such an experience or state of affairs would be *good* (or bad).'

For the present purpose I shall group the first two together under the name of *Judgments of Obligation*. I shall call the third kind *Judgments of Value*. Now this brings us to a fundamental difference of opinion which it is essential to notice if we are to have any intelligent discussion on such questions as we have before us.

Some people hold that there is one and only one *ultimate* obligation, and that this involves an essential reference to *value*. According to them the one ultimate obligation is to secure the increase and to prevent the decrease of the present amount of good, and to secure the diminution and check the increase of the present amount of evil. All other obligations, such as the duty to keep one's promises or to obey the laws of one's country, are derivative from this one. They are obligations if and only if they are, in the actual circumstances, the most efficient way of fulfilling the one ultimate obligation to conserve and increase good and to check or diminish evil. Otherwise they are wrong. I shall call this the *Teleological Theory of Obligation*.

This theory can, of course, take many different forms. I shall not attempt to distinguish more than two of them, which I will call the *Universalistic Form* and the *Restricted Form*. According to the universalistic form of the theory a person has no special obligation to produce good and diminish evil in one person or community rather than in another. Suppose you have two alternative courses of action open to you. By one of them you will improve the condition of your own countrymen, and by the other you will improve the conditions in another country instead. Then it is your duty, on this view, to avoid the former action and to do the latter, provided that the improvement which you will effect in the foreign country is in the least degree greater than that which you would effect in your own country. According to the *restricted* form of the teleological theory your ultimate obligation still is to conserve and increase good and to check and diminish evil. But you have a stronger obligation to increase the good and diminish the evil in certain persons and

234

communities, to which you stand in certain special relations, than you have towards other persons and communities to which you do not stand in these relations. On either form of the theory the one and only ultimate obligation is that of *Beneficence*. On the universalistic form of it there is only the general obligation to be as beneficent as you can in the circumstances in which you are placed. On the restricted form of it the appropriate strength and direction of the obligation of beneficence is in part determined by the special relations in which the agent stands to certain individuals, institutions, and communities.

Now many people would reject the teleological theory of obligation. They would hold that there are *many* ultimate obligations, and that they do not all involve an essential reference to value. They admit that I am under a general obligation to be beneficent to human beings as such; and they assert that I am also under more special and stringent obligations to be beneficent to my parents, my benefactors, my fellow-countrymen, and so on. But they say that there are many other obligations which are not reducible to beneficence at all, whether general or special. E.g. if a person asks me a question to which I know the answer, the mere fact that I am in this state and that he and I are in this situation gives him a claim on me to receive a *true* answer. On this view there is an obligation of truth-speaking which is not reducible to any obligation of beneficence and which may conflict with one's general or special obligations of beneficence. And there may be other obligations, e.g. an obligation to obey the laws of one's country, which may conflict with the obligation of truth-speaking and with the special and the general obligations of beneficence. I propose to call this theory the *Pluralistic Theory of Obligation*.

On the pluralistic theory a person who is called upon to act in one way or another, or to abstain from action, in a given situation may be subject to many different and conflicting claims or obligations of varying strength, arising out of various factors in his past history and various relations in which he stands to various persons, institutions, and communities. Whichever alternative he chooses he will fulfil some of these component obligations, and in doing so he will necessarily break others which conflict with the former. In such cases the right action is one which makes the best compromise between the several conflicting claims, when due weight is given to their number and their relative urgency. But no general principles can be suggested for deciding what is the best compromise.

Now I cannot attempt here to decide between the universalistic form of the teleological theory, the restricted form of it, and the pluralistic theory. I will content myself with two remarks about them. (1) *Prima facie* the pluralistic theory is in accord with common sense, and the universalistic form of the teleological theory is flagrantly at variance with common sense. And, if we reject the universalistic form of the teleological theory, it seems doubtful whether we can consistently rest in the restricted form of it. It looks as if the restricted form were an unstable compromise between the pluralistic theory and the universalistic form of the teleological theory. (2) However this may be, it is essential to be clear in one's own mind as to which theory one is going to assume before one can argue intelligently about the question at issue. Facts which might prove conclusively, on the universalistic form of the teleological theory, that a man ought not to fight for his country might lead to no such consequence if one held that a citizen is under a special obligation of beneficence to his own nation. And their force would be still further diminished if one held that a man is under a strong direct obligation to obey the laws of his country, good or bad, simply because he is a citizen of it.

It remains to say something about the other kind of ethical propositions, viz. Judgments of Value. Here again there is a profound difference of opinion on a fundamental question. Some people hold that there is one and only one kind of subject of which the adjectives 'intrinsically good' and 'intrinsically evil' can properly be predicated, viz. experiences. And they hold further that there is one and only one characteristic of experiences which makes them good or evil. I will call this the *Monistic Theory of Value*. It might conceivably take many different forms, according to what characteristic of experiences was held to be the one and only good-making or bad-making characteristic. But in practice, I think, nearly everyone who holds the monistic theory of value assumes that the one and only good-making or bad-making characteristic of experiences is their hedonic quality in its two opposed forms of pleasantness and unpleasantness. So, for the present purpose, we may identify the monistic theory of value with the *Hedonistic Theory of Value*.

On this theory, whenever we call a community or an institution or a person or a disposition or an action 'good' or 'bad', we are making a mixed ethical statement. Suppose, e.g. that we call a certain person 'good'. We mean simply and solely to assert the two following propositions. (*a*) That his nature is such that he tends in most circumstances to have, or to produce in others, experiences which are predominantly pleasant. And (*b*) that such experiences are, for that reason and to that extent, good.

Now many people would unhesitatingly reject the Hedonistic Theory of Value in whole or in part. Some would hold that persons can be good or evil in the same ultimate sense in which experiences can be. Some would go further, and would hold that this is true also of certain collective wholes, composed of intimately interrelated persons, e.g. nations. Again, even those who hold that nothing but experiences can be intrinsically good or evil may hold that there are other good-making and bad-making characteristics of experiences beside their pleasantness and their unpleasantness. Anyone who holds any of these views may be said to accept the *Pluralistic Theory of Value*.

Once again I shall not attempt to decide between the rival theories. I will content myself with the following remarks. (1) *Prima facie* the hedonistic theory is flagrantly at variance with common sense. The common-sense view is *prima facie* that persons, at any rate, can be intrinsically good or evil as well as experiences, and that there are many characteristics beside pleasantness and unpleasantness which make experiences intrinsically good or bad. (2) If a pluralistic theory of value is admitted, a person who accepts the teleological theory of obligation is faced at the second move with the same kind of problem as faces an adherent of the pluralistic theory of obligation at the first move. He will not, indeed, have to try to find the best compromise between a number of ultimate and conflicting obligations of various degrees of urgency. But he will have to aim at producing the best compromise between a number of ultimate kinds of value and disvalue. He may, e.g. have to weigh the nett value of a state of heroic self-sacrifice accompanied by misery and intellectual stupidity against that of a state of clear-sighted and cool selfishness accompanied by comfort. And no general principle can be offered for conducting the comparison. The only person who can avoid such difficulties is one who combines the universalistic form of the teleological theory of obligation with the hedonistic theory of value. And both the elements in this combination seem *prima facie* far too simple to be true. (3) Whatever may be the truth about these rival theories of value, this at least is certain. It is essential to be clear in one's own mind as to which theory one is going to assume before one can argue intelligently about the question at issue. Facts which might prove conclusively, on the hedonistic theory of value, that a man ought not to fight for his country might lead to no such consequence if it were held that heroic self-sacrifice gives value to the persons who practise it just as pleasantness gives value to pleasant experiences. And their force might be still further diminished if it were held that a nation is a persistent collective entity of a peculiar kind, with a characteristic value or disvalue of its own which is determined by the actions and dispositions of its citizens.

This completes what I have to say about the general conditions which govern all rational discussion about such questions as we have before us. I will summarize them as follows. (1) The factual and the ethical premises must be clearly distinguished; any mixed ethical premises must be analysed into their purely factual and their purely ethical components; and the instantial and the nomic factual premises must be separately stated. (2) The theory of obligation which is being assumed by any disputant must be explicitly stated. We must know whether he assumes the pluralistic theory or the teleological theory. And, if he assumes the latter, we must know whether he assumes the universalistic or the restricted form of it. (3) The theory of value which is being assumed by any disputant must be explicitly stated. We must know whether he assumes the hedonistic theory or the pluralistic theory. And, if he assumes the latter, we must know whether he holds that only experiences can have intrinsic value or disvalue, or that only experiences and persons can have it, or that experiences and persons and societies can have it. Unless these conditions are fulfilled, there can be no rational *argument*; there can be only emotional hot-air emitted in argumentative form.

When these conditions have been fulfilled I do not believe

that there is much room for argument on such questions except on the purely factual side. We may be able to alter a man's opinions about the probable consequences of fighting or refusing to fight when his country is involved in war, by showing him particular facts which he had overlooked, or by convincing him, from empirical evidence, of laws or tendencies which he had not suspected. But there are no arguments by which we can alter his opinions as to what circumstances do and what do not impose obligations on him, or as to the kinds of thing which can have intrinsic value or disvalue, or as to the characteristics which do and those which do not confer intrinsic value or disvalue on the things which possess them. If he is a pluralist about obligation, we cannot by argument alter his opinions about the relative urgency of the various conflicting obligations which he believes to be incumbent on him. If he is a pluralist about value, we cannot by argument alter his opinions as to the various degrees of goodness or badness conferred by the various characteristics which he believes to be good-making or bad-making. We can clear up confusions and indicate possible sources of prejudice; but, when we have done this, we have done all that argument can accomplish in such matters, and, if we still differ, we must agree to do so.

My next business is to try to restate the question in a perfectly clear and concrete form. I shall assume that the war in question is an important one, in the sense that there is real uncertainty as to whether England will win or lose it, and that the loss of it would certainly entail on England such disastrous consequences as accrued to the defeated nations after the war of 1914 to 1918. I shall assume that conscription is in force. And I shall assume that 'we' means persons liable under the act to military service, and not exempted by the authorities because of special usefulness in some other form of war-work, such as munition-making. The question is whether such persons, in such circumstances, ought to obey this law or to refuse to obey it. Of course a very similar question would arise for those specially skilled persons, such as research-chemists, who would be exempted from military service in order to apply their special skill to other forms of war-work. Ought they to refuse both to fight and to exercise their abilities in arming those who are fighting?

Now I have no idea what is the right answer to this question, and, if I had, I should not be able to prove it to people who accepted different ethical principles and premisses from those which I accept. I am not sure indeed that it is the kind of question to which there is an answer, even laid up in Heaven, as Plato might say. I shall therefore content myself with making a few remarks which are, I think, relevant to it.

(1) There are three and only three cases in which no difficulty can arise. (i) A person may be persuaded that the war in which his country is engaged is the least evil alternative open to it in the circumstances, and he may hold that he has a direct or derived obligation to obey the laws of his country. Such a person will presumably hold that he ought to fight if he is ordered to do so. (ii) A man may hold that there is a direct obligation not to take or help in taking human life, and that this is so urgent that it overrides all other obligations, direct or derivative, which conflict with it. Such a man will have no difficulty in deciding that he ought not to fight, no matter how good the cause may be and even if he admits that war is the only way to bring about a great good or avoid a great evil. (iii) A man may hold that there is a direct obligation to obey the laws of his country, and that this is so urgent that it overrides all other obligations which may conflict with it. Such a man will have no difficulty in deciding that he ought to fight, no matter how bad the cause may be and even if he thinks that war is an inefficient means of securing good or avoiding evil. The second and the third of these opinions seem to me absurd. I do not believe that there is any one obligation which is of such unique urgency that it overrides all other obligations, direct or indirect, that may conflict with it. Therefore the only case that seems to me to be of interest is that of a man who holds that war in general, or this war in particular, is wrong, and who does not hold that there is an overwhelming obligation either to refrain from taking human life or to obey the laws of his country.

(2) The following fact is very important, and is liable to be overlooked. If one believes that war in general, or a certain particular war, is wrong, this may be a conclusive reason for trying to prevent one's country getting into it and for trying to get one's country out of it if it has entered upon it. But, except on the universalistic form of the teleological theory of obligation,

it is *not* a conclusive reason for refusing to fight for your country when, in spite of your efforts, it is engaged in war. There is nothing particularly paradoxical in this. If one is a member of an ordinary partnership or committee, it is often one's duty loyally to help in carrying out a policy which one believes to be wrong and which one has conscientiously opposed while it was still under discussion. No doubt, if the conflict is too extreme, it becomes one's duty to dissolve the partnership or to resign from the committee. But it is just at this point that the analogy breaks down. For you cannot really do anything analogous to resigning from your country. If you are to go on living in England at all during the war, you will be dependent for your food and for such protection as you enjoy on the army, the navy, and the air force; i.e. on the fact that there is a majority of persons of military age whose consciences are less sensitive than yours or work in a different way. Plainly there is a *prima facie* obligation not to put yourself in this situation of one-sided dependence on what you must regard as the wrong actions of people who are less virtuous or less enlightened than yourself. This complication would be avoided if the conscription-law imposed the death penalty for refusal to undertake military or other war service. I am inclined to think that this ought to be done, and that really conscientous objectors to military service should welcome it.

(3) Refusal to fight in a war is one of those actions whose effects vary greatly with the proportion and the distribution of those who practise them. If a *majority* of persons of military age in *both* belligerent countries simultaneously refused to fight, it would be an extremely good thing, since it would automatically bring the war to an end without either victory or defeat. If a considerable proportion of such persons in England refused to fight, whilst few if any in the enemy country did so, the result would be the defeat of England. Under the conditions of modern war a complete and early defeat might be better even for the defeated country than victory after prolonged fighting. But it is not worth discussing either of these alternatives, because it is as certain as anything of this kind can be that nothing like them will in fact be realized. The actual situation will certainly be that only a quite negligible proportion of those liable to military service, either in England or in any country with

which England is likely to be at war, will refuse to fight. The intending refuser can safely assume that, if he refuses, he will be in a tiny minority, and that his action will make no appreciable difference to the duration or the outcome of the war.

Now there are two remarks to be made about this. (i) It is a mistake to suppose that, because refusal *would be* right if most people in both countries were going to refuse, therefore it *will be* right in the actual case where only very few people in either country will refuse. No legitimate inference can be made to what is right in the actual case from what would be right in the widely different hypothetical case. The rightness or wrongness of an action depends, *inter alia*, on the circumstances in which it is done; and one extremely relevant circumstance in the present case is the extent to which other people will perform similar actions.

(ii) Since the large-scale effects of refusing to fight are likely to be negligible, the individual who is debating whether he ought to refuse can confine his attention to the probable effects on himself and his circle of friends and relations when considering the utility or disutility of refusal. This is, no doubt, a great convenience for him. But he will have to reflect that he owes this convenience, as he will owe his food and protection, to the fact that he can count on most other people doing what he judges to be wrong and deciding to fight. Unless he holds the universalistic form of the teleological theory of obligation and the hedonistic theory of value, he may suspect that it is not altogether fitting that his honour should be rooted in the fortunate dishonour of most of his contemporaries.

In conclusion I would make one remark to those who are convinced that they ought not to fight for their country in the next war or are not convinced that they ought to. They can avoid most of their difficulties by suicide; and, on the whole, this is the course which I should recommend to those of them who do not think that there is an overwhelming obligation not to take one's own life. Of course it is possible that we survive the death of our present bodies, and it is alleged that the position of the suicide in the next life is less eligible than that of the non-suicide. But there is no conclusive evidence for the first proposition, and no evidence at all that the position of the suicide is worse than that of the victim of any other form of violent death.

The next life, if there be one, must be bad indeed if it is worse than this life will be in time of war. And the gas in your oven is no less deadly and far more merciful than that which you will encounter on the battlefield or in the streets of your own town if it should be bombed.

CONSCIENCE AND CONSCIENTIOUS
ACTION

AT the present time[1] Tribunals, appointed under an Act of
Parliament, are engaged all over England in dealing
with claims to exemption from military service based
on the ground of 'conscientious objection' to taking part
directly or indirectly in warlike activities. Now it is no part of
the professional business of moral philosophers to tell people
what they ought or ought not to do or to exhort them to do
their duty. Moral philosophers, as such, have no special information, not available to the general public, about what is right
and what is wrong; nor have they any call to undertake those
hortatory functions which are so adequately performed by
clergymen, politicians, leader-writers, and wireless loud-
speakers. But it *is* the function of a moral philosopher to reflect
on the moral concepts and beliefs which he or others have; to
try to analyse them and draw distinctions and clear up confusions in connexion with them; and to see how they are interrelated and whether they can be arranged in a coherent system.
Now there can be no doubt that the popular notions of 'conscience' and 'conscientious action' are extremely vague and
confused. So I think that, by devoting this paper to an attempt
to elucidate them, I may succeed in being topical without being
impertinent.

I shall begin by trying to describe what I understand by 'conscience', in the widest sense of the word. I have no doubt that it
is often used in certain narrower senses, which I shall indicate in

[1] Written in 1940.

due course. I think that failure to recognize this ambiguity often leads to misunderstandings and disputes which are mainly verbal.

All civilized languages which I know or have heard of contain adjectives like 'right' and 'wrong', 'good' and 'evil', or their equivalents. This shows that human beings from the earliest times have had certain experiences which they took to be cognitions of acts, intentions, motives, etc., as having certain characteristics, viz. *moral* ones, which can take opposed forms. Again, retrospection assures most of us that we too have had such experiences when we have contemplated certain actions, dispositions, or characters, whether our own, or those of other real people, or those of fictitious persons in novels or plays. I am not at present concerned with the question whether there really are moral characteristics and whether we really do cognize them. I am concerned only with the plain psychological and historical fact that most of us, and most of our human predecessors back into prehistoric times, have had experiences which they took to be cognitions of such characteristics in acts, dispositions, characters, etc. I shall call these experiences 'ostensibly moral cognitions'.

It is an equally plain psychological fact that, when a human being contemplates an action or disposition or character in which these moral characteristics seem to him to be present, he is liable to feel certain kinds of emotion which he would not otherwise feel. All languages have words like 'remorse', 'feeling of guilt', 'feeling of obligation', 'moral indignation', and so on; and most of us know what such words indicate from our own experiences of such emotions. I propose to call these 'morally directed emotions'.

Here I must interpolate some remarks in order to ward off possible misunderstandings. We must notice that nothing ever has or could have *only* moral characteristics, any more than a word could have *only* meaning without any particular sound or visible form. Anything that has moral characteristics will also have certain non-moral ones; and, what is more, its moral characteristics will always depend upon certain of its non-moral ones. If I am told that a certain act was wrong, it is always sensible for me to ask: 'Why? What *made* it wrong?' And the answer that I expect would be an indication of some characteristic which can be fully described and understood without the use of any moral term, e.g. that it was an intentionally misleading answer to a question, that it was an intentional infliction of unnecessary pain, and so on. I propose to call these non-moral characteristics on which moral characteristics depend 'right-making', 'good-making', and so on.

Now emotions may be and often are felt towards acts, experiences, etc., in respect of their non-moral characteristics. Suppose, e.g. that a friend grants me a favour unfairly at the expense of another person because he likes me and does not like him. I shall tend to view this act with a non-morally directed emotion of complaisance in respect of its non-moral characteristic of being an act of special love and favour towards myself. But I shall tend also to view it with a morally-directed emotion of disapproval in so far as it is an act of unfairness towards my rival. It is, I think, quite possible to feel a non-morally directed dislike for an act in respect of those very right-making characteristics which give it a rightness which calls forth one's moral approval. Our attitude towards certain acts of stern justice towards their sons by typical Roman fathers is of this mixed kind.

It follows from all this that we may often think that we are feeling an *unmixed* morally directed emotion, when what we are really feeling is a mixture of morally and non-morally directed emotion. And we may sometimes mistake a purely non-moral emotion, such as fear of discovery and punishment or malice, for a morally directed emotion, such as remorse or righteous indignation. But the possibility and even the frequency of such mistakes has no tendency to show that there are not specifically moral emotions. The very fact that we recognize that we are liable to make these mistakes, strongly suggests that there are specifically moral emotions.

Lastly, it is an equally plain psychological fact that the belief that a certain course of action would be right does exercise a certain attraction or compulsion on most people and thus provides them with a motive-component for doing it. Still more obvious is it that the belief that a certain course of action would be wrong exercises a certain repulsion or inhibition on most people and thus provides them with a motive-component against doing it. Sometimes every other feature in alternative A is such as would make one prefer it to B. To do A might benefit me and other people, and to do *B* might injure me and other people. But to do *A* would involve breaking a promise which I gave, after due consideration, to a person who is now dead and therefore cannot release me. If I believe that it is wrong to break a promise given under those conditions, this one feature in *A* may make me reject it and choose *B*. I am not at present considering such cases from an ethical point of view; all that I am concerned with here is the psychological fact that they happen and are perfectly familiar. All civilized languages have words like 'ought', 'duty', 'obligation', etc. All these words refer to the fact that the supposed rightness of an action gives rise to a motive-component for doing it, and that the supposed wrongness of an action gives rise to a motive-component against doing it, and that these specifically *moral* motive-components may conflict with others which arise from one's belief about the non-moral characteristics of the action. I shall refer to these psychological facts as 'moral motivation'.

Here again we must notice that non-moral motive-components, based on the attractiveness or repulsiveness which an action derives from the non-moral characteristics which we believe it to have, will generally co-exist and co-operate with components of moral attraction and moral repulsion. In consequence of this a person may often think that he is being moved by purely moral motives when really his total motive for choosing or rejecting an alternative contains both moral and non-moral motive-components. And we may sometimes mistake a purely non-moral motive, such as desire for comfort or safety, for the moral motive of desire to do what is right as such. But the possibility and even frequency of such mistakes has no tendency to show that there is not moral motivation.

We may sum up these facts by saying that the vast majority of sane adult human beings are capable of ostensibly moral cognition, of morally directed emotion, and of moral motivation. Now every such person is also capable of *reflexive* cognition, i.e. of contemplating himself, his experiences, dispositions, intentions, motives, and actions, from various points of view. To say that a person 'has a Conscience', when this phrase is used in its widest sense, is equivalent to asserting the following three closely connected propositions about him. (1) That he has and exercises the cognitive power of reflecting on his own past and future actions, and considering whether they are right or wrong; of reflecting on his own motives, intentions, emotions, dispositions, and character, and considering whether they are morally good or bad; and of reflecting on the relative moral value of various alternative ideals of character and conduct. (2) That he has and exercises the emotional disposition to feel certain peculiar emotions, such as remorse, feeling of guilt, moral approval, etc., towards himself and his own actions, dispositions, etc., in respect of the moral characteristics which he believes these to have. (3) That he has and exercises the conative disposition to seek what he believes to be good and to shun what he believes to be bad, as such, and to do what he believes to be right and avoid what he believes to be wrong, as such.

I propose to describe this as 'the phenomenological sense' of the phrase 'having a conscience'. I think that the most sceptical of speculators about morals would hardly deny that most people nowadays and throughout the course of history have 'had a conscience', in this phenomenological sense. Let us consider where ethical scepticism would be relevant to this question. The most radical form of scepticism would deny that adjectives like 'right', 'morally good', 'obligatory', etc., really stand for characteristics. Its advocates would allege that sentences in which such words occur as grammatical predicates are really interjections or commands masquerading as statements about certain peculiar characteristics of actions, dispositions, persons, etc. If so, those experiences which seem to most people to be cognitions of moral characteristics cannot really be so; for there will be no such characteristics to be cognized. But it can hardly be denied that there are experiences which *seem* to be cognitions of moral characteristics. If there were not, it is impossible to see why moral sentences in all languages should have been couched in the indicative form with a moral adjective as grammatical predicate. So I do not think that such an ethical sceptic, if he knew his business, would attempt to deny that there are *ostensibly* moral cognitions, and this is all that is involved in the cognitive part of the definition of 'having a conscience', in the phenomological sense of that phrase.

If there are no ethical characteristics, it cannot be their presence in the actions, etc., which we contemplate, that moves our emotions. But that would not affect our definition. Granted

248

that a person believes that there are moral characteristics, and believes that such and such of them are present in certain objects which he contemplates, there is no reason why this belief (however false or baseless it may be) should not evoke in him specifically moral emotions towards those objects. The ethical sceptic will, indeed, have to regard those emotions rather as a disbeliever in ghosts might regard the fear which a superstitious person would feel in a room which he believes to be haunted. But any reasonable person would admit that, even if ghosts do not exist, a specific kind of fear is felt by persons who believe in ghosts when they are in places which they believe to be haunted. What is more, a disbeliever in ghosts might himself feel such a fear in such circumstances, though he would judge it to be unreasonable. Similarly an ethical sceptic might himself continue to feel morally directed emotions, though he would have to regard them as unreasonable. And he should have no difficulty in admitting that most human beings do so. Therefore this kind of ethical sceptic need not deny that the emotional condition for having a conscience, in the phenomenological sense of that phrase, is fulfilled by most people.

Precisely similar remarks apply to the question of moral motivation. We are moved by our *beliefs* about the characteristics of things, regardless of whether those beliefs be true or false, well or ill founded. Since it can hardly be denied that most people believe themselves to be aware of moral characteristics in the actions, dispositions, etc., which they contemplate, the doctrine that all such beliefs are in principle mistaken is quite consistent with the contention that most people are susceptible to moral motivation.

An independent attack could, no doubt, be made on the applicability of the second and third clauses in our definition of 'having a conscience'. It might be contended that, whether we cognize moral characteristics or not, our beliefs in the presence of such characteristics never evoke any specific emotion and never influence our actions. Our emotions, it might be said, are evoked and our actions are influenced *only* by what we believe about the *non-moral* characteristics of what we are contemplating. But we proceed either to deceive ourselves or to try to deceive others about the direction of our emotions and the nature of our motives.

I think that this kind of scepticism is usually based on some general theory of human action, such as psychological hedonism, which would rule out the possibility of specifically moral emotion and motivation. I need only say that all such general theories rest on certain rather subtle verbal confusions, and may safely be rejected. A more empirical basis for such scepticism is the admitted mixture of non-moral emotions and motives with moral ones, and the admitted possibility of mistaking one of the former for one of the latter in any particular case. As I have already said, it does not seem to me that the facts about mixture and about mistakes and sophistications are adequate to support the sweeping negative conclusions which have been based on them, in face of the strong *prima facie* evidence for moral motivation and moral emotion.

I see no reason, then, to qualify my assertion that, in the phenomenological sense of the phrase, practically every sane adult human being 'has a conscience', whatever may have been the case with himself as an infant or with his prehistoric ancestors. Of course an individual may happen to live in an environment in which his conscientious dispositions are hardly ever excited or are constantly suppressed. They may then atrophy or become warped, as any other set of dispositions would be likely to do under similar circumstances.

We must now notice some important negative facts about having a conscience, in the sense defined. (1) To say that a person has a conscience, in this sense, neither entails nor excludes that this person holds any particular theory about the nature of goodness or rightness or moral obligation. It neither entails nor excludes that he holds any particular theory about what makes good things good or right acts right. And it neither entails nor excludes that he holds any particular theory about the nature and sources of our moral knowledge and belief. A plain man, with no theories on any of these subjects, can have a conscience and act conscientiously. So too can persons who hold the most varied theories on these points; a man can be a conscientious Utilitarian, a conscientious Intuitionist, a conscientious Hegelian, or what not. All that is necessary is that he shall believe that, in some way or other, he can form a reasonable opinion about the rightness or wrongness, goodness or badness, of various courses open to him, and that his opinions on such matters shall be capable of evoking his emotions and influencing his decisions.

(2) The fact that most people have consciences, in the sense defined, does not, so far as I can see, establish or refute any particular ethical theory. This is, of course, quite a different point from the one which we have just been discussing. It is one thing to say, e.g. that a person could equally well have a conscience whether he accepted or rejected Utilitarianism. It is quite another thing to say that a person could equally well have a conscience whether Utilitarianism be true or false. I assert that, on my definition of 'having a conscience', both these statements are true, and that they would be equally true if any other ethical theory were substituted for Utilitarianism.

Now there is no doubt that the phrase 'to have a conscience' has often been used in a narrower sense than this. I propose now to consider the more important of the narrower senses in which it has been used. In order to do this I must begin with a very brief account of the moral situation in which we appear *prima facie* to find ourselves. It is roughly as follows.

We seem to be under an obligation to do what we can to maintain and increase the amount of good and to diminish the amount of evil, of every kind, in the lives of other persons whom we can affect appreciably by our actions. Let us call this a 'teleological obligation'. *Prima facie* it seems that we have other obligations, not derivable from it, which limit it and may conflict with it, e.g. the mere fact that a person has made a promise seems to be enough to impose on him an obligation to keep it unless the promisee should release him. This obligation appears to be independent of any good that may be produced or evil that may be averted or diminished in others by keeping the promise. We seem to be under an obligation to keep it even when we have strong reason to believe that the consequences would be better for all concerned if we were to break it. Again, there seem to be non-teleological obligations which bear upon the direction and range of our teleological obligations. Granted that one has a duty to do good to others, it seems obvious to most people that a man has a more urgent duty to do good to his parents or his benefactors than to complete strangers.

Now there seem to be a number of non-teleological obligations, e.g. to answer questions truly, to keep one's promises, and so on. And they are liable to conflict, not only with our teleological obligation, but also with each other. E.g. a person may have made a certain promise and he may afterwards be asked a certain question. And it may be impossible to keep the promise and answer truly. In order to keep the promise he must tell a lie, and in order to answer truly he must break the promise. The only remaining alternative is to refuse to answer the question; but in many cases refusal to answer would, for all practical purposes, be equivalent to answering in a certain way and betraying a confidence which one had promised to keep.

Now there is an important epistemological difference between teleological and non-teleological obligations. Suppose I am in a situation where several alternative actions are open to me, and that I am trying to fulfil the teleological obligation to produce as much good or as little evil as I can in others. In order to discover my duty I shall have to consider elaborately the probable remote consequences of the various alternative courses of action. Now this involves a great deal of wholly *non-moral* reflexion on the properties of things, the dispositions of persons, the laws of nature, and so on. The conclusions of such reflections will generally be highly uncertain, and one's capacity to conduct them successfully will depend on the extent of one's knowledge about non-moral facts and the degree of one's capacity for reasoning about physical, psychological, social, economic, and political matters. The *moral* insight that is needed will be concerned only with estimating and comparing the goodness and badness of the consequences which one thinks it likely that the various alternative courses of action would produce. Suppose, on the other hand, I am in a situation where non-teleological obligations are predominant, such as truth-telling and promise-keeping. Then in most cases the ascertainment of the relevant non-moral facts is perfectly simple and straightforward and can be performed without any expert knowledge or technical skill and instruction. If one has made a promise and is asked a question, there is generally not the least difficulty in being certain as to what answers would be lies and what answers would be breaches of promise. Here, then, almost the whole of the cognition involved is specifically *moral*; it is concerned with seeing that making a promise, as such, imposes an obligation to keep it; that answering a question, as such, imposes an obligation to answer it truthfully; and with estimating the relative urgency of these two obligations in cases where they conflict.

It is not surprising, therefore, that many people should be inclined to use the word 'conscience' in such a way that conscience, on its cognitive side, is confined to the task of intuiting non-teleological obligations and estimating their relative urgency.

Suppose we take 'conscience' in this narrower sense. Then it will follow that, if Utilitarianism be true, no one has a conscience. For the essence of Utilitarianism is that there are no non-teleological obligations. And, if there are none, no one can intuit them and estimate their relative urgency; though non-Utilitarians may mistakenly think that they do so. According to the Utilitarian, what makes it obligatory to keep a promise is not the mere fact that the promise has been made. What makes it obligatory, when it is so, is that we are under the obligation to produce as much good and as little evil as possible by our actions, and that experience has shown that promise-keeping on the whole leads to better consequences than promise-breaking. And similar remarks apply, *mutatis mutandis*, to all the alleged non-teleological obligations.

I am not at present concerned to discuss the truth or falsity of Utilitarianism, so I will confine myself to the following three remarks.

(i) In deciding what he ought to do in any situation, a Utilitarian would have to consider carefully, not only what the consequences of various alternative actions would probably be, but also what kinds and amounts of good and evil would attach to each of these consequences if it were realized. It seems inconvenient to use the word 'conscience' in such a way that intuition and comparison of *goods and evils* would not be a function of conscience, whilst intuition and comparison of *non-teleological obligations* would be so.

(ii) Suppose that Utilitarianism is false, and that there are non-teleological obligations. It can hardly be denied that there is *also* the teleological obligation to produce as much good and as little evil as one can. The mistake of Utilitarianism would be to hold that this is the *only* obligation, and to fail to see that there are others, equally fundamental, which limit it and may conflict with it. Truth-speaking and promise-keeping will be duties not reducible to beneficence, but beneficence will still be one duty among others. Therefore, in deciding what one ought to do in a given situation, it will often be necessary to consider the relative urgency of the teleological obligation of beneficence and certain non-teleological obligations, such as truth-telling and promise-keeping. In order to estimate the urgency of the obligation of beneficence it will be necessary to enter into precisely the same kind of calculations as Utilitarians consider to be necessary in every case, since this urgency will plainly depend on the nature and amount of good to be produced or evil to be averted by one's actions. It seems to me that it would be highly inconvenient to use the word 'conscience' in such a way that it was part of the function of conscience to compare the urgency of various non-teleological obligations, but was no part of its functions to compare the urgency of non-teleological obligations with that of teleological ones or to compare that of two or more teleological ones with each other.

(iii) Nevertheless, the considerations which have now been brought to our notice do suggest that the following explanatory sentences should be added to our definition of 'having a conscience'. We must distinguish between the *purely factual* and the *purely ethical* considerations which are involved in any attempt to decide what we ought to do in a given situation. Both factors enter in all cases. The purely factual elements are generally (though by no means always) obvious, even to quite ignorant and simple people, when only non-teleological obligations are in question; but, when teleological obligations have to be seriously considered, they may be highly complex and uncertain and may demand technical knowledge and skill of an advanced kind. Now conscience, as such, is concerned directly only with the purely ethical factors. The operation of forecasting the consequences of various alternative actions, as distinct from estimating the goodness or badness of these consequences, could be performed as well or better by a person who had no conscience. But, although this intellectual process cannot itself be assigned to conscience, it is an essential condition without which conscience cannot do its own proper work in situations of any complexity. A person who is trying to find out what he ought to do is not using his conscience properly if he fails to inform himself as fully and accurately as possible of all the relevant facts, or if he omits to apply his utmost care and skill to the task of fore-casting the remote and the indirect consequences of the alternatives under consideration.

When the word 'conscience' is used in such a way that conscience, in its cognitive aspect, is confined to intuiting and balancing non-teleological obligations, I shall say that it is used 'in the intuitional sense'. I have now tried to show that this is an inconveniently narrow sense. But the word is often used in senses which are even narrower than this, and I will now consider some of them.

It is held by some people that certain kinds of non-teleological obligation are so urgent that a person ought not under any conceivable circumstances to do an action which would infringe any of them. This claim has been made, e.g. for the obligation to answer a question truthfully if at all. Now it seems to me that the word 'conscience', and phrases which contain it, are often used in such a way as to imply that a person cannot have a conscience unless he holds this opinion, and that his conscience is in operation only on occasions when his action or his refusal to act is based on his belief that one of these unconditional obligations is involved. I should consider it most undesirable that the word should be used in this narrow way. For the opinion in question is almost certainly mistaken; and, even if it were true, it has been rejected by many people who, in any ordinary use of language, have been scrupulously conscientious, such as John Stuart Mill. It would plainly be unfortunate to use the word 'conscience' in such a way that no one could be said to have a conscience unless he were mistaken on an important point of moral theory, and that no one could be said to be following his conscience except when he was under the influence of this delusion. The utmost that can be granted to the intuitionist is that we can see directly that certain relationships, as such, impose certain component obligations on us, and that some of them are so urgent that any act which would conflict with any of these has a very strong tendency to be wrong. In certain cases this is true, not only of all the *actions* open to one, but also of the only remaining alternative, viz. *refusal to act*. If we care to say that, in such cases all the alternatives are wrong, we can do so; but we shall then have to admit that we ought to choose that alternative (be it one of the actions or refusal to act) which is the *least wrong.* And in complex cases there is not the faintest reason to believe that we have intuitive knowledge as to which one this is.

It remains to notice one further narrowing of the word 'conscience'. Sometimes it is used in such a way that a person would be said to be following his conscience only in so far as he bases his decision about what he ought to do on some alleged divine revelation. In many cases, I think, this amounts to little more than the previous usage decorated with theological frillings. The pronouncements of conscience about what is unconditionally wrong are regarded as, in some sense, the voice of God speaking in and to the individual; and so the agent can take them to be infallible without arrogating too much for himself. In other cases, however, the situation is quite different. Certain actions are regarded by the individual as unconditionally right or unconditionally wrong, not because he sees this for himself by direct inspection, but because he believes that God has given a ruling on the matter either in inspired writings or in the traditions of a divinely founded and directed Church.

I will now leave the notion of conscience, and pass to that of a conscientious action. Conscience, as I have defined it, is a system of cognitive, emotional, and conative *dispositions*, and it is only when these dispositions are in operation that we have conscientious action.

The question whether an action is conscientious or not is mainly a question about the agent's motives in doing it. We must clear up the notion of motive a little before we can give a satisfactory definition of 'conscientious action'. Suppose that an agent is contemplating a certain possible course of action in a given situation. He will have various beliefs and expectations about its qualities, its relations, and its consequences, e.g. he may believe that it would be unpleasant to himself, that it would please his mother, and that it would be a breach of a promise made to his father, and so on. Some of these beliefs and expectations will attract him towards doing the action, some will repel him from doing it, and others may leave him unmoved. I call any belief about an action which attracts one towards doing it a 'motive-component *for* the action', and any belief about it which repels one from doing it a 'motive-component *against* the action'. Suppose that a certain action is in fact chosen and performed. Then I say that the agent's 'total motive *in* doing the action' was the resultant of all the motive-components for doing it and all the motive components against doing it. And I say that he did it '*because of*' the former, and '*in spite of*' the latter.

Now suppose that there were several components for doing a certain action, and several against doing it, and that it was in fact done because of the former and in spite of the latter. Let us call the former a, b, and c, and the latter u, v, and w. Now consider, e.g. the component a. We can ask ourselves the following question about it. Would a have been sufficient, in the absence of b and c, to induce the agent to do this action in spite of the components u, v, and w against doing it? Or did the component a need to be supplemented by b or by c or by both in order to overcome the influence of u, v, and w? If and only if the first alternative is true, we can say that a was 'a *sufficient* motive-component for doing the action'. Next we can raise the following question. Would bc have been sufficient, in the absence of a, to induce the agent to do the action in spite of the components u, v, and w against doing it? Or did bc need to be supplemented by a in order to overcome the influence of u, v, and w? If, and only if, the second alternative is true, we can say that a was 'a *necessary* motive-component for doing the action'. Lastly, suppose that a had been the only component for doing the action. Then we could say that 'the action was done *purely* from the motive a'.

We can now apply these general considerations to the particular case of conscientious action. An action is conscientious if the following conditions are fulfilled. (i) The agent has reflected on the situation, the action, and the alternatives to it, in order to discover what is the right course. In this reflection he has tried his utmost to learn the relevant facts and to give each its due weight, he has exercised his judgment on them to the best of his ability, and he has striven to allow for all sources of bias. (ii) He has decided that, on the factual and ethical information available to him, the action in question is probably the most right or the least wrong of all those which are open to him. (iii) His belief that the action has this moral characteristic, together with his desire to do what is right as such, was either (*a*) the *only* motive-component for doing it, or (*b*) a *sufficient and necessary* motive-component for doing it. If the first alternative is fulfilled, we can say that his action was '*purely* conscientious'. If the second is fulfilled, we can say that it was '*predominantly* conscientious'. The following would be an example of a predominantly conscientious action. Suppose that a person, after reflection, decides that the right action for him is to undertake military service. Suppose that the two motive-components which induce him to undertake this action, in spite of fear, love of comfort, etc., are his belief that it is right, together with his desire to do what is right as such, and his dislike of being thought cowardly by his friends. Then the action is predominantly conscientious if (*a*) his desire to do what is right, as such, *would* have sufficed to overcome his fear and his love of comfort even in the absence of his dislike of being thought cowardly, whilst (*b*) his dislike of being thought cowardly *would not* have sufficed to overcome those motive-components in the absence of his desire to do what is right, as such. In such a case we can say that the non-conscientious component for doing the action which the agent believes to be right is indeed present but is superfluous and insufficient. It would be absurd to refuse to call the action 'conscientious' merely because a superfluous and insufficient non-conscientious motive-component for doing it happened to co-exist with the sufficient and necessary conscientious motive-component for doing it.

We come now to a much more difficult and doubtful case. Suppose that the agent's belief that the action is right, together with his desire to do what is right as such, is sufficient, but not necessary, to induce him to do it, in spite of the components against doing it. This would be illustrated by our old example if we varied it in the following way. We must now suppose that the agent's dislike of been thought cowardly *would* have sufficed to overcome his fear and his love of comfort and *would* have induced him to choose the course of action which he believes to be right, even if his belief that it is right and his desire to do what is right, as such, had been absent. The situation may be described as follows. The non-conscientious motive-component for doing the action is still superfluous; but now we must say that the conscientious component for doing it is equally superfluous. Each is sufficient, and therefore neither individually is necessary; all that is necessary is that one or other of them should be present. If you confine your attention to the *sufficiency* of the conscientious motive-component, you will be inclined to say that the action *is* conscientious; if you attend only to the *super-fluity* of this component, you will be inclined to say that it is *not* conscientious.

We pass now to another difficult and doubtful case. Suppose now that the agent's belief that the action is right, together with his desire to do what is right as such, is necessary but not sufficient to induce him to do it in spite of the components against doing it. This would be illustrated by the following modification of our old example. We must now suppose (*a*) that the agent's belief that it is right for him to undertake military service, together with his desire to do what is right as such, would not have sufficed, in the absence of his dislike of being thought cowardly, to overcome his fear and his love of comfort; and (*b*) that the latter motive-component, in the absence of the former, would also not have sufficed to overcome his fear and his love of comfort. Each of the two motive-components for doing the action is now necessary, and therefore neither of them individually is sufficient. If you confine your attention to the *indispensability* of the conscientious motive-component, you will be inclined to say that the action *is* conscientious; if you attend only to its *insufficiency*, you will be inclined to say that it is *not* conscientious.

I will group together purely and predominantly conscientious actions, in the sense defined above, under the name of '*fully* conscientious actions'; and I will group together the two doubt-ful cases, which we have just been discussing, under the name of '*semi-conscientious* actions'. The two kinds of these can then be distinguished as (i) actions in which the conscientious motive-component is sufficient but superfluous, and (ii) actions in which the conscientious motive-component is indispensable but inadequate.

If a person does an act which he believes to be less right or more wrong than some other act open to him at the time, he does it in spite of his desire to do what is right, as such. Any action of this kind may be called '*contra-conscientious*'.

It is plain that a great many of our deliberate actions are neither fully conscientious, nor semi-conscientious, nor contra-conscientious; for many are done without considering them and the alternatives to them from the standpoint of rightness and wrongness. Such actions may be called '*non-conscientious*'. A non-conscientious action may be such that, if the agent had considered it and the alternatives to it from the standpoint of rightness and wrongness, he would have judged it to be the most right or the least wrong of the alternatives open to him. And it may be that he would then have done it for that reason alone or for that reason combined with others which are superfluous and insufficient. If both these conditions are fulfilled, we may say that this non-conscientious action was '*potentially* conscientious'. In a similar way we could define the statement that a certain non-conscientious act was '*potentially* contra-conscientious'.

I have now completed the task of analysis and definition, and I will conclude my paper with a few remarks about conscientious action, as defined above. (1) There is a very important sense of 'ought' in which it is true to say that a person ought always to do the alternative which he believes, at the time when he has to act, to be the most right or the least wrong of all those that are open to him. (There are, undoubtedly, other senses of 'ought' in which this would not be true; but we are not concerned with them here.) For this sense of 'ought' to be applicable it does not matter how ignorant or deluded the agent may be about the relevant facts, how incompetent he may be to make reasonable inferences from them, nor how crazy or perverted his judgments about right and wrong, good and evil, may be. But, the more fully this is admitted, the more obvious does the following complementary fact become. The most right or the least wrong act open to other individuals or to a society, in certain cases, may be to prevent a conscientious individual from doing certain acts which he ought, in this sense, to do, and to try to compel him to do certain acts which he ought, in this sense, to refrain from doing. Moreover, if other individuals or the authorities in a society honestly believe that the most right or the least wrong action open to them is to treat a certain conscientious individual in this way, then they *ought*, in the very same sense, to do so. What is sauce for the conscientious goose is sauce for the conscientious ganders who are his neighbours or his governors. This fact is often obscured because many people inadvertently or dishonestly confine their attention to cases, such as the trial of Socrates or of Christ, in which subsequent generations have held that the individual was not only conscientious but also correct in his ethical opinions, whilst the tribunal which condemned him was either not conscientious or was mistaken in its ethical opinions. It may be salutary for such persons to widen their purview by envisaging the case of a high-minded Indian civilian conscientiously securing the capture and execution of a high-minded Thug for conscientiously practising murder.

(2) It is sometimes said that, when an individual sets up his conscience against the general opinion of his society or of mankind, he is claiming 'moral infallibility'. If he knows his business, he is doing nothing of the kind. In order for it to be his duty, in the present sense, to do a certain alternative, all that is necessary is that he should think it *probable*, after considering the question to the best of his ability, that this alternative is more right or less wrong than any of the others which are open to him. Since he has to enact one of the alternatives, it does not matter in the least whether this probability is high or low. Nor does it matter whether the difference in rightness or wrongness is great or small. In considering the question, it is his duty to give full weight to the fact that most members of his society or most of the human race have formed a certain opinion about it. If he is a wise man, he will attach very great weight to this fact. But if, in spite of having done so, he comes to a contrary opinion, he ought, in the present sense, to act upon it, no matter how far short of complete conviction his opinion may fall.

(3) The last remark that I have to make is this. A *purely* conscientious action, in the sense defined above, must be a very rare event. It is hardly credible, e.g. that either undertaking or refusing military service could be a purely conscientious act, in that sense; for everyone fears death and wounds and everyone dislikes to be thought cowardly.

Now the definitions of 'predominantly conscientious' act, and of the two kinds of 'semi-conscientious' act, all have the following peculiarity. They all involve the notion of what *would* have happened if certain conditions had been other than they in fact were. This notion of the consequences of unfulfilled conditions always enters whenever the question of sufficiency and dispensability is raised. It follows that an individual can seldom be rationally justified in feeling a very strong conviction that an action of his was conscientious; for, in order to decide this question, he has to form an opinion as to how he would have acted in the *absence* of certain motive-components which were in fact *present*. It seems to me that *a fortiori* it must be almost impossible for anyone to decide rationally as to whether another person's action is conscientious or not.

If I am right in this, the Tribunals have been given a task which is, from the nature of the case, incapable of being satisfactorily performed. This, so far as it goes, is a strong ground against allowing exemption from military service on grounds of conscience and against setting up Tribunals at all. There are, no doubt, other reasons which point in the opposite direction; and Parliament has decided that, in the present state of public opinion in England, the balance of advantage is in favour of allowing exemption on such grounds, and has therefore set up Tribunals to consider claims. It only remains for us to watch with sympathy and interest the efforts of these well-meaning men to deal with questions to which God alone can know the answer.

INDEX OF NAMES AND TITLES

INDEX

Bristol, 29, 50
British Academy, vii, viii, 108
'British Solomon', 125
Brixton, 95
Browning, R., 93
Bruno, G., 144, 157
Brunswick, Duke of, 168
Bull Hotel (Cambridge), 95
Burton Coggles, 3
Butler, H. M., 60
    Joseph, 170

Cabbalists, 146
Caesar, C. J., 176, 202
Caius College (Cambridge), 169
Cambridge, 94, 112, 205
Cambridge Historical Journal, viii
Cambridge University, 8, 9
    History of Science Committee, ix
    Press, vii
Cambridge Women's Training College, 103-4
Canterbury, Archbishop of, 50, 124
Carlyle, T., 98
Carolina, 37
Caroline of Anspach, 170
Carr, Rev. Wm., 50
Cavendish Professorship of Physics (Cambridge), 55
Chadwick, J. A., 107
Character of a Trimmer (Halifax), 229
Characteristics (Shaftesbury), 33
Charles II, King, 7, 32, 33-4, 91
Charles Dickens (Chesterton), 112
Charon Court (house), 29
Chesterfield, 4th Earl of, 78
Chesterton, G. K., 112
Chew Magna, 29
Chipley, 44
Christ, J., 124
Christ Church (Oxford), 30
    Dean of, 33-4
Chrystal, Professor, 102
Church of England, 62, 90, 124
Clark, Mr. (of Grantham), 4
Clarke, Edmund (of Chipley), 44
Clarke, John, 169
    Dr. S., controversy with Leibniz, 170-91
    life of, 168-9
Clausewitz, K. von, 127
Clifford, W. K., 68, 102
Clifton College, 70, 73, 89

Clough, A. H., 95
    Miss, 60
Collins, Anthony, 44
Colsterworth, 3
Colonial Office, 95
Commentary to Hegel's Logic (McTaggart), 71
Commercium Epistolicum, 12
Commissionership of Appeals, 35
    Trade and Plantations, 47
Concept of Mind (Ryle), ix
Condillac, E. de, 136
Conduitt, Catharine, 11
    John, 11
Conservative Party, 98
Contemporary British Philosophy, 82
Convention Parliament, 8, 9
Copernicus, 146
Corpus Christi College (Cambridge) 95
'Corsican Ogre', 140
Cotes, Roger, 13
Council of the Senate (Cambridge), 60
Cox, Homersham, 102
Critique of Pure Reason (Kant), 39
Crofts, Mary (*see* Mrs. Sidgwick senior), 49, 50
Cudworth, R., 44
Cumberland, 49
Cunningham, Wm., 56

Dakyns, H. G., 51, 52, 61
Dale, Rev. H., 50
D'Alembert, J., 141
Dante, 79
Darwin, Charles, 52, 124
Darwinians, 124
Davos, 60
De Augmentis (Bacon), 120
Defence of Freethinking in Mathematics (Berkeley), 27
de Maistre, J., 124
Democritus, 134, 154
De Motu (Newton), 7
Dent, 49
Descartes, R., philosophy of, 154-67
    references to, ix, 15, 39, 40, 42, 87, 120, 123, 141, 144
Development of European Polity (Sidgwick), 61
Dialectic of Existence (McTaggart), 82
'Diamond' (Newton's dog), 9

264

INDEX

Dickens, Charles, 112
Discourse on Method, (Descartes), 157
Downing College (Cambridge), 96
   Street, No. 10; 62
Dorsetshire, 29
Dryden, J., 31
Dürer, A., 106
Dynamic (Clifford), 102

Economic Journal, 103
Economics, Special Board of (Cambridge), 59
Edgworth, F. Y., 103
Edinburgh University, 9
Einstein, Professor A., 25
Elements (Euclid), 4
Eliot, George, 112
Encyclopaedia (Hegel), 82
Encyclopaedia Britannica, 56
Encyclopaedists, 124, 141
England, 73, 89, 91, 239, 241–2, 244
Englishmen, 220
Enneads (Plotinus), 82
Essay on Human Understanding (Locke) 35, 38–44
Essex, 44, 48, 62
Ethics (Spinoza), 71, 82
Etonians, Old, 220
Evans's House (Rugby), 51
Ewald, Professor, 52
Exeter College (Oxford), xi
   House, 32

Fascism, 90
Fell, Dr., 33–4
Fielding, H., 37, 46
Fifth Monarchy Men, 31
Filmer, Sir R., 35
Finland, xi
Fitzwilliam Museum (Cambridge), 99
Flamsteed, J., 10, 12, 13
Forerunners, or Anticipations of the New Philosophy (Bacon), 121
France, 32
Friendship's Garland (Arnold), 98

Gabriel, 150
Galen, 134
Galileo, his contributions to science, 18–20, 155–7
   other references to, 21, 25, 26, 159, 164, 165

Garter King of Arms, 78
Gaul, 202
General Board of Studies (Cambridge), 57, 58
George, Prince (of Denmark), 10
Germany, xi, 52–3, 57
'Ghost-in-the-Machine Theory', ix–x
Glasgow, 14
Gotobed, James, 95
Gouda, 35
Grantham (King's School), 3–4
Greeks, 118
Green, T. H., 51, 59, 61
Grote, John, 54
Guenellon, 33
Guericke, O. von, 186

Hadley, J., 15
Halifax, 1st Marquess of, 229
Hallelujah Chorus, 101
Halley, E., 7, 8, 12–13, 24
Hanover, 168, 170
Harlow, 44
Harrovians, Old, 220
Harvey Road (Cambridge), 113
Heaton, Barbara Keymer (Mrs. W. E. Johnson), 106
Hegel, G. F. W., 72–5, 76–8, 85, 87, 89, 91
Hegelianism, 54
Heppenstall, 99
Herschell, Sir J., 28
Hervey, Lord, 93, 170
Hibbert Journal, vii
High Lever, 48
Hilbert, D., 110
Hillside (house), 55, 56, 60
Hipparchus, 145
Hobbes, T., 35–6, 37, 71, 123, 159
Holland, 33, 34, 39, 44
Hooke, R., 6, 7, 8, 12, 13, 16
Hume, D., 38, 39, 71, 89, 142
Huntingdonshire, 94
Huxley, T. H., 52
Huygens, C., 16
Hyères, 99, 100, 103

India, 46
International Congress of Philosophy (1900), 107
Ireland, 59–60
Italy, 90, 154

INDEX

INDEX

INDEX

INDEX

Stoke, 3
Stoke Rochford, 14
Stone Gappe (house), 50
Stout, G. F., 102, 104
Strauss, D. F., 52
Studies and Exercises in Formal Logic
(Keynes), 105, 113
Studies in Hegelian Cosmology (McTaggart), 71, 78–80
Studies in Hegelian Dialectic (McTaggart), 71, 75–8
Sunderland, 2nd Earl of, 34
Sunning Hill, 31
Super Flumina Babylonis (Swinburne),
62
Sutton Wick, 29
Swinburne, A. C., 93
Switzerland, 101, 106
Sylva Sylvarum (Bacon), 120
Symonds, J. A., 60
Synthetic Society, 62

Taranaki, 70
Tawney, 54
Telesius, 123
Temple, Frederick, 52
Temporis Partus Masculus (Bacon),
134
Tennyson, 1st Baron, 95
Terling, 62
Thackeray, W. M., 112
The Grove (Cambridge), 96
Theoria, viii
Theory of Logical Equations (Johnson),
107
Thevenot, 33
Thomas, Dr., 31
Thompson, W. H., 60
Thomson, Sir J. J., 133
Thoughts on Education (Locke), 33,
44, 46
Tower of London, 33
Treatise on Fluxions (Maclaurin), 14,
27
Treatise on Probability (Keynes), 105,
107–8, 109
Trevelyan, Sir G. O., Bart., 61

Trigonometry (Johnson), 102, 107
Trinity College (Cambridge), 4, 5,
8, 28, 30, 49, 51, 53, 54, 56, 60, 70,
73, 87, 89, 92, 168
    (Dublin), 67
Trollope, A., 112
Truro, Bishopric of, 50
Turner, Edmund, 14
Two Notable Corruptions of Scripture
(Newton), 9
Tycho Brahe, 146, 157

Union Society (Cambridge), 70, 93
United States of America, 90
Uppsala University, x

Vane, Sir Walter, 30
Venice, 14

Wallace, Edgar, 46
Walpole, Horace, 4th Earl of Orford, 93
Ward, J., 58, 61, 71, 97
Watson, R., 96
Wellington College, 50
Westcott, B. F., 59
Westminster Abbey, 14
    School, 29–30
Westmorland, 49
Weyl, Professor H., 110
*What does Mr. Johnson mean by a
Proposition?* (Joseph), 109
Whiggism, 90–1
William II, *Kaiser*, 34
William III, King, 11, 35, 46, 47
Wills (family), 29
Wittgenstein, L., 110
Woolsthorpe, 3, 14, 23
Wordsworth, Wm., 95, 112
Wren, Sir C., 8, 10
Wrington, 29
Wüstenfeld, Professor, 52

Yarborough, Dr., 169
Yonge, Charlotte, 112
Yorkshire, 49, 50

INDEX OF SUBJECTS

INDEX

Curves, cubic, Newton's classification of, 12
  rectification of by Fluxions, 12

Deferents, 145
Desires, egoistic, classification of, 219–21
  inter-relations of, 221–3
  extra-verted and introverted, 220–21
  self-centred, 221
  self-referential, 221
  self-regarding and other-regarding, 221
  pluralism v. monism of ultimate, 218, 230–1
Determinables and determinates, 109
Determination, complete, 209, 210
Determining Correspondence, Principle of, 83
Determinism, definition of, 210–11
  McTaggart's defence of, 81–2
Dialectical Method, McTaggart's account of, 76–8, 79, 82
Diffraction, 17
Dispositional premisses, 207
Dissimilarity of the Diverse, Principle of, 177
Distribution, Sidgwick's *a priori* principles of, 64–5
Divine Right of Kings, 35
Duties, *prima facie*, conflicts of, 63–4

Eccentrics, 145
Economics, Johnson's contributions to, 102–3
Education, Locke's views on, 44–6
Educational policy, Sidgwick's, 58–9
Egoism, psychological, 219–30
  summary on, 228–30
  various forms of, 223 *et seq.*, 228–9
Element, fifth, 146
Elements, doctrine of, 146–7
Elimination by negative instances, 138–40
Elliptic orbits, Newton's work on, 7
Emission-theory of light, Newton's attitude to, 17–18
Epicycles, 145
Epistemic conditions (Johnson), 109
Epistemology and ontology, 43–4

Equinoxes, precession of, Newton's explanation of, 13
Essence and existence, 148
Eternity, 175
  McTaggart's doctrine of, 85
Ether, 17
Ethics, Bacon's views on, 122–3
Existence, knowledge of, Locke's views on, 41
Experiment, Bacon's views on, 125–6, 137
  Descartes' views on, 164
Extension, Descartes' views on, 161

'First Philosophy or Wisdom' (Bacon), 127–8
'Fits of easy transmission' (Newton), 17
Fluxions, and differential calculus, 25–8
  applied to rectification of curves, 12
  controversy as to priority, 12, 27
  later history of, 13, 27–8
  logically correct formulation of, 13–14
Force, Newton's definition of, 21
Form and stuff, 148–50
'Formula of Interpretation' (Bacon), 138
Forms, Bacon's metaphysic of, 128–33
Free Will, 215–16

Geometry, analytical, 158–9
  Newton's early weakness in, 4
God, Descartes' views on, 161–2
  his choice of the best possible world, 175–6
  his relation to Space and Time, 175
  Locke's views on, 41
  postulated by Sidgwick, 65–6
  sensorium of, 171
Gravitation, Descartes' views on, 166
  Leibniz's views on, 172
  Newton's first notions of, 5
  universal, Newton's proof of, 22–5
Great Instauration, Bacon's plans for, 120–1

Happiness, desire for one's own greatest, 219, 220

271